Caring for Preschool Children, 2nd Ed.

A Competency-Based Training Program

Volume I

Diane Trister Dodge

Derry G. Koralek

Peter J. Pizzolongo

TEACHING STRATEGIES INC.

Washington, DC

Published by

Teaching Strategies, Inc.
P.O. Box 42243
Washington, DC 20015

Distributed by

Gryphon House Inc.
P.O. Box 207
Beltsville, MD 20704

ISBN: 1-879537-25-7 (Volume I)

Library of Congress Card Catalog Number: 96-61070

Contents

Acknowledgments

Caring for Preschool Children has a long history and therefore we have many individuals to acknowledge and thank. The primary basis for this publication is a training program developed by the authors for the U.S. Navy and the U.S. Army Child Development Services Programs. Carolee Callen, then Head of the Navy Child Development Services Branch, originally conceived of the idea of a standardized, self-instructional training program for child care staff. In 1986 the Navy contracted with Creative Associates International, Inc., a Washington, DC-based consulting firm where the authors then worked, to develop a comprehensive training program. M.-A. Lucas, Chief of Child Development Services in the U.S. Army, funded an adaptation of the training program to support training in Army child development centers. We are indebted to these two individuals, their Headquarters staff, and the staff at Army and Navy child development centers who reviewed all drafts of the materials developed under this contract and provided us with constructive and helpful suggestions that greatly improved the program.

During the development of this training program, in its original format for military child care settings and as revised by Teaching Strategies in 1989, several early childhood educators worked with us and provided expert advice. In particular, we want to thank Dr. Jenni Klein, whose considerable knowledge and vast practical experience made her contributions exceptionally valuable. Dr. Joan Lombardi reviewed the training materials from the perspective of the Child Development Associate (CDA) Standards and showed us where changes and additions were needed. On individual modules, we are grateful for the contributions of Laura Colker, Marilyn Goldhammer, Dr. Trudy Hamby, Bonnie Kittredge, Cynthia Prather, and Lillian Sugarman.

Since 1989, *Caring for Preschool Children* has been implemented in early childhood programs across the country and used as the text for college courses. It served as the basis for two new sets of materials—*Caring for Children in Family Child Care* and *Caring for Children in School-Age Programs.* Our experiences in developing the new materials led us to the decision to update this original work and publish a second edition.

We are especially grateful to Emily Kohn who edited the manuscript; Debra Al-Salám who served as production manager; Jennifer Barrett O'Connell who created the art work for our new cover and the graphics in each module; Ayesha Khwaja Husain who designed the cover and layout of the book and also assisted with production; and to Larry Bram who kept us all on track.

And finally, we want to acknowledge the many early childhood educators we have worked with over the years from whom we have learned a great deal. We have undoubtedly adapted and expanded on many of their excellent ideas; this training program is richer as a result.

It is our hope that this second edition of *Caring for Preschool Children* will have a positive impact on the quality of early childhood programs by giving staff developers and teachers a practical and comprehensive tool to support their important work.

Orientation

Welcome to *Caring for Preschool Children*, a personalized training program designed to help you acquire the skills and knowledge you need to provide a high-quality program for preschool children. Whether you are new to the profession or have years of experience, this training program offers practical information on topics central to teaching preschool children. Throughout these materials we use the term *teacher* to mean any adult who works with young children in a classroom setting, including mentor teachers, lead teachers, teacher aides, teacher assistants, caregivers, and volunteers. We use the term *trainer* to refer to the individual who is guiding your participation in this training program.

Several features of *Caring for Preschool Children* make it unique.

- The materials are appropriate for new as well as experienced teachers.

- You take responsibility for your progress through the training program, with guidance and feedback provided by a trainer.

- The training program is individualized; you work independently, according to your own schedule, and at your own pace.

- The information presented in the modules is practical and of immediate use in your daily work with children.

- Many of the learning activities ask you to observe children to learn about their skills and interests. Observation is a key way to get to know children and to plan ways to respond to each child as an individual.

- Your completed learning activities become a professional resource and record of your growth and competence.

How the Training Program Can Help You

Caring for Preschool Children is designed to provide specialized training to help you achieve a high-quality preschool program. The modules in this training program describe the typical developmental stages of children ages three to five and include many examples of how you can apply this knowledge to plan and implement your program. The more you know about children, the more effective you can be in establishing a positive relationship with each child, a relationship that supports learning and skill development.

Working with young children is a rewarding profession, one in which you can constantly grow and feel challenged. As an adult, you bring years of experience to the task of teaching preschool children. Once you begin this training program, you will find you already have many skills addressed in the modules. Completing the modules will enable you to extend and expand on the skills and knowledge you already have. The training will help you to meet the profession's standards and to become a more competent teacher.

Caring for Preschool Children can help you achieve a nationally recognized credential that acknowledges your skills as a teacher of preschool children. The training program is based on the Child Development Associate (CDA) Competency Standards, as defined by The Council for Early Childhood Professional Recognition (The Council) in Washington, DC. There are 13 CDA functional areas that define the skills and knowledge of competent teachers. (See pages 7-8 for definitions of each functional area.) Each of the modules in *Caring for Preschool Children* addresses one of the functional areas. Teachers who demonstrate that they have acquired the skills and knowledge outlined in the CDA Competency Standards can apply for a credential from The Council. Contact the Council at 1-800-424-4310 for more information about the requirements for a CDA credential.

The Role of the Trainer

An important part of this training program is the feedback and support you receive from a trainer. The trainer might be a colleague, mentor teacher, supervisor, education coordinator, college instructor, or other individual who can observe you at work and provide meaningful feedback to encourage your professional development. Although the modules are designed to be self-instructional, you will benefit most if you have an experienced trainer who can review and discuss your responses to learning activities, answer questions, and comment on your interactions with children and families. A trainer can provide feedback on site at the program, during a phone conference, via electronic mail (e-mail), or in a group meeting.

How the Training Program Works

When you have completed this Orientation, your next step is to complete the self-assessment. This is not a test. It is designed to introduce the major topics covered in each module so you can meet with your trainer to develop a module completion plan. To complete this plan, you select three modules to work on first. Then you determine a tentative schedule for completing the entire training program.

To learn more about your current skills, ask your trainer to conduct several observations of you as you work with children. Observation is an important training tool. Trainers use observations to give you feedback on your progress in applying the skills and knowledge gained as you work on the modules. You and your trainer can review the observation notes and the results of the self-assessment as you develop your individualized module completion plan.

You might choose to begin with a module of particular interest precisely because you have already acquired many of the relevant skills. Or, you might begin with a module that addresses a training need identified through the self-assessment or your trainer's observations. If you are using this training program as a part of course or seminar, your trainer might ask you to begin with a specific module so that you can participate in group meetings with others who are working on the same module. A program director might ask teachers to begin with a module that addresses a program need, such as improving partnerships with parents.

You can expect to spend about four to six weeks on each module. Generally, it takes 12 to 18 months to complete the training program. For each module, you will follow a consistent sequence of steps. These steps are described in the following paragraphs.

The **overview** introduces the topics addressed in the module and defines three major skills teachers must have. For each skill, you review concrete examples depicting teachers demonstrating their competence and a short situation illustrating teachers applying their skills. You answer questions following each situation. The last section of the overview asks you to relate the topic to your own experiences.

Complete the overview.

The **pre-training assessment** is a list of the key skills competent teachers should possess in each area. You indicate whether you use a skill regularly, sometimes, or not enough. Review your responses on the pre-training assessment, then identify three to five skills to improve or topics you wish to learn more about. Before beginning the learning activities, you discuss the overview and the pre-training assessment with your trainer.

Do the pre-training assessment.

Each module has four to six **learning activities.** The activities begin with objectives—statements of what you will learn—and several pages of information about the topic. After completing the reading, you apply what you learned by answering questions; completing a checklist; trying out suggested practices; planning, implementing, and evaluating an activity; or observing children and using your notes to plan an individualized program. Directions for applying your knowledge are in shaded text. When you have completed each learning activity, you arrange a time to meet with your trainer to discuss the activity and to receive feedback. For some activities, you also meet with colleagues or a child's family to discuss what you did and what you learned.

Complete each learning activity.

After you have completed all the learning activities in the module, you **summarize your progress** by reviewing the pre-training assessment and describing your increased knowledge and skills. You then meet with your trainer to discuss your progress and to determine whether you are ready to schedule your knowledge and competency assessments.

Summarize your progress.

Your trainer will give you the **knowledge and competency assessments**. On the knowledge assessment, you must achieve a score of 80 percent before going on to a new module. For the competency assessment, your trainer observes you working with children to assess your competence in the functional area. Some competency assessments must take place at a specific time—for example, the competency assessment for Module 11, Families, should take place at drop-off or pick-up time, when parents are present. After you have completed both assessments you and your trainer discuss whether you have successfully completed the module. If you need to spend more time on the module, your trainer may suggest activities to help you gain the skills needed to demonstrate competence.

Complete the assessment process.

Before You Begin

Take a few minutes to review the glossary on the following page. It defines the terms used throughout the training program. The glossary is followed by the definitions of the CDA functional areas, a bibliography of suggested resources, and a list of publishers and distributors of resources. You may find the recommended resources in your program's library, or you may want to collect some for your own professional library. The self-assessment begins on page 17.

When you are ready, take the self-assessment and begin planning your training.

Glossary

Child development

All the stages a child passes through as he or she gains social, emotional, physical, and cognitive skills.

Child Development Associate (CDA)

A person who has been assessed by The Council for Early Childhood Recognition (The Council) and judged to be a competent early childhood professional.

CDA Credentialing Program

The process used by The Council to assess the competence of early childhood professionals. Assessment and credentialing are based on performance in 13 functional areas. (See definition below.) The CDA credential is accepted by the early childhood profession nationwide.

Competencies

Those tasks, skills, attitudes, and values needed to provide a high-quality preschool program. Competencies differ from knowledge in that competencies describe a teacher's actions and performance.

Competency assessments

The performance-based section of the assessment process. For the competency assessments, teachers demonstrate their skills while working with children.

Developmentally appropriate practice

Program environment, activities, routines, and adult interactions with children that reflect children's individual characteristics and stages of social, emotional, physical, and cognitive development. Developmentally appropriate practice is age, individually, and culturally appropriate.

Environment

The indoor and outdoor space regularly available for the program. It includes furniture, materials, equipment, the schedule and routines followed, and the interactions of children and adults.

Functional areas

The 13 major categories of tasks or functions, as defined by The Council, that are used as the framework for this training program. Each module addresses a functional area in which a staff member must demonstrate competence in order to complete the training program.

Knowledge assessment

The paper-and-pencil exercises of the assessment process, testing knowledge of the concepts presented in the module.

Observation

The act of systematically watching and objectively taking notes on what a child says and does. Observation notes are used to learn more about a child in order to offer a program that reflects the child's current needs, strengths, and interests.

Pre-training assessment

A tool used at the beginning of each module by a teacher and a trainer to identify what skills the teacher has and where more training is needed.

Functional Areas of the Child Development Associate Competency Standards[*]

Safe

Provide a safe environment to prevent and reduce injuries.

Healthy

Promote good health and nutrition and provide an environment that contributes to the prevention of illness.

Learning Environment

Use space, relationships, materials, and routines as resources for constructing an interesting, secure, and enjoyable environment that encourages play, exploration, and learning.

Physical

Provide a variety of equipment, activities, and opportunities to promote the physical development of children.

Cognitive

Provide activities and opportunities that encourage curiosity, exploration, and problem-solving appropriate to the developmental levels and learning styles of children.

Communication

Communicate with children and provide opportunities and support for children to understand, acquire, and use verbal and nonverbal means of communicating thoughts and feelings.

Creative

Provide opportunities that stimulate children to play with sound, rhythm, language, materials, space, and ideas in individual ways to express their creative abilities.

Self

Provide physical and emotional security for each child and help each child to know, accept, and take pride in himself or herself and to develop a sense of independence.

Social

Help each child to feel accepted in the group, help children learn to communicate and get along with others, and encourage feelings of empathy and mutual respect among children and adults.

[*]The Council for Early Childhood Professional Recognition, Washington, D.C.

Guidance

Provide a supportive environment in which children can begin to learn and practice appropriate and acceptable behaviors as individuals and as a group.

Families

Maintain an open, friendly, and cooperative relationship with each child's family, encourage their involvement in the program, and support the child's relationship with his or her family.

Program Management

Use all available resources to ensure an effective operation.

Professionalism

Make decisions based on knowledge of early childhood theories and practices, promote quality in child care services, and take advantage of opportunities to improve competence both for personal and professional growth and for the benefit of children and families.

Bibliography

It would be impossible to list all of the excellent resources for early childhood professionals. Here are some favorites—old and new. Except for the first category, which is relevant to all modules, the books are listed by the module they are most closely tied to; however, many could be listed in more than one category.

General

Ages and Stages, Karen Miller (Marshfield, MA: TelShare, 1985). This clearly written guide describes the stages children pass through as they develop physically, emotionally, and intellectually. Descriptions of children's behavior are accompanied by suggestions on ways teachers can respond so as to encourage growth and development.

The Creative Curriculum for Early Childhood, 3rd Ed., Diane Trister Dodge and Laura J. Colker (Washington, DC: Teaching Strategies, Inc. 1992). This comprehensive curriculum is appropriate for children in preschool and kindergarten. It offers practical strategies based on child development theory for setting the stage and promoting learning in ten interest areas: Blocks, House Corner, Table Toys, Art, Sand and Water, Library, Music and Movement, Cooking, Computers, and Outdoors.

Developmentally Appropriate Practice in Early Childhood Programs Serving Children from Birth Through Age 8, Sue Bredekamp, Ed. (Washington, DC: National Association for the Education of Young Children, 1987). This publication defines standards of quality in programs serving children up to age eight. Included are descriptions of strategies teachers can use to support growth and development.

Developmental Profiles: Pre-Birth Through Eight, 2nd Edition, K. Eileen Allen and Lynn Marotz (Albany, NY: Delmar Publishers, Inc., 1994). Included in this helpful book are a discussion of child development principles and concepts and chapters devoted to each age group. The chapter on the preschooler provides separate developmental profiles and growth patterns for three-, four-, and five-year-old children.

Health and Safety

Caring for Our Children, National Health and Safety Standards: Guidelines for Out-of-Home Child Care Programs, American Public Health Association and American Academy of Pediatrics (Washington, DC and Elk Grove Village, IL 1992). This volume defines the standards and rationale for ensuring children's health and safety in child care programs.

Cup Cooking and Cup Cooking Starter Set, Barbara Johnson and Betty Plemons (Lake Alfred, FL: Early Educators Press, 1985). Children can prepare the single-serving recipes in this book with little assistance from adults. Simple illustrations explain the steps involved in measuring and mixing ingredients.

Healthy Young Children: A Manual for Programs, 1995 Edition, Abby Shapiro Kendrick, Roxane Kaufman, and Katherine P. Messenger, Eds. (Washington, DC: National Association for the Education of Young Children, 1995). This comprehensive manual, includes three separate chapters devoted to maintaining a safe environment, promoting transportation safety, and handling emergencies.

Learning Through Cooking: A Cooking Program for Children Two to Ten, Nancy J. Ferreira (Palo Alto, CA: R & E Research Associates, 1982). This resource offers recipes, explains the skills and concepts learned through cooking, and includes sample forms for planning and evaluating cooking projects.

Model Child Care Health Policies, Pennsylvania Chapter, American Academy of Pediatrics (Washington, DC: National Association for the Education of Young Children, 1993). These model policies provide an excellent starting point for writing health policies. The policies are available on a computer disk so that programs can adapt and reproduce them.

ABCs of Safe and Healthy Child Care, U.S. Department of Health and Human Services, Public Health Service, and Centers for Disease Control (Atlanta, GA: Centers for Disease Control, 1996). Formerly titled, *What You Should Know About Contagious Diseases in Day Care Settings*, this publication contains a practical and descriptive listing of all major childhood illnesses, how they are spread, and measures for prevention.

Learning Environment

Caring Spaces, Learning Places: Children's Environments That Work, Jim Greenman (Redmond, WA: Exchange Press Inc., 1988). This book shows how to set up environments that make creative use of space and respond to children's developmental needs. It is richly illustrated with photographs of children using indoor and outdoor spaces.

Hug a Tree, Robert E. Rockwell, Elizabeth A. Sherwood, and Robert A. Williams (Beltsville, MD: Gryphon House, 1983). Readers of this book will learn to make use of the outdoor environment in a variety of ways. Each outdoor learning experience has a suggested age level, a clear description of the activity, and suggestions for follow-up learning.

The Outside Play and Learning Book, Karen Miller (Beltsville, MD: Gryphon House, 1989). A comprehensive and creative collection of outdoor activities, this book offers practical suggestions for making good use of the outdoor environment in all seasons.

Places and Spaces for Preschool and Primary (Indoors) and *Places and Spaces for Preschool and Primary (Outdoors)*, J. Vergeront (Washington, DC: National Association for the Education of Young Children, 1988). These two books include sketches and patterns for building safe and creative play structures.

Play and Playscapes, Joe L. Frost (Albany, NY: Delmar Press, 1992). The author provides detailed descriptions of a variety of equipment found on playgrounds and explains how to create exciting outdoor environments for young children.

The Right Stuff for Children Birth to 8: Selecting Play Materials to Support Development, Martha B. Bronson (Washington, DC: National Association for the Education of Young Children, 1988). This book is a thorough guide to appropriate play materials. The chapter for preschool and kindergarten children describes typical developmental characteristics and suggests materials to encourage different kinds of activities.

Physical

Easy Woodstuff for Kids, David Thompson (Beltsville, MD: Gryphon House, 1981). This woodworking primer shows how children can be creative using sticks, branches, and wood leftovers and scraps. The book includes detailed instructions for each project.

Feeling Strong, Feeling Free: Movement Exploration for Young Children, Molly Sullivan (Washington, DC: National Association for the Education of Young Children, 1982). This author presents a step-by-step approach to planning movement activities for children up to age eight. She describes the value of movement experiences and how to plan and introduce them to children.

Kid Fitness, Kenneth H. Cooper, M.D., M.P.H. (New York, NY: Bantam Books, 1991). This book focuses on the physical development of children. It includes tips for encouraging children to participate in appropriate fitness activities and follow diets based on good nutrition. Although written for parents, there is much useful information for teachers.

Cognitive

The Complete Block Book, Eugene F. Provenzo, Jr., and Arlene Brett (Syracuse, NY: Syracuse University Press, 1983). This beautifully illustrated book combines the history of blocks with theory and ideas for practical use with children. It includes many photographs of children using blocks.

The Block Book, E. S. Hirsch, Ed. Revised Edition (Washington, DC: National Association for the Education of Young Children, 1996). Newly revised, this illustrated classic describes how and what children can learn using blocks—math concepts, science, social studies, self-awareness, and more.

Earthways, Simple Environmental Activities for Young Children, Carol Petrash (Beltsville, MD: Gryphon House, 1992). Most of the activities presented in this book make use of materials found in nature. Children can learn to understand and value the plants and animals that share their world.

Mudpies to Magnets: A Preschool Science Curriculum and *More Mudpies to Magnets*, Robert A. Williams, Robert E. Rockwell, and Elizabeth A. Sherwood (Beltsville, MD: Gryphon House, 1987 and 1990). Each book describes numerous hands-on science experiments for young children, including clear directions and materials needed.

Scaffolding Children's Learning: Vygotsky and Early Childhood Education, Laura E. Berk and Adam Winsler (Washington, DC: National Association for the Education of Young Children, 1995). This book will be of interest to experienced teachers who want to learn more about Vygotsky's views on child development and how to apply them with children in their classrooms.

Young Children and Computers, Charles Hohmann (Ypsilanti, MI: High/Scope Press, 1990). This book describes developmentally appropriate ways to introduce computers in a preschool classroom. Included are guidelines for selecting software, setting up a computer area, and incorporating computers in the curriculum.

Creative

Dribble-Drabble, Art Experiences for Young Children, Deya Brashears (Fort Collins, CO: DMC Publications, 1985). This is a collection of art activities and recipes appropriate for preschool children.

Growing Up Creative, Teresa Amabile (New York, NY: Crown Publishers, 1989). Written for parents, this book explains Amabile's theories about creativity and offers strategies for encouraging children's creativity.

Kids Create, Laurie Carlson (Charlotte, VT: Williamson Publishing, 1990). This book describes art and craft projects for children ages three through nine. It provides illustrated instructions for a wide variety of activities that allow children to exercise their creativity.

Make Mine Music, Tom Walther (Boston, MA: Little Brown, and Company, 1981). This resource presents the view that everyone can make music. It includes ideas for making musical instruments from materials commonly found in our everyday environment.

Mudworks, Creative Clay, Dough, and Modeling Experiences, Mary Ann Kohl (Bellingham, WA: Bright Ring Publishing, 1989). There are over 100 open-ended ways to engage children in modeling experiences described in this book. The clearly written recipes are presented in a format that gives appropriate guidance to adults.

Please Don't Move the Muffin Tins: A Hands-Off Guide to Art for the Young Child, Bev Bos (Roseville, CA: Turn-the-Page Press, 1984). This is a wonderful collection of developmentally appropriate art experiences for young children.

Preschool Art, It's the Process, Not the Product!, Mary Ann Kohl (Beltsville, MD: Gryphon House, 1994). As the title suggests, this book offers a selection of open-ended art activities that allow children to fully experience the process of creating something rather than the product itself.

Communication

Emerging Literacy, Dorothy S. Strickland and Lesley Mandel Morrow, Eds. (Newark, DE: International Reading Association, 1989). Each of the 12 chapters in this book was written by a different expert on children's literacy development. Learning literacy is presented as a continuous process that begins when parents and providers expose infants to oral and written language and continues throughout childhood.

Literacy Learning in the Early Years, Linda Gibson (New York: Teachers College Press, 1989). This author is a teacher-researcher who combines a theoretical perspective with examples from observations of teachers and children. Learning to read and write is viewed as an ongoing process that begins in infancy. The book's four parts are organized according to age level.

More Than the ABCs: The Early Stages of Reading and Writing, Judith A. Schickendanz (Washington, DC: National Association for the Education of Young Children, 1986). A practical book filled with ideas for organizing the environment so that children experience reading and writing as a meaningful part of their lives.

Story S-t-r-e-t-c-h-e-r-s: Activities to Expand Children's Favorite Books and *More Story S-t-r-e-t-c-h-e-r-s*, Shirley C. Raines and Robert J. Canady (Beltsville, MD: Gryphon House, 1989 and 1991). Filled with activities providers can use to extend children's enjoyment of their favorite books. Five active learning experiences are described for each of 90 books.

Young Children and Picture Books: Literature from Infancy to Six, M.R. Jalongo (Washington, DC: National Association for the Education of Young Children, 1988). An excellent book for teachers on what constitutes high-quality literature and art for young children and how children benefit from good books.

Self, Social, and Guidance

Alike and Different: Exploring Our Humanity with Young Children, Bonnie Neugebauer, Ed. (Washington, DC: National Association for the Education of Young Children, 1992). The articles collected in this book offer thoughtful advice and approaches to meeting the needs of all children. Also addressed are diversity issues related to staffing, living in a changing world, and resources.

Anti-Bias Curriculum: Tools for Empowering Young Children, Louise Derman-Sparks and the A.B.C. Task Force (Washington, DC: National Association for the Education of Young Children, 1989). This book contains many practical suggestions for helping adults understand how we unintentionally convey biases to children and how to minimize, deal with, and even eliminate those biases.

Beyond Self-Esteem: Developing a Genuine Sense of Human Value, Nancy E. Curry and C. N. Johnson (Washington, DC: National Association for the Education of Young Children, 1990). Part I of this book describes how children of different ages develop a sense of self and self-esteem. Part II presents strategies for encouraging children to develop strong, positive identities.

Common Sense Discipline, Grace Mitchell and Lois Dewsnap (Marshfield, MA: TelShare Publishing, 1995). Through real-life stories about children, this book demonstrates a developmentally appropriate approach to guidance. The authors look for the reasons for certain behaviors and suggest individualized strategies parents and teachers can use to promote self-discipline.

Early Violence Prevention, Tools for Teachers of Young Children, Ronald G. Slaby, Wendy C. Roedell, Diana Arezzo, and Kate Hendrix (Washington, DC: National Association for the Education of Young Children, 1995). This book combines research results with teaching guidelines to help prevent violent behaviors in young children. It presents techniques for helping children understand their feelings and provides alternatives to aggression, such as conflict resolution.

First Feelings, Milestones in the Emotional Development of Your Baby and Child, Stanley Greenspan (New York: Viking Penguin, Inc., 1985). Dr. Greenspan, child psychiatrist and author, reviews the stages of normal emotional development for children. He offers suggestions for parents on how to handle typical problems and challenges. Teachers can adapt these strategies in their work with young children.

Greater Expectations: Overcoming the Culture of Indulgence in America's Homes and Schools, William Damon (New York: The Free Press, 1995). Written in response to what the author believes has been an overemphasis on misguided efforts to promote self-esteem, Damon advocates providing children with meaningful challenges, moral guidance, and opportunities to serve others. He stresses the importance of the quality of interactions between adults and children.

Parents, Please Don't Sit on the Kids, Clare Cherry (Belmont, CA: David S. Lake Publishers, 1985). The author offers practical suggestions for guiding children's behavior. She explains why some techniques work with young children and others do not.

Roots and Wings: Affirming Culture in Early Childhood Programs, Stacy York (Minneapolis: Redleaf Press, 1991). This resource defines a framework for multicultural education and shows how it is related to quality early childhood programs. The author defines the stages through which children pass as they become aware of differences and develop prejudices. She discusses the effects of prejudice on young children from diverse cultures.

Starting School: From Separation to Independence, Nancy Balaban (New York: Teachers College Press, 1985). This book explains how children experience and cope with separation and provides practical suggestions for supporting children and families in the child care setting.

Teaching Young Children in Violent Times: Building a Peaceable Classroom, Diane E. Levin (Cambridge, MA: Educators for Social Responsibility, 1994). This very practical resource is filled with ideas for creating classrooms where preschool through third grade children can learn peaceful alternatives to the violent behaviors they see in the media and in real life.

Your Child's Self-Esteem, Dorothy Corkille Briggs (Garden City, NY: Dolphin Books, 1975). This early childhood classic focuses on the importance of self-image, how it develops, and how adults can support children's self-esteem.

Families

A Parent's Guide to Early Childhood Education, Diane Trister Dodge and Joanna Phinney (Washington, DC: Teaching Strategies, Inc., 1990). Written for parents and available in English, Spanish, and Chinese, this booklet can help teachers explain to families how children learn through developmentally appropriate preschool experiences.

Teacher-Parent Relationships, Jeannette Galambos-Stone (Washington, DC: National Association for the Education of Young Children, 1987). This book provides useful strategies for building relationships between teachers and families. The author describes how the relationship grows and changes over time and discusses how to handle common problems in supportive ways.

Program Management

The Crisis Manual for Early Childhood Teachers, Karen Miller (Beltsville, MD: Gryphon House, 1995). This comprehensive resource begins by defining the role of teachers in responding to crises that affect children and families. Subsequent chapters describe resources and strategies for specific types of crisis. The final section addresses how teachers can plan a curriculum that can respond to crises.

Emergent Curriculum, Elizabeth Jones and John Nimmo (Washington, DC: National Association for the Education of Young Children, 1994). This book illustrates the curriculum planning process by telling the story of a year in an early childhood classroom. Using this approach, the authors create a vivid picture of teachers planning a program that reflects individual and developmental goals for children.

Observing the Development of the Young Child, Janice J. Beaty (Columbus, OH: Charles E. Merrill, 1986). This book focuses on observing six major aspects of development—social, emotional, physical, cognitive, language, and creative—in children ages two through six. It includes a skills checklist with specific behaviors that teachers can observe.

Observing and Recording the Behavior of Young Children, 3rd ed. (New York: Teachers College Press, 1983). Observing is the key to understanding individual children and planning ways to respond. This classic provides an excellent introduction to the purposes and techniques of observing children in all areas of development.

A Place for Me: Including Children with Special Needs in Early Childhood Programs, P. Chandler (Washington, DC: National Association for the Education of Young Children, 1994). This book allows teachers to acknowledge and address their feelings about the challenges of caring for children with special needs. The book also provides practical ideas for working with parents, preparing the environment, and helping all children appreciate themselves and others.

The Portfolio and Its Use: Developmentally Appropriate Assessment of Young Children, Cathy Grace and Elizabeth F. Shores (Little Rock: Southern Association on Children Under Six, 1992). This book discusses why portfolios are a developmentally appropriate method for assessing young children's progress, defines the contents of a typical portfolio, and explains how portfolios can be used for evaluation and for communication with families.

Engaging Children's Minds: The Project Approach, Lilian G. Katz and Sylvia C. Chard (Washington, DC: National Association for the Education of Young Children, 1989). This overview of the project approach—a teaching technique that encourages children to conduct an in-depth study of a specific topic—will help teachers address children's skills, backgrounds, and interests in the planning process.

Reaching Potentials: Appropriate Curriculum and Assessment for Young Children, Volume I, Sue Bredekamp, Ed. (Washington, DC: National Association for the Education of Young Children, 1992). This volume presents the NAEYC curriculum and assessment guidelines and discusses how to use them in screening and assessment and for curriculum planning. Separate chapters describe strategies for helping children with special needs, minority children, and linguistically diverse children reach their potential.

Professionalism

*A to Z: The Early Childhood Educator's Guide to the Interne*t, ERIC Clearinghouse on Elementary and Early Childhood Education (Urbana, IL: University of Illinois, 1996). This guide was written for early childhood professionals to explain the benefits of using the Internet to share ideas, solve problems, and learn about resources on working with children and families. Readers learn how to use Internet mail groups and sites for early childhood educators and how to use ERIC on the Internet.

Beginner's Bibliography—1994, Carol Copple, Ed. (Washington, DC: National Association for the Education of Young Children, 1994). This is an annotated list of recommended resources for teachers of young children.

Ethical Behavior in Early Childhood Education, Expanded Edition, Lilian G. Katz and Evangeline H. Ward (Washington, DC: National Association for the Education of Young Children, 1991). This book includes descriptions of dilemmas faced by teachers and the NAEYC Code of Ethics. Teachers can use the situations described to start discussions about how to handle difficult situations at their programs.

Speaking Out: Early Childhood Advocacy, Stacie G. Goffin and Joan Lombardi (Washington, DC: National Association for the Education of Young Children, 1988). This resource helps demystify advocacy by providing practical ideas and examples of ways to influence policies for children, families, and professionals who work with children.

Publishers and Distributors of Resources

The following organizations are publishers and distributors of resources for early childhood professionals. Write or call to receive copies of their most recent catalogs.

Association for Childhood Education International (ACEI), 11501 Georgia Avenue, Suite 315, Wheaton, MD 20902, (1-800-423-3563). ACEI offers resources and support for meeting the developmental needs of children from infancy through early adolescence.

Bank Street Bookstore, Bank Street College of Education, 610 West 112th Street, New York, NY 10025 (1-800-724-1486). Through its catalog, the college bookstore offers a broad selection of materials, organized by curriculum themes that are appropriate for young children.

Creative Education Surplus, 1000 Apollo Road, Eagen, MN 55121 (1-800-886-6428). This is a good source for a wide variety of surplus items children can use for crafts and other projects.

Educational Resources Information Center (ERIC) Clearinghouse on Elementary and Early Childhood Education, University of Illinois, 805 West Pennsylvania Avenue, Urbana, IL 61801-4897 (1-800-583-4135). ERIC provides information on the development, care, and education of children birth through early adolescence through database, information services, publications, and the Internet.

Gryphon House, P. O. Box 207, Beltsville, MD 20704-0207 (1-800-638-0928). This company publishes and distributes resources for child care professionals and books for young children.

Kaplan Companies, 1310 Lewis Clemmons Road, Lewisville, NC 27023 (1-800-452-7526). This company distributes equipment, supplies, and print and audiovisual resources for early childhood professionals.

National Association for the Education of Young Children (NAEYC), 1509 16th Street, NW, Washington, DC 20036-1426 (1-800-424-2460). NAEYC publishes numerous reasonably-priced resources on topics of interest to teachers. If you join NAEYC, you will receive their journal, *Young Children*, which has a wealth of articles on caring for children ages birth through eight.

Redleaf Press, Resources for Child Caring, 450 North Syndicate, Suite 5, St. Paul, MN 55104-4125 (1-800-423-8309). This organization offers a wide variety of resources on general and specific child care topics.

Teachers College Press, Teachers College, Columbia University, New York, NY 10027 (1-800-575-6566). This press publishes and distributes books, videos, and assessment tools for early childhood professionals.

Teaching Strategies, Inc., P.O. Box 42243, Washington, DC 20015 (1-800-637-3652). Teaching Strategies publishes this book as well as a complete range of curriculum and training materials for programs serving children from birth through middle childhood.

Self-Assessment

Competencies	I Do This:	Regularly	Sometimes	Not Enough

1. Safe

a. Maintaining indoor and outdoor environments that reduce and prevent accidents and injuries ☐ ☐ ☐

b. Planning for and responding to accidents and injuries ☐ ☐ ☐

c. Helping children develop habits that reduce and prevent accidents and injuries ☐ ☐ ☐

2. Healthy

a. Maintaining indoor and outdoor environments that promote wellness and reduce the spread of disease ☐ ☐ ☐

b. Helping children develop habits that promote good hygiene and nutrition ☐ ☐ ☐

c. Recognizing and reporting child abuse and neglect ☐ ☐ ☐

3. Learning Environment

a. Organizing indoor and outdoor areas that encourage play and exploration ☐ ☐ ☐

b. Selecting and attractively displaying materials and equipment ☐ ☐ ☐

c. Planning and implementing a schedule, routines, and transitions that meet children's needs ☐ ☐ ☐

Competencies	I Do This Regularly	Sometimes	Not Enough

4. Physical

a. Providing materials, equipment, and opportunities for gross motor development ☐ ☐ ☐

b. Providing materials and opportunities for fine motor development ☐ ☐ ☐

c. Reinforcing and encouraging children's physical fitness ☐ ☐ ☐

5. Cognitive

a. Creating an environment that encourages children to explore and discover ☐ ☐ ☐

b. Interacting with children in ways that help them develop confidence in their ability to think and solve problems ☐ ☐ ☐

c. Providing opportunities for children to construct knowledge about their world ☐ ☐ ☐

6. Communication

a. Encouraging children to listen and speak ☐ ☐ ☐

b. Helping children use language in meaningful ways ☐ ☐ ☐

c. Providing materials and experiences that support emerging literacy skills ☐ ☐ ☐

Competencies	I Do This:	Regularly	Sometimes	Not Enough

7. Creative

a. Arranging the environment to encourage exploration and experimentation ☐ ☐ ☐

b. Offering a variety of materials and activities that promote self-expression ☐ ☐ ☐

c. Interacting with children in ways that encourage and and respect original ideas and expressions ☐ ☐ ☐

8. Self

a. Developing a positive and supportive relationship with each child ☐ ☐ ☐

b. Helping children accept and appreciate themselves and others ☐ ☐ ☐

c. Providing opportunities for children to be successful and feel competent ☐ ☐ ☐

9. Social

a. Helping children learn to get along with others ☐ ☐ ☐

b. Helping children understand and express their feelings and respect those of others ☐ ☐ ☐

c. Providing an environment and experiences that help children develop social skills ☐ ☐ ☐

Competencies	**I Do This:**	**Regularly**	**Sometimes**	**Not Enough**

10. Guidance

a. Providing an environment that encourages self-discipline ☐ ☐ ☐

b. Using positive methods to guide individual children ☐ ☐ ☐

c. Helping children understand and express their feelings in acceptable ways ☐ ☐ ☐

11. Families

a. Communicating frequently with parents to share information about their child's experiences and development ☐ ☐ ☐

b. Offering a variety of ways for parents to participate in their child's life at the program ☐ ☐ ☐

c. Providing support to families ☐ ☐ ☐

12. Program Management

a. Learning about each child's culture, language, family, skills, needs, and interests ☐ ☐ ☐

b. Working as a team to offer an individualized program ☐ ☐ ☐

c. Following administrative policies and procedures ☐ ☐ ☐

Competencies

	I Do This:	Regularly	Sometimes	Not Enough

13. Professionalism

a. Continually assessing your own performance ☐ ☐ ☐

b. Continuing to learn about caring for children ☐ ☐ ☐

c. Applying professional ethics at all times ☐ ☐ ☐

Module Completion Plan

Review your responses to the self-assessment with your trainer. What do you feel are your strengths, interests, and needs? Decide which areas you would like to work on first. Select three modules to begin with and set target dates for their completion. (Your trainer can let you know how much work is involved for each module.) Record the module titles and target completion dates below. You may also wish to determine a tentative schedule for completing *Caring for Preschool Children*.

Module	Target Completion Date

Tentative schedule for completion of the *Caring for Preschool Children* Training Program:

Module	Date

Teacher	Date	Trainer	Date

Overview

Keeping children safe involves:

- Maintaining indoor and outdoor environments that reduce and prevent accidents and injuries
- Planning for and responding to accidents and injuries
- Helping children develop habits that reduce and prevent accidents and injuries

---

Adults feel safe when they are in control of situations. Knowing how to prevent accidents and injuries and what to do if accidents and injuries occur helps adults feel in control.

Adults and children feel safe when they are in control.

To feel safe, children must trust adults to see that no harm comes to them, and to know what to do when accidents occur. As children become more independent, they learn that they can take steps to control their environment. As a result, they are better able to explore their world safely.

Risk-taking is common among preschoolers who have learned to trust their environment. Their sense of independence and initiative makes them eager to participate in activities without direct adult supervision. Many preschool children try to challenge themselves, their parents, and their teachers. Because risk-taking may lead to accidents, children need help to pursue these challenges safely. Accidents are the leading cause of death among children. However, national studies indicate that 95 percent of these accidents are preventable.

Preschool children often take risks.

As a teacher, you have a professional responsibility to keep children safe. As stated in the Code of Ethical Conduct of the National Association for the Education of Young Children (NAEYC) (Principle 1.1):[1]

Teachers are responsible for protecting children.

> Above all we shall not harm children. We shall not participate in practices that are disrespectful, degrading, dangerous, exploitive, intimidating, psychologically damaging, or physically harmful to children.

There are three ways in which teachers can help keep children safe. First, you can create and maintain classroom and outdoor areas that are free from conditions that might cause accidents or injuries. These play spaces should provide structure and clear limits so active preschoolers can safely explore and take risks. Secondly, you can—and should—become familiar with your program's established procedures to ensure children's safety on a daily basis and during emergencies. When you

---

[1] Stephanie Feeney and Kenneth Kipnis. *Code of Ethical Conduct and Statement of Commitment.* Washington, D.C.: NAEYC, 1990, p.5.

follow these procedures in a calm manner during drills and actual emergencies, you help children learn how to keep themselves safe. Third, as you guide children to be self-disciplined individuals who can solve problems and think ahead, you help them develop habits that promote their own safety. For example, they learn how to use materials and equipment safely and anticipate what might happen if they don't.

Listed on the following pages are three sets of examples showing how teachers demonstrate their competence in keeping children safe. Following each set of examples is a short reading and two questions to answer. When you have finished this section, compare your answers with those on the answer sheet at the end of the module. If your answers are different, discuss them with your trainer. There can be more than one good answer.

Maintaining Indoor and Outdoor Environments That Reduce and Prevent Accidents and Injuries

Check indoor and outdoor areas daily and remove any hazardous materials.

Follow recommended adult-child ratios of 1:8 for a group of 16 or 1:9 for a group of 18 preschoolers.

Check daily to see that all electrical outlets are covered and electrical cords are placed away from water, traffic paths, and children's reach.

Check materials and equipment daily for broken parts, loose bolts, or jagged edges; make sure that imperfect materials and equipment are repaired or replaced.

Arrange the room so that there are no long or open spaces that tempt children to run and so that there are clear fire exits.

Check safety equipment monthly to ensure it is in an easy-to-reach place and in good condition.

Work with colleagues to supervise all children at all times.

Ms. Kim notices three-year-old Jill across the room climbing on a box. It is sagging with her weight. "Ms. Richards," Ms. Kim says, alerting the teacher on that side of the room. Quickly, Ms. Richards moves to Jill's side. "Jill," she says, calmly, "I'm going to help you climb down off that box. It isn't a safe place for climbing, because it isn't strong enough to hold you. I am going to put this box away so children won't climb on it. Do you want to help me?" Jill and Ms. Richards carry the box to the closet. "Thank you for helping make our room safer," says Ms. Richards. "Now, would you like to climb on the climber? It's a good place for climbing."

1. **How did Ms. Kim and Ms. Richards work together to make the program safer?**

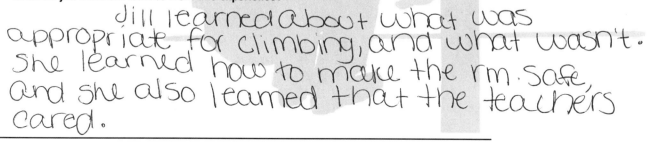

ms. Kim made ms. Richards aware of Jill, and ms. Richards went over to Jill. ms. Richards calmly spoke to Jill and helped her down.

2. **What do you think Jill learned from this experience?**

Jill learned about what was appropriate for climbing, and what wasn't. She learned how to make the rm. safe, and she also learned that the teachers cared.

Responding to Accidents and Emergencies

Develop and post accident and emergency procedures.

Make sure the telephone is easy to reach and is working properly.

Know where to find parents' emergency telephone numbers.

Respond quickly and calmly to children in distress.

Maintain current emergency information on all children.

Know and follow established procedures for leading children to safety during fire and other hazard drills and in real emergencies.

Mr. Lopez and his group of four-year-olds are walking into the building when Andy trips and scrapes his knee. "You scraped your knee a little," explains Mr. Lopez as he helps Andy to his feet. When they get back to the room, Mr. Lopez takes Andy to the office while Ms. Thomas and a volunteer stay with the other children. They get the first-aid kit off the shelf. Mr. Lopez opens the kit and reviews the chart taped to the inside lid that describes how to treat minor injuries. Mr. Lopez puts on latex gloves, then washes Andy's knee with soap and water. Andy winces. "You're being brave," says Mr. Lopez. "I know this stings a bit, but your knee needs to be clean so it will heal." At Andy's request, he puts a bandage on the scrape. Andy helps stick it in place. Finally, Mr. Lopez takes Andy back to the room. "You're all set and ready to play again," he says. He fills out an accident report form and writes a note on the daily chart so at the end of the day he will remember to tell Andy's parents to read and sign the accident report.

1. **How did Mr. Lopez know what to do?**

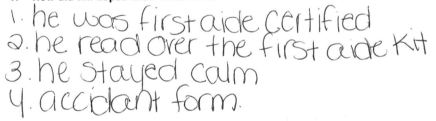

1. he was first aide certified
2. he read over the first aide kit
3. he stayed calm
4. accidant form.

2. **What did Mr. Lopez do to reassure Andy?**

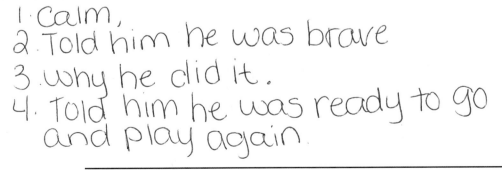

1. calm,
2. Told him he was brave
3. why he did it.
4. Told him he was ready to go and play again

Helping Children Develop Safe Habits

Take safety precautions in a calm and reassuring manner without overprotecting children or making them fearful.

"Carlos, the pecan shells are splintering when you smash them and might hurt someone. Use the hammer for wood."

Convey to children in actions and words that the program is a safe place and that they will be protected.

"Judson, I'll stand next to the slide if that will help you feel better about going down."

Involve children in making safety rules for indoor and outdoor equipment, materials, and activities.

"Before we use our new loft we need to make some rules for climbing and jumping safely."

Remind children of safety rules and emergency procedures using diagrams, pictures, and words.

"Hold your funnel over the water table so the water doesn't spill. Someone might slip and fall if the floor gets wet."

Demonstrate proper ways to use potentially dangerous materials and equipment.

"I'm cutting with a sharp knife, so I make sure my other hand is away from the blade."

Teach children how to observe safety when taking neighborhood walks and field trips.

"Let's make sure everyone has a partner and knows which group they are in for our trip."

Use positive guidance techniques to respond immediately when children are involved in unsafe activities.

"It hurts Teresa when you drive into her ankles. If you want to pass, ask her to please move onto the grass."

Point out potential hazards so children will learn how to prevent accidents.

"Roxanne, please help me trim the loose strings on the edge of this rug so nobody gets a foot caught and trips."

Five-year-old Kirsten builds a structure as high as her head. "I want to build my house bigger than I am," she says to the other children in the block area. Ms. Williams hears Kirsten's announcement and walks to the block area. "None of the children have built a building taller than they are, yet, Kirsten. Let's talk about how to do that safely," she says. "It's only a problem if someone knocks it and it falls," says Kirsten. "I know!" volunteers Amanda, "Take some tape and make a circle around the building so no one gets too close. Then it won't fall." "Good problem solving," says Ms. Williams. "You'll have to let the other children know." They decide that they need to write a "Safety in the Block Area" chart, with pictures and words, so all will know the guidelines. Kirsten says, "We can talk about what to put on our safety chart at group time today."

1. **How did Ms. Williams let the children know that the program is a safe place?**

   Circle around the block structure. Discussed what to do.

2. **How were the children learning to keep themselves safe?**

   By putting up a tape, and sign.

Your Own Need for Safety

Feeling safe is a basic human need.

Everyone needs to feel safe. When we know that we are protected from harm, we can function well. Safe environments make us feel secure, relaxed, confident, and able to enjoy ourselves. When we do not feel protected, we may be fearful and anxious.

The increasing violence in many communities today, especially random, unpredictable violence makes many of us feel unsafe. Children have the same fears as adults. They see violence on television and too often experience it in their homes and neighborhoods. Safety is an important issue for everyone.

When you are in charge of your environment, you can make it a safer one. You probably have experienced times when you were doing something that was potentially dangerous, and you did things to make that activity safer. Do you remember times when you:

- climbed a ladder while someone held it to keep it stable;

- parked your car at night in a well-lit area of the shopping mall; or

- carefully unplugged a lamp with a frayed cord and had the wiring replaced?

Learning about safety begins in childhood.

You have learned about safety through experience. When you were a child, the important adults in your life may have controlled your environment to keep it safe and helped you develop habits concerning safety. As you grew older, you learned what you could do to minimize dangerous situations.

Think of a situation where you didn't feel safe and describe it below.

What could you have done to reduce or prevent an accident or injury?

What can you learn from this experience that will help you keep children safe?

As you work through this module you will learn how to set up and maintain a safe environment. Safety is important in all aspects of your work with young children—whether you are guiding learning, encouraging creativity, or promoting self-discipline. Keeping children safe is one of your most important responsibilities.

When you have finished this overview section, complete the pre-training assessment. Refer to the glossary at the end of this module if you need definitions of the terms used.

Pre-Training Assessment

Listed below are the skills that teachers use to make sure children are safe. Think about whether you do these things regularly, sometimes, or not enough. Place a check in one of the boxes on the right for each skill listed. Then discuss your answers with your trainer.

Maintaining Indoor and Outdoor Environments That Reduce and Prevent Accidents and Injuries

	I Do This:	Regularly	Sometimes	Not Enough
1.	Check indoor and outdoor areas daily and remove any hazardous materials.	☒	☐	☐
2.	Follow required recommended adult-child ratios of 1:8 for a group of 16 or 1:9 for a group of 18 preschoolers.	☒	☐	☐
3.	Check daily to see that all electrical outlets are covered and electrical cords are placed away from water, traffic paths, and children's reach.	☒	☐	☐
4.	Check materials and equipment daily for broken parts, loose bolts, or jagged edges and make sure they are repaired or replaced.	☒	☐	☐
5.	Arrange the room so that there are no long or open spaces that tempt children to run and so that there are clear fire exits.	☐	☒	☐
6.	Check safety equipment monthly to ensure it is in an easy-to-reach place and in good condition.	☒	☐	☐
7.	Work with colleagues to supervise all children at all times.	☒	☐	☐
8.	Develop and post accident and emergency procedures.	☒	☐	☐

Responding To Accidents and Emergencies

	I Do This:	Regularly	Sometimes	Not Enough
9.	Make sure the telephone is easy to reach and is working properly.	☒	☐	☐
10.	Know where to find parents' emergency telephone numbers.	☒	☐	☐
11.	Respond quickly and calmly to children in distress.	☒	☐	☐
12.	Maintain current emergency information on all children.	☒	☐	☐
13.	Know and follow established procedures for leading children to safety during a fire and other hazard drills and in real emergencies.	☒	☐	☐

Helping Children Develop Safe Habits

		Regularly	Sometimes	Not Enough
14.	Take safety precautions in a calm and reassuring manner without overprotecting children to make them fearful.	☒	☐	☐
15.	Convey to children in actions and words that the program is a safe place and that they will be protected.	☒	☐	☐
16.	Involve children in making safety rules for indoor and outdoor equipment, materials, and activities.	☒	☐	☐
17.	Remind children of safety rules and emergency procedures using diagrams, pictures, and words.	☒	☐	☐

Helping Children Develop Safe Habits

(continued)

	I Do This:	Regularly	Sometimes	Not Enough
18. Demonstrate proper ways to use potentially dangerous materials and equipment.		☐	☒	☐
19. Teach children how to observe safety rules when taking neighborhood walks and field trips.		☒	☐	☐
20. Use positive guidance techniques to respond immediately when children are involved in unsafe activities.		☒	☐	☐
21. Point out potential hazards so children will learn how to prevent accidents.		☒	☐	☐

Review your responses, then list three to five skills you would like to improve or topics you would like to learn more about. When you finish this module, you can list examples of your new or improved knowledge and skills.

I need to Demonstrate proper ways of using dangerous material & Equipment w/ the children because I usually try and just keep the children away from those things.

Arranging rooms are difficult for me, because I don't know how much room to give them, or how much room, is too much or too little.

Begin the learning activities for Module 1, Safe.

Learning Activities

I. Using Your Knowledge of Child Development to Keep Children Safe

---

In this activity you will learn to:

- Recognize some typical behaviors of preschool children
- Use what you know about children to keep them safe

Almost every new activity has an element of risk, and almost every risk can be minimized through preparation and anticipation of potential hazards. Early childhood teachers have dual, and sometimes conflicting, responsibilities to children. They must keep them safe while also providing challenges that encourage development of cognitive, socio-emotional, and physical skills. Whether selecting materials, arranging the environment, guiding learning, or responding to accidents and injuries, teachers must think of ways to encourage children to take risks, while at the same time showing them how to do so safely. To carry out these responsibilities successfully, teachers think about what preschool children are like, what they can do, and what skills they are still developing.

Teachers can help children learn how to take risks safely.

You can expect preschoolers to run, climb, and jump whenever they have a chance to do so. Sometimes they will perform these actions on a dare: "Who can jump farthest . . . run fastest . . . climb highest?" To prevent accidents, you and your colleagues need to work together to make sure that active play areas are continually supervised. Daily and monthly safety checks will help you maintain an uncluttered environment, free from potentially dangerous items, and with plenty of room for children to move their bodies. In addition, children will be less likely to run inside, jump off tables, or climb on shelves when the daily schedule offers time for active play, both indoors and out.

You can prevent accidents through supervision and regular safety checks.

Most preschoolers enjoy playing and working with others. However, social interactions take a lot of energy, especially for the younger preschoolers who may have little experience with group life. Accidents tend to happen when children are tired from active play, long activities, or from being in a large group or a noisy room. You can arrange the day's activities to keep children from becoming too tired. Alternate vigorous activities with more quiet ones. When you see that a child seems weary, suggest a quiet play activity so the child can recoup lost energy.

Tired children are more likely to have accidents.

Preschool children show a lot of initiative—they are curious learners who are trying to make sense of their world. To find out how things work, children take objects apart and put them back together; they may use materials in ways other than intended. Look for toys and other materials that are well-constructed and durable enough to withstand children's play and explorations.

Select materials with children's safety in mind.

Preschoolers can use their thinking skills to learn safe ways to play.

Preschoolers can make plans and think before acting, but frequently forget to do so. Although they are beginning to understand cause and effect, they may not consider what might happen if they ride a tricycle too fast, climb up the slide, or splash water on the floor under the sink. Teachers can help children think about keeping themselves safe by asking them to help make safety rules; offering frequent and positive reminders of rules and limits; and asking questions that help children understand how accidents happen: "What might happen if . . .?" "Why do you think you fell . . .?" "What can we do . . . ?"

Some other strategies for encouraging preschool children to think about taking risks safely include the following.

- Stand near the equipment children are using and praise the children's safe actions. "Tricia, you remembered how to stay safe. You looked to make sure nobody was in the way and you said, 'I'm going to jump.'"

- Provide constant, close supervision over active games and for activities such as cooking and woodworking that involve use of potentially hazardous equipment.

- Participate with the children, not in conversations with other teachers.

- Step in quickly to turn unsafe practices into safe ones: "Use the step stool, not the table." "Hold the knife by the handle, not the blade."

Applying Your Knowledge

The chart on the next page lists some typical behaviors of children in the preschool years, ages three to five. Included are behaviors relevant to children's safety. The right column asks you to identify ways that teachers can use this information about child development to keep children safe. Try to think of as many examples as you can. As you work through the module you will learn new strategies for keeping children safe, and you can add them to the chart. You are not expected to think of all the examples at one time. If you need help getting started, turn to the completed chart at the end of the module. By the time you complete all the learning activities, you will find that you have learned many ways to keep children safe.

Using Your Knowledge of Child
Development to Keep Children Safe

What Preschool Children Are Like	How Teachers Can Use This Information to Keep Children Safe
They have lots of energy and run, hop, and jump.	*Set up the indoor and outdoor areas so children can move freely without bumping into each other or the furniture and equipment. Limit running to the outdoor area or a supervised hallway and offer frequent, positive reminders: "Walk inside". Provide energy outlets indoors such as a climber or a movement activity.*
They may have accidents when they are tired or over-excited.	rotate w/ activities. one activity could be loud, and exciting but the next activity should be a quiet one to relax the children.
They ride tricycles and other moving equipment.	make sure they know to watch where they are going, so they don't run other children over. & I always make sure shoes are tied so they don't get caught on the peddles.
They slide, swing, and climb on equipment. *Safety zones cushioning inspect equip.*	make sure rules are known: Slide, 1. 1 at a time going down the slide, and don't go up the slide just down. 2. Don't walk in front of the swings, when someone is on it. 3. Be careful climbing.
They throw, kick, and catch objects.	Don't kick or throw objects where other children are playing. Before swinging a bat, make sure nobody is near you. make sure the balls are soft, so nobody gets hurt.

Using Your Knowledge of Child Development to Keep Children Safe

What Preschool Children Are Like	How Teachers Can Use This Information to Keep Children Safe
They can use tools such as knives, scissors, and woodworking equipment. *supervision, storage, safety equip.*	Show the children how to use them the correct way. How to walk w/ scissors & a knife are also important.
They perform toileting routines independently. *clean spills*	Children need to flush the toilet, and wash their hands properly afterwards. w/ soap + dry them w/ paper towel
They begin to understand cause and effect. *what if*	Let the children experience these things on their own, but be next to them to make sure they are alright.
They like to take risks and face challenges. *set limits praise*	You also need to let the children experience these but you need to protect them, so be close by, and make sure things are safe by them.
They poke, handle, and squeeze objects to discover what they are and what they can do. *storage, inspect toys, equip.*	make sure they are safe, and let the children experience new things.

When you have completed as much as you can do on the chart, discuss your answers with your trainer. As you proceed with the rest of the learning activities, you can refer back to the chart and add examples of how teachers keep children safe.

II. Creating and Maintaining a Safe Environment

In this activity you will learn to:

- Set up indoor and outdoor environments that are safe for preschool children
- Use daily and monthly safety checklists to identify potential hazards in the indoor and outdoor areas

---

One of the most effective ways to keep children safe is to provide a safe environment. Your choice of toys, materials, and equipment and the way you arrange your space can prevent and reduce accidents and injuries.

Creating a safe environment can prevent accidents.

In setting up a safe environment, you must be prepared for the unexpected. Because children don't always think ahead and see the consequences of their actions, you have to do it for them as you set up your space.

Providing sufficient space for children's play and activities is clearly the first step in providing a safe environment. *The National Health and Safety Performance Standards, Guidelines for Out-of-Home Child Care Programs,*[2] suggests a minimum of 35 square feet per child that is free of furniture and equipment. This usually translates to a minimum of 50 square feet per child, measured wall-to-wall, not including space dedicated to sick child care, offices, staff rooms, halls, the kitchen, and so on. Some of the other safety requirements found in *The Guidelines* include the following.

Know the guidelines for keeping children safe.

- Closets that are accessible to children must have an internal release mechanism that can be opened by a child inside the closet.

- Bathroom doors should be fitted with hardware so that the doors can be opened from both inside and outside.

- Strings or cords on window shades or blinds that are within children's reach must be less than six inches in length to prevent strangulation.

- Plastic bags and Styrofoam must be stored out of children's reach to prevent choking and suffocation.

- Carpeting should be clean, in good repair, nonflammable, and nontoxic.

- Furniture used by children should be durable and child-sized.

---

[2] *National Health and Safety Performance Standards, Guidelines for Out-of-Home Child Care Programs*, a joint collaborative project of the American Public Health Association and the American Academy of Pediatrics, supported by Maternal and Child Health Bureau, Department of Health and Human Services, published by National Center for Education in Maternal and Child Health, Arlington, VA, 1992.

- A-B-C type fire extinguishers should be clearly visible. Instructions for use should be posted on the unit or nearby. All staff should learn how to use the extinguishers.

- Properly functioning smoke detectors should be installed 6 to 12 inches below the ceiling and 40 feet apart; batteries must be less than one year old.

- Exits and escape paths should be easy to see and free from any items that obstruct traffic.

- Steps and footstools should be nonslip, with steps no higher than the user's knee.

- Teachers should assume that all plants are potentially poisonous and place them out of children's reach. They should contact the poison control center to learn whether a specific plant is poisonous.

Ask your supervisor for information on your program's guidelines for environmental safety and the licensing requirements that your program must meet. Many of these requirements are designed to keep preschoolers safe.

Consider these tips for making indoor interest areas and activities safe.

When setting up the interest areas in your room, use low dividers or shelves so you and your colleagues can easily see all children at all times. Display and store materials on low, open shelves, not in chests with heavy lids that can fall on children. Place heavy toys on bottom shelves so children won't pull down heavy items on themselves. Make sure each area has enough room for children to engage in the kinds of activities that take place there. Create clear traffic paths so children don't get in each other's way. Provide a sufficient quantity of safe, developmentally appropriate play materials so children do not have to wait for a long time to use desired items. Regularly examine toys, furniture, and equipment to make sure they are:

- sturdy

- in good repair (no loose parts or chipped paint)

- nonflammable

- nontoxic

- free of sharp edges, points, corners, and splinters

- unbreakable

- free of paint containing lead or other poisonous materials

- hypo-allergenic

- free of small removable parts (with diameters less than 1-1/4 inches) that children might swallow

The following suggestions apply to individual interest areas.

Sand and water: Locate away from electrical outlets and cords. Use newspapers, drop cloths, or towels to control spills; have a mop, towels, and sponges nearby; limit the number of children using the area at one time.

House corner: Set up so the wall(s), shelves, and furniture create three sides. Remove drawstrings and shorten sleeves and hems of adult clothes so children don't get caught or trip while walking. Check furniture regularly to make sure it is in good repair.

Cooking: Set up near a source of water and a fire extinguisher. Use a work surface that is at children's level. Regularly check the cords and functioning of electric appliances and place them near outlets. Teach children safe ways to use child-sized knives and closely supervise activities.

Woodworking: Open this area only when a teacher is available to offer close supervision to a very small group of children. Provide sturdy, real tools that children can use with success, and have children wear safety goggles.

Blocks: Enclose on three sides. If you locate the block area in a corner you have two sides enclosed and just need a shelf. Set up in a large space with a level floor, preferably, covered with indoor-outdoor carpeting. Place tape on the floor to define a "no building zone." Store blocks on low, open, labeled shelves with the largest ones on the bottom. Set and post guidelines for the height of structures.

Table toys: Make sure all play materials meet the standards set by the U.S. Consumer Product Safety Commission—no sharp points or edges, no pieces small enough to be swallowed, and no pieces that can be used as projectiles. Use labeled storage containers so children can easily put items away. Teach children to check the floor regularly so they don't trip over small items such as loose beads or Legos.

Art: Locate near a source of water. Adjust open easels to children's height and fasten them securely. Use nontoxic supplies only. Store scissors with the points facing down. Provide sponges and towels for wiping up spills. Art materials should be certified as safe by organizations such as The Art and Craft Materials Institute.

Whether you use an outdoor play area at your program or a neighborhood park, it must have certain features that promote the safety of preschool children. The following list describes characteristics of safe playgrounds. [3]

- A fence encloses the area, is in good repair, and is free of splinters.

- Traffic paths are clearly defined and separate from other areas.

[3] Based on Collins Management Consulting, Inc., *Head Start Facilities Manual* (Washington, DC: Department of Health and Human Services), 1995) pp. 25-26 and 48-49; and Diane Trister Dodge and Laura J. Colker, *The Creative Curriculum for Early Childhood, Third Edition* (Washington, DC: Teaching Strategies, Inc., 1992) pp. 338-340.

- The area drains well.

- The area has 80 to 100 square feet per child.

- Bathrooms and a telephone are located nearby.

- The area is arranged so teachers can see all the children, all the time.

- The area is arranged so all children, including those with mobility impairments, can move about safely and participate fully.

- Equipment is securely anchored to the ground.

- Each piece of equipment is surrounded by a 6-foot wide safety zone.

- Equipment is in good repair and free of splinters, rough surfaces, frayed cables, worn ropes, and chains that could pinch.

- There are 10 to 12 inches of shock-absorbing cushioning (wood mulch, sand, or pea gravel) under and around equipment.

- Openings in equipment are less than three or greater than nine inches wide, so children can't get stuck.

- Climbing structures are no more than six feet high.

- Slides have:

  - a platform that can hold several children at a time;

  - handrails to support children as they sit at the top of the slide;

  - sides at least four inches high for the entire length of the sliding surface;

  - a bottom parallel to the ground to reduce speed and make it easier to stand; and

  - an open area where they end.

- Metal slides are located in the shade.

- Swings are located toward a corner or edge of the playground and have:

  - seats made of a lightweight flexible material-rubber, canvas, plastic;

  - tightly closed S-hooks used for suspension; and

  - no animal or rope swings, trapeze bars, or exercise rings.

- Tire swings are separated from conventional swings.

- Sand boxes are covered to keep out cats and other animals.

Use safety checklists regularly.

Teachers must also be sure that the wheeled toys children use outdoors are safe. Tricycles and other riding toys should be spoke-less, steerable, and have a low center of gravity. Riding toys should be the appropriate size for the children in the class, and children should wear safety helmets while riding. The program should provide plastic liners so children can share helmets.

A safe environment must be maintained. Because children use materials and equipment continuously, wear and tear can make a once safe item or area dangerous. To maintain a safe environment, teachers must stay one step ahead of the children. They continually check toys and equipment for sturdiness, make sure that exit paths stay clear, and remove unsafe items to be repaired.

Applying Your Knowledge

In this learning activity you use daily and monthly safety checklists to assess your indoor and outdoor environments. There is space on each checklist to add additional items required by licensing regulations or your program's safety guidelines. Next, you use the checklists to identify items that need your attention and describe steps you can take to improve the safety of your indoor and outdoor areas.

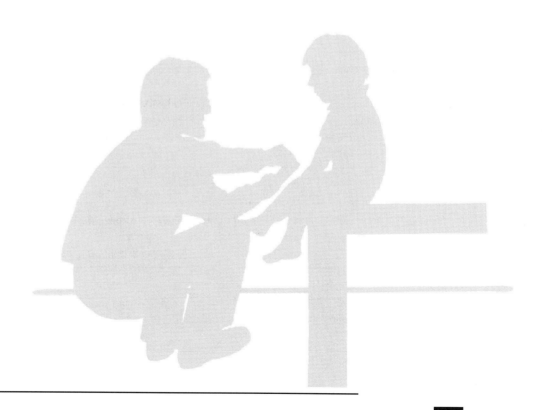

r Safety Checklist

Check Daily

Safety Conditions	Satisfactory or Not Applicable	Needs Attention
1. The written schedule states the times each teacher will supervise areas and activities so children are monitored at all times.		
2. The room is free of clutter.		
3. Electrical outlets are covered and cords are out of children's reach and away from water and traffic paths.		
4. Toxic materials and cleaning supplies are stored in their original labeled containers in a place inaccessible to children.		
5. Furniture has no sharp edges or corners at children's eye level.		
6. Inclines are clearly marked.		
7. Storage units are stable and secured; drawers and doors are closed.		
8. Steps and platforms are padded and have protective railings.		
9. Steps, climbers, and lofts have padding underneath and protective railings.		
10. Scissors, knives, and other sharp objects are out of children's reach.		
11. The room contains no highly flammable furnishings or decorations.		
12. Each area has enough space for children to work and play.		
13. There are timers, signs, and planning boards to help children take turns and follow occupancy limits for interest areas.		
14. Equipment and furniture are properly anchored or secured.		
15. Carpets are securely attached and have no frayed edges.		
16. Floors are dry.		
17. Exit signs are in working order.		
18. Exit doors and traffic paths are clearly marked and free of clutter.		

Safety Conditions	Satisfactory or Not Applicable	Needs Attention
19. Staffing patterns meet required child-adult ratios at all times.		
20. Electric fans are mounted securely and are out of children's reach.		
21.		
22.		
23.		

Check Monthly

24. Blocks and other wooden items are smooth and splinter-free.		
25. Moving parts (wheels, knobs) are securely fastened and working properly.		
26. Scissors and knives children use are sharp enough for easy cutting.		
27. Hinges, screws, and bolts on furniture and equipment are securely fastened.		
28. Electrical wires are not frayed.		
29. Radiators and hot water pipes are covered or insulated.		
30. The smoke detectors are 6 to 12 inches below the ceiling 40 feet apart, working properly, and have batteries less than one year old.		
31. The fire extinguishers are properly located and fully charged.		
32. The emergency plans are posted.		
33. An emergency drill is held each month.		
34. The telephone is accessible and working properly.		
35. Parents' emergency numbers are up to date.		
36. outlets/safety plugs		
37. First aide + CPR training		
39.		

Outdoor Safety Checklist

Check Daily

Safety Conditions	Satisfactory or Not Applicable	Needs Attention
1. The area is securely fenced, and gate latches are locked and may be opened only by adults.		
2. Play equipment is free of splinters, rough surfaces, frayed cables, worn ropes, and chains that could pinch.		
3. There is shock-absorbing cushioning (10-12 inches of wood mulch, sand, or pea gravel) under and around climbers, slides, and swings.		
4. No objects or obstructions are under or around equipment where children might fall.		
5. Play areas are free of broken glass, debris, standing water, and loose gravel (on asphalt).		
6. Safety zones are marked around swings and slides. Teachers remind children what the marks mean.		
7. Riding paths are clearly marked, gently curved, and separate from other areas.		
8. There is adequate space for the day's activities and equipment is arranged to avoid collisions.		
9. playground adjacent to school		
10. Sunny + shady places.		
11.		

Check Monthly

Safety Conditions	Satisfactory or Not Applicable	Needs Attention
13. Screws, nuts, and bolts on climbing and other equipment are securely fastened and do not stick out.		
14. Metal equipment is free of rust or chipped paint.		
15. All equipment is securely affixed to the ground.		
16. Tricycles and other wheeled toys are in good repair (screws tightened, free of rust, etc.).		
17. The sandbox cover is free of splinters and in good repair.		
18.		
19.		
20.		

Use the completed checklists to identify and list the items that you found in need of attention. Then describe the steps you can take to improve the safety of your environment.

Items Needing Attention	Steps to Improve the Safety of the Environment	Date Completed

Discuss your steps for improving your program's environment with your trainer and your colleagues. Make the changes, and check them off as they are completed. With your colleagues, develop a schedule for conducting daily and monthly safety checks of the indoor and outdoor environments.

III. Handling Accidents and Emergencies

In this activity you will learn to:

In this activity you will learn to:

- Prepare for accidents and other emergencies
- Follow your program's procedures for dealing with accidents and emergencies

Even the most safety-conscious and well-prepared teacher will have to deal with accidents and emergencies from time to time. How would you respond if a child fell off the climber? If the building lost power during a rainstorm? If you smelled smoke? Because accidents and emergencies can occur at any time, it makes sense to get ready for them before they happen. Part of keeping children safe is knowing and following the program's policies and procedures for responding to accidents and emergencies. The more familiar you are with these procedures, the more quickly and effectively you can respond.

Responding to Children's Injuries

Most accidents preschoolers have result in minor injuries—bumped heads or sore knees—requiring only soothing words and perhaps a bandage. For minor injuries such as cuts and bruises, your program probably has an accident injury form you must complete. Be sure to inform parents of the incident when they pick up their children at the end of the day and ask them to read and sign the form. In addition, let your supervisor know about the accident.

Sometimes, children's injuries are serious enough to require medical assistance on site and perhaps taking a child to the hospital. Follow your program's procedures for seeking emergency medical assistance right away if the child is unconscious, if a wound continues to bleed even when direct pressure is applied, or if the child has a severe reaction to an insect bite or sting. The American Red Cross recommends calling for medical assistance immediately if a child has any of the following symptoms or conditions:[4]

Stay calm and follow proper procedures.

- looks or acts very ill or seems to be getting worse quickly

- has neck pain when the head is moved or touched

- has a stiff neck or severe headache

[4] *National Health and Safety Performance Standards, Guidelines for Out-of-Home Child Care Programs*, a joint collaborative project of the American Public Health Association and the American Academy of Pediatrics, supported by Maternal and Child Health Bureau, Department of Health and Human Services, published by National Center for Education in Maternal and Child Health, Arlington, VA, 1992.

- has a seizure for the first time

- acts unusually confused

- has uneven sized pupils (black centers of the eyes)

- has a blood-red or purple rash made up of pinhead-sized spots or bruises that are not associated with injury

- has a rash or hives or welts that appear quickly

- breathes so fast or hard that he or she cannot play, talk, cry, or drink

- has a severe stomachache causing the child to double up and scream

- has a stomachache (without vomiting or diarrhea) after a recent injury, blow to the abdomen, or hard fall

- has stools that are black or have blood mixed through them

- has not urinated in more than 8 hours; has dry mouth and tongue

- has continuous clear drainage from the nose following a hard blow to the head

Be sure to call the child's parents as soon as you complete the emergency call.

Your program should have a plan for emergency transportation to the closest hospital or health care facility. If you must accompany a child in the ambulance, be sure to bring with you the child's signed medical history and emergency authorization forms. Most programs ask parents to complete forms authorizing emergency medical care and providing the names and phone numbers of emergency contacts. The director or a colleague should contact the child's parents and ask them to meet you at the hospital as soon as possible.

First-Aid Procedures

First aid is the immediate care you provide to a child who is injured or ill. It is a way to manage the situation until further medical care can take place. In cases of drowning, electric shock, and smoke inhalation, cardiopulmonary resuscitation (CPR) is used to clear the patient's throat and help him or her to breathe. Many early childhood programs require teachers and other staff to take first-aid and CPR training and to update their skills and knowledge annually.

Every early childhood program should maintain at least two well-stocked first-aid kits—one to be used at the program and one to take on field trips. Keep first-aid supplies in a closed container that is accessible to all staff but out of children's reach. Restock the kits after each use and check them every month to make sure all items are still in place. A basic first-aid kit contains the following items:[5]

- recently published first aid guide (Red Cross or equivalent)

- index cards or note pad and pens

- flashlight

- coins to make emergency calls (at least $1.00)

- disposable, nonporous gloves

- sealed packages of alcohol wipes or antiseptic

- water

- antibacterial soap

- boxes of sterile gauze pads (2" X 2" and 4" X 4")

- rolls of flexible 2" roller gauze (2" and 4")

- bandage tape

- assorted small bandages (extras of the 1" size)

- a triangular muslin bandage

- blunt tip scissors

- tweezers

- thermometer

- a large, clean container (1- to 2-quart) for use in flushing eyes

- eye irrigation saline solution

- eye dressing

[5] *National Health and Safety Performance Standards, Guidelines for Out-of-Home Child Care Programs*, a joint collaborative project of the American Public Health Association and the American Academy of Pediatrics, supported by Maternal and Child Health Bureau, Department of Health and Human Services, published by National Center for Education in Maternal and Child Health, Arlington, VA, 1992.

- cold pack

- plastic bags to make ice packs

- safety pins

- syrup of Ipecac and poison control center phone number (see discussion below under poison emergencies)

- additional supplies for a child with special health needs (e.g., a bee sting kit or antihistamine for a child with severe allergy, honey or sugar for a child with diabetes, or an inhalator for a child with asthma)

It is also a good idea to keep extra blankets, pillows, and ice packs on hand.

Follow these steps when giving first aid.

If you must administer first aid, try to remain calm so you can think clearly and act appropriately. Reassure the child. Ask other children to move away from the victim so you can carry out the necessary first aid in a clear area. While you attend to the injured child, have someone else call 911 for assistance. If more than one person is hurt, begin by administering first aid to the person who seems to be in the greatest danger. When giving first aid, remember these important rules.

- Do no harm. Harm might occur if you fail to treat the injury or if you make the injury worse.

- Do not move a hurt child except to save a life. Moving the child might cause further injury.

1. **Find out what happened.**

   What caused the injury?

   How?

   Who is hurt?

   Is there still danger?

2. **Check for life-threatening problems.**

   Is the child conscious?

   If not, is the child breathing (chest moving and air coming out of nose or mouth)?

   If the child is not breathing, lift only the child's jaw and give four quick breaths of mouth-to-mouth resuscitation. Is there a pulse in the neck? If not start CPR.

If the child is conscious, ask questions such as, "What's your name?" to help determine the child's condition. Keep checking breathing and pulse.

Wash any wounds to reduce chances of infection.

3. **Decide whether to call an ambulance.** If you have any doubt about the child's well-being, call an ambulance. Then call the child's parents.

4. **Check for injuries.** Start at the head and work down. When medical personnel arrive, they will ask you for this information.

5. **Regroup.** Check the condition of any other injured children. Calmly explain to everyone present that you are taking care of the injured child.

6. **Complete an accident report form.** Follow procedures for reporting the accident and give copies of the form to the parents.

If the child is not breathing, use the following techniques:

Follow these CPR steps if a child is not breathing.

- Clear the throat with a finger sweep and wipe out any fluid, vomit, mucus, or foreign body.

- Place the victim on his or her back.

- Straighten neck (unless neck injury is suspected) and lift the victim's jaw.

- Pinch the child's nostrils closed and give slow, steady breaths into the mouth.

- Breathe at 15 puffs per minute. Use only enough air to move the child's chest up and down.

If there is no pulse or heartbeat, use the following technique:

- Place the victim on a firm surface.

- Depress 1/3 of the breastbone with the heel of your hand at 80 compressions per minute. There should be 5 compressions to one respiration.

- Call an ambulance immediately if this procedure is not successful.

If a child is choking, place the child on his or her back. Kneel down and place the heel of your hand on the child's abdomen in the midline between the navel and the rib cage. Apply a series of 6 to 10 rapid inward and upward abdominal thrusts, until the foreign object is expelled. Use two hands to apply the thrusts while the child is sitting, standing, or lying down. If this procedure is not successful, call an ambulance as quickly as possible.

Use these techniques if a child is choking.

Follow these procedures when responding to burns.

If a child has extensive burns, electrical burns, and burns of any size on his or her face, hands, feet, or genitalia, the first thing to do is to call an ambulance.

If burns are caused by heat, respond as follows:

- Immerse the burned area in cool water or apply cool (50° to 60° F) compresses to burns on a child's trunk or face to relieve the pain.

- Do not break blisters.

- Use aluminum foil as an emergency covering because it will not stick to the burn.

Respond as follows for extensive burns:

- Keep the patient flat and warm.

- Remove clothing from the burn area if it comes off easily; if not, leave it alone.

- Apply cool, wet compresses to the injured area (not more the 25 percent of the body at a time).

- Do not use ointments, greases, or powders.

For electrical burns, respond as follows:

- Do not use your bare hands.

- Disconnect the power source if possible or pull the child away from the source using wood or cloth (these will not conduct electricity).

- Apply CPR if necessary.

Learn how to respond to a poison emergency.

A poison emergency occurs when a toxic substance touches someone in a harmful way. This can happen when someone swallows a toxic substance, gets chemicals in the eyes, or touches or breathes toxic fumes. The following common substances might be poisonous: cleaners and laundry products; hair care products; prescription and over-the-counter drugs; art supplies; plant food and lawn care chemicals; cigarettes; liquor; paint and paint removal products; and workroom supplies. None of these should be accessible to children.

Whenever you suspect or know that a child has been poisoned, call the poison control center or a medical clinic immediately. Tell the individual answering the phone what product or chemical the child was exposed to (have the container with you when you make the call). Tell the person how much the child took or was exposed to and how long ago the accident took place.

Although the first-aid kit should include syrup of ipecac, a substance that induces vomiting, it should not be administered until someone has checked with the child's physician or the poison control center in your community. Using ipecac is not always advisable. Some poisons, such as drain cleaner or lye, can do serious damage to the esophagus if vomited. After receiving syrup of ipecac, the child must go to a hospital for medical evaluation.

Responding to Fires

Every month, teachers should hold an emergency drill so all the children and adults will know what to do if they must quickly leave the building during a fire or other emergency. The program's emergency procedures should be posted in every classroom so all adults can work as a team to lead the children to safety. It is helpful to designate specific staff responsibilities in advance. Emergency responsibilities might include administering first-aid if needed, overseeing the evacuation of the building, accounting for all children and adults, and calling 911.

It is important to know when and when not to use a fire extinguisher. Do not try to fight fires that spread beyond the spot where they started. For example, you can probably put out a grease fire in a frying pan, but if it gets out of control or threatens to block an exit, you and the children should get out of the building immediately. Use an extinguisher after all the children are safely out of the building and in the care of a responsible person and only if the following conditions exist.

Know when it is appropriate to use a fire extinguisher.

- You can get out fast if your efforts aren't working.

- You are nearby when the fire starts, or you discover the fire soon after it has started.

- The fire is small and confined to a space such as a trash can, cushion, or small appliance.

- You can fight the fire with your back to an exit.

- The extinguisher is in working order, and you can: stand back about 8 feet; aim at the base of the fire, not the flames or smoke; and squeeze or press the lever while sweeping from the sides to the middle.

If you have the slightest doubt about whether to fight the fire or get out, get out of the building and call the fire department. Your safety is more important than the property you might save.

If in doubt, get out!

If the building is filled with smoke, have the children crawl under the smoke to get to safety. If a child's clothes catch fire, tell him or her to drop and roll. You can practice this procedure during one of your emergency drills. Apply cold water to burns immediately and cover the injury with a loose bandage or clean cloth.

Responding to Other Emergencies

Flood, landslides, tornadoes, hurricanes, earthquakes, and other weather-related emergencies may occur with little or no warning. If you know what to do, you can act swiftly. Contact local authorities or the National Weather Service to learn about the recommended precautions and responses to weather-related emergencies. Review your program's plans for responding to these events. Discuss and role-play with the children how everyone should respond in a real emergency.

Learn how to respond during weather-related emergencies typical to your area.

The National Weather Service recommends the actions described below in case of lightning storms, tornadoes, and earthquakes.

Lightning storms. To avoid being outdoors in a lightning storm, get weather information before taking children away from the program center. If you are caught in a lightning storm, move to shelter as quickly as possible, preferably in a vehicle or in a low area under small trees. Observe these precautions.

- Stay out of metal or wood sheds.

- Do not stand on a hilltop.

- Avoid being the tallest object in the area.

- Stay away from isolated trees and from items made of metal—pipes, rails, fences, and wire clotheslines.

- Do not cluster together—but spread out and keep several yards apart.

- Stay away from water.

If your hair stands on end, you are in **immediate danger**—drop to your knees and curl your head forward. Make your body as small as possible. When someone is struck by lightning, he or she carries no electrical charge and may be handled safely. Even if the person is feeling fine, immediate medical attention is recommended. Keep the person warm and elevate his or her legs.

Tornadoes. Tornadoes can arrive with little warning. If you are in a building and time permits, practice these precautions.

- Move to a basement or storm shelter.

- If there is no basement, go to a small room, closet, or bathroom in the center of the building and stay away from windows.

- If you are in a high-rise building, move to the center of the building, preferably to a stairwell. Do not open or stay near windows.

If outdoors, have the children lie down in a low area and cover their heads with their arms. If in a vehicle, stop immediately. Get the children out and have them lie face down with their heads covered.

Earthquakes. If your program is located in an area where earthquakes are likely, keep a transistor radio in your room and practice with the children what to do if there is an earthquake.

If inside, stay there and get away from the windows. Have the children cover their heads and the backs of their necks with pillows, magazines, or books. Children can get under tables or stay inside a strong doorway. If outside, stay there and keep away from high buildings, walls, power poles, and similar objects.

After the earthquake, wait for additional shocks. Do not light matches or turn on any lights because you could cause a fire. Keep your head and face protected as you check on the children. Administer first aid if needed. Turn on your transistor radio and listen for emergency instructions.

Applying Your Knowledge

In this learning activity you review your program's established procedures for responding to accidents and evacuating children and staff in case of fire or other emergencies. Then answer the questions on accident and emergency procedures that follow.

Emergency and Accident Procedures

What would you do if a child cut his or her leg during outdoor play?

1. put on rubber gloves
2. wash the cut off
3. Ask the child if they would like a bandage

While I was doing all of this I would be talking to the child, and calming them, down if they were crying.

What would you do if a child had a seizure?

remove all objects

turn child on side

Call 911, and parents. Sit w/ the child, and have the other children move away.

Who informs parents if their child has a minor injury? When are the parents informed?

The teacher informs them, when they come to pick-up their child, and they have to sign an injury report form.

Who calls for emergency medical assistance if a child has a serious injury? What is the procedure for contacting the child's parents?

One person/adult stays w/ the injured child while another adult goes to get medical assistance. Call them, and tell them to meet you at the hospital.

To which hospital would the program take a seriously injured child? How would the child be transported?

To the closest hospital.
The child should be transported
by ambulance.

What would you do if a fire started during a cooking activity?

1. get the children out.
2. see if it was safe for me to put the fire out w/ a fire extinguisher.
3. if not get out and call the fire department.

What is your emergency evacuation plan? What would you do if the planned evacuation route was blocked?

Always have two planned routes out of the building, if one is blocked you can use the other way.

What emergencies (weather-related or otherwise) might affect your program? What are the procedures for preparing for and handling these emergencies.

* fire > planned route out of building
* injuries > 1st Aide + CPR
* weather > shelter or basement

Discuss your answers with your trainer. If you have questions about what to do in an emergency, review your program's emergency procedures and discuss them with your supervisor.

IV. Ensuring Children's Safety Away from the Program[6]

In this activity you will learn to:

• Keep children safe while walking near traffic

• Plan and implement field trips with children

The preschool years are a time when children expand their understanding of the world around them. One of the ways you can support children's growing interest in their community is by planning walks in the neighborhood and field trips to interesting places. Remember, however, that taking children away from the program involves an element of risk. You and the children might have to cross busy streets, travel in cars or vans, or take public transportation to new and unfamiliar locations. You can minimize the risks to children's safety by teaching children how to cross streets and walk near traffic, and by following the program's procedures for conducting safe field trips.

Walking Safely Near Traffic

There are many good reasons why you and the children might take a neighborhood walk. A nearby park might offer the children a new and challenging environment. A particular walk might provide an opportunity to explore a new concept or skill: a listening walk; a walk to collect seeds in the fall; or a visit to a local store to purchase something the group needs or to learn about the community.

Preschool children are capable of learning and following rules about walking in traffic safely. Before taking a walk with children, review and discuss the following safety guidelines.

- Obey the crosswalk signals—"Walk" and "Don't Walk."

- Cross at the corner and stay within the crosswalk.

- Never walk out from between parked cars.

- Always walk on the sidewalk.

- Look left, right, and left again before crossing, even when the light is green or the signal says "Walk."

[6] Strategies in this section are based in part on Abby Shapiro Kendrick, Roxane Kaufmann, and Katherine P. Messenger, editors, *Healthy Young Children, A Manual for Programs* (Washington, DC: National Association for the Education of Young Children, 1988), pp. 57 and 85-90.

During your neighborhood walks, follow these rules consistently and talk to children about what you are doing. "There's the corner where we will cross the street." Post pictures of traffic warning signs (stop lights, stop signs, crosswalks) in the classroom and discuss them with the children. Point out these signs when you are on a walk and talk about how they help keep people safe.

Try these suggestions for ensuring children's safety when walking near traffic.

- Use a knotted clothesline or rope to keep the group together and have each child hold onto a knot.

- Make the walk fun by singing a song, looking for objects or shapes, or playing "Follow the Leader."

- Know which children may need close attention on a walk and be sure one adult is assigned to be close by at all times.

- Return to the program if children seem tired, frustrated, or are misbehaving.

Planning Safe Field Trips

Field trips often expose children to new and unfamiliar places. For preschoolers, trips should be to nearby sites and should last no more than a few hours. For example, most preschoolers are ready for a morning trip to the Children's Museum to see a specific room or exhibit. An all-day trip would be too tiring and overwhelming for this age group.

The children are likely to be excited and apprehensive about an upcoming field trip. Some children may be fearful about leaving the program, disrupting the normal routine, and going to a strange place. They may worry that their parents won't know where to find them. You, too, may be nervous about supervising the children in an unfamiliar location. If you are driving, you might be anxious about getting to and from the place or about parking. If you are taking public transportation, you might worry about children getting separated from the group. For all these reasons, it is important to plan ahead and take precautions to ensure children's safety on field trips.

Prior to each trip, you and your colleagues can divide up the planning tasks and then report back to each other.

Take these steps before a field trip.

- Recruit volunteers—parents, senior citizens, students from early childhood courses at a local college or high school—to help supervise the children. Be sure volunteers are always accompanied by someone from the program.

- Obtain signed permission slips for each trip so parents know when their children will be leaving the program and where they will be going.

- Go over the route to be sure you have correct directions and have allocated adequate time for travel and the visit.

- Check the first-aid kit and replace missing or outdated items. Provide a first-aid kit for each vehicle and/or group of children.

- Prepare a trip folder with a list of emergency phone numbers, signed parent emergency forms (be sure information is current), signed permission slips, and information about the site.

- If you will be traveling by car, make sure you have a seat belt for each child and adult.

- If you will be traveling by public transportation, have a plan for paying fares and getting all the children on and off the vehicle.

- If possible, visit the site in advance, travelling there using the same route you will follow on the trip. Look for potential problems such as detours, one-way streets, or parking restrictions. Adjust the trip schedule if needed.

- While at the site, locate the telephones, restrooms, shelters for poor weather, and where to go for emergency assistance.

- Make tags or badges for each child stating the name and telephone number of your program.

- Prepare children for the trip by discussing what you will see and do. Involve children in setting safety rules. Give children clear instructions about what to do if they get separated from the group.

Follow your plans while on the field trip.

The planning you do before a field trip goes a long way in making you feel relaxed and in control. Children will sense this and be reassured by your calm manner. You also set an example for children by following safety rules yourself. On the day of the trip, use a checklist to remind yourself of what to do at each stage. Include the following items and others relevant to your program.

Before you leave the program:

- Review the trip folder to make sure it is complete.

- Give each group or vehicle a first-aid kit.

When traveling by car or van:

- Place one and only one child in a securely adjusted seat belt.

- Remove sharp or heavy objects from inside the vehicle—these can become deadly projectiles in a sudden stop.

- Remind children to keep seat belts buckled and arms and heads inside.

When traveling by bus or subway:

- Review the procedures for getting on and off the vehicle.

- Remind children to stay seated and keep arms and heads inside.

On your way to and from the site:

- Use travel time to talk about scenes along the way, what you expect to see when you arrive at your destination, and to remind children of the safety rules.

- If children become unruly or undo their seat belts, pull off the road and stop. Do not try to discipline children while driving. Let children know that the rules must be followed.

- Never leave children in a vehicle without adult supervision.

While you are at the site:

- Check prearranged procedures on arrival.

- Closely supervise all children all the time.

- Pay attention to children's behavior. If children seem tired or frustrated cut the visit short and return to the program.

When you leave the site:

- Account for everyone. Count children and adults at least twice.

- Once again, make sure everyone is wearing a seat belt.

- Review the safety rules.

Ensuring children's safety is especially challenging when you are away from the program. Following the suggestions in this learning activity will help you meet the challenge.

Applying Your Knowledge

In this learning activity, you review your program's policies and procedures for ensuring children's safety on field trips and when walking in the neighborhood. After recording them on the form that follows, you can compare them to the suggestions in this activity and list safety precautions you want to add.

ing Children Away from the Program

What are your program's policies and procedures for taking children on neighborhood walks?

What does your program require you to do before taking a field trip?

What are the policies and procedures for keeping children safe on field trips?

How can you improve the procedures and planning process to more effectively ensure children's safety away from the program?

Discuss your answers with your trainer and colleagues. Implement the ideas that will improve your program's safety practices.

V. Helping Children Learn to Keep Themselves Safe

> **In this activity you will learn to:**
>
> - Teach children how to stay safe throughout the day
> - Develop safety rules with children

The first step in teaching children safety is to show them—by your actions—how you prevent accidents. Children need to see adults acting in safe ways:

- walking, not running, in the room;

- sitting, not standing, on chairs;

- using a step stool to reach a high cupboard; and

- keeping their hands away from sharp objects during woodworking and cooking.

When you or a colleague are using a potentially dangerous item or taking a risk, talk to the children about what's happening and why.

> "Mr. Chanute is changing the light bulb over the water table. He's moving the water table out of the way. Now he can set up the step ladder right under the light. Now, he's opening up the ladder and fastening the safety latches. The latches help to keep the ladder steady so he won't fall. Mr. Lopez will stand nearby to pass Mr. Chanute the new bulb and to be ready to help, if needed. . . ."

There are numerous opportunities throughout the day to explain and demonstrate the safe way to use materials, play games, and carry out routines. Here are some suggestions for teaching children to do things the safe way:

Teach children about safety during daily activities.

Explain to children what they can do, rather than what they cannot. Offer reminders as often as needed. "The area behind the orange cones is the safety zone for the slide. You can kick your ball on the grass."

Be consistent in applying rules and offer praise to the children who follow them. "Drew, I see you remembered to wear a safety helmet while riding your trike."

When necessary, step in to assist a child in following the rules. "I can't let you build any higher than this because the blocks might fall down and hurt you or one of the other children."

Remove the child from the situation if he or she continues to break a safety rule, and explain why he or she is being removed. "Nellie, put the scissors down. I told you twice to stop waving the scissors in the air because someone could get hurt."

Show children how to use equipment properly (for example, how to hold a saw and where to place one's hands when sawing a board).

Involve children in cleanup routines so they will learn that potentially hazardous equipment should be stored safely. "Thank you for placing the knives in the basket. I'll put them on top of the cabinet until I can wash and put them away."

Preschool children are beginning to understand cause and effect, which helps them recognize how accidents happen and what can be done to prevent them. They can make predictions and talk about past, present, and future events. Using simple language, you can talk with children about dangerous situations and remind them of previous situations in which children did or did not stay safe. "Do you remember what happened last week when Mara and Tony ran around the room? They bumped into each other and banged their heads." You can also demonstrate, using concrete objects and experiences, the correct ways to use materials and equipment.

Children can help develop safety rules.

Most preschoolers can understand and follow safety rules, though they are likely to need frequent reminders. The children in your group are more likely to understand and remember to follow safety rules they themselves have helped set. To develop safety rules with children, you might start a discussion by saying:

- "Tell me about . . ."

- "What could happen when . . . ?"

- "What might happen if . . . ?"

For example, assume you are planning a cooking activity that involves use of an electric skillet. Before the activity, you can meet with the children to set some rules for safe use of the skillet. You might say, "Tell me about cooking with skillets." The children will offer several different comments: "It's fun," and "It gets really hot." Then ask, "What might happen if you put your hand on a hot skillet?" "You would get burned," a child answers. Now you can lead the group in developing the following rules for using the skillet:

- Keep your hands off the skillet.

- Use a pot holder to hold the handle.

- Only one child can use the skillet at a time.

By participating in similar discussions, children learn that there are things they can do to keep themselves safe. As teachers offer reminders of safety rules while supervising activities, children begin to develop the skills and sound judgment needed to keep themselves safe.

Applying Your Knowledge

In this learning activity you work with a small group of children to develop safety limits for an indoor or outdoor interest area. Review the example, then begin the activity.

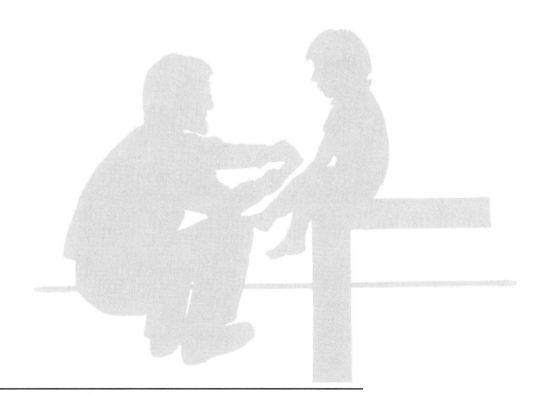

Developing Safety Rules with Children

(Example)

Area: *Woodworking*   **Age(s):** *4-5 years*   **Date:** *September 10*

What do you think are the safety hazards in this area?

Children could get hurt using the tools. They could cut themselves with saws, hit their fingers with the hammers, or pinch their fingers with the vises and pliers. They might get splinters from the wood, even though we check the wood before putting it out. Children could swallow nails and other small items. If they don't wear safety goggles they could get something in their eyes.

How did the children answer your "tell me about..." questions?

Rion said, "It's fun." Sabrina said, "You can hammer your finger." Kim said, "You can make things." Cynthia said, "You can saw something you shouldn't."

How did the children answer your "what might happen if..." and "what could happen when..." questions?

Sabrina said, "You could hammer your finger, if you're not watching what you're doing." Cynthia said, "You could cut your finger with the saw, if your hands aren't in the right place."

What safety limits did you and the children develop?

Only two children may use the woodworking area at a time.

One adult must be in the area when children are working.

Wear safety goggles to protect our eyes.

Use vises or C-clamps to hold tools or equipment.

Keep nails, wood, and tools out of our mouths.

Put tools back on their hooks after using them.

Area: _____   **Age(s):** _____   **Date:** _____

What do you think are the safety hazards in this area?

How did the children answer your "tell me about . . ." question?

How did the children answer your "what might happen if . . ." and "what could happen when . . ." questions?

What safety limits did you and the children develop?

Discuss your responses with your trainer. Because keeping children safe is a team effort, you should also discuss this activity with your colleagues.

Summarizing Your Progress

You have now completed all of the learning activities for this module. Whether you are an experienced teacher or new to the profession, this module has probably helped you develop new skills for keeping children safe.

Before you go on, take a few minutes to summarize what you've learned.

- Turn back to Learning Activity I, Using Your Knowledge of Child Development to Keep Children Safe, and add to the chart specific examples of what you learned about keeping children safe during the time you were working on this module. Compare your ideas to those in the completed chart at the end of the module.

- Next, review your responses to the pre-training assessment for this module. Write a summary of what you learned, and list the skills you developed or improved.

If there are topics you would like to know more about, you will find recommended readings listed in the Orientation.

Your final step in this module is to complete the knowledge and competency assessments. Let your trainer know when you are ready to schedule the assessments. After you have successfully completed these assessments, you will be ready to start a new module. Congratulations on your progress so far, and good luck with your next module.

Answer Sheets

Maintaining Indoor and Outdoor Environments That Reduce and Prevent Accidents and Injuries

1. **How did Ms. Kim and Ms. Richards work together to make the program safer?**

   a. *When Ms. Kim spotted Jill climbing on a box, she alerted Ms. Richards, who was closer to Jill.*

   b. *Ms. Richards responded quickly to Ms. Kim's warning and calmly moved in to help Jill climb down.*

   c. *Ms. Richards asked Jill to help her put the box in the closet so children wouldn't climb on it.*

   d. *Ms. Richards suggests that Jill climb on the climber.*

2. **What do you think Jill learned from this experience?**

   a. *She learned that she could safely climb on the climber, but not on the box.*

   b. *She learned that Ms. Richards would keep her safe.*

   c. *She learned that she could help Ms. Richards make the room safer for all the children.*

Responding to Accidents and Emergencies

1. **How did Mr. Lopez know what to do?**

   a. *He used the chart taped to the inside lid of the first-aid kit, that described how to treat minor injuries.*

   b. *The program had accident report forms and a daily chart to record information.*

2. **What did Mr. Lopez do to reassure Andy?**

   a. *He told Andy that he was being brave.*

   b. *He explained that he was cleaning the knee so it would heal.*

   c. *He took him back to the room and told him his injury had been taken care of and that he was now safe and ready to play.*

Helping Children Develop Safe Habits

1. **How did Ms. Williams let the children know that the program is a safe place?**
   a. *She walked calmly to the block area.*

   b. *She encouraged Kristen to recognize the possible danger of her structure.*

   c. *She and the children discussed how to build high buildings in a safe way.*

2. **How were the children learning to keep themselves safe?**
   a. *They discussed how to build tall structures safely.*

   b. *They decided they need a safety chart for the block area.*

   c. *They planned to talk about what to put on the safety chart during group time.*

Using Your Knowledge of Child Development to Keep Children Safe
(p. 37)

What Preschool Children Are Like	How Teachers Can Use This Information to Keep Children Safe
They have lots of energy and run, hop, and jump.	*Set up the indoor and outdoor areas so children can move freely without bumping into each other or the furniture and equipment. Limit running to the outdoor area or a supervised hallway and offer frequent, positive reminders: "Walk inside". Provide energy outlets indoors such as a climber or a movement activity.*
They may have accidents when they are tired or over-excited.	*Follow a schedule that provides a balance between quiet and active times and times spent alone, in small groups, and with the whole class. Pay attention to children's actions and feelings and suggest an activity at a quieter pace if needed. Use a flexible approach to routines so children can rest or sleep if they are tired.*
They ride tricycles and other moving equipment.	*Designate hard surfaces for riding. Provide tricycles and safety helmets sized to fit the children. Discuss with children safe ways to ride trikes, pull wagons, and so on.*
They slide, swing, and climb on equipment.	*Make sure equipment is sturdy and has adequate cushioning beneath. Mark off areas around swings and at the base of slides that must be kept clear so children aren't knocked down.*
They throw, kick, and catch objects.	*Provide an area where children can throw and kick soft objects without hurting others. Remind children to kick and throw balls and bean bags, not sand, toys, and other items that could cause injuries.*

Using Your Knowledge of Child Development to Keep Children Safe
(p. 38)

What Preschool Children Are Like	How Teachers Can Use This Information to Keep Children Safe
They can use tools such as knives, scissors, and woodworking equipment.	*Use butter knives for meals and sharp child-sized knives for cooking. Provide sturdy tools children can use with success. Store tools when not in use. Demonstrate how to use tools safely and involve children in setting safety rules. Limit the number of children in cooking and woodworking at one time and offer close supervision.*
They perform toileting routines independently.	*Supervise handwashing, brushing teeth, and using the toilet. Provide nontoxic liquid soap in an easy-to-use pump. Remind children to keep water in the sink and ask them to help mop up spills. Test the water to make sure it is hot enough for handwashing but not so hot that children get burned.*
They begin to understand cause and effect.	*Involve children in discussing and setting safety rules and limits—for example, height limits for block structures. Use positive statements as reminders. Point out potential hazards and discuss what might happen if they are not removed or avoided.*
They like to take risks and face challenges.	*Closely supervise areas, activities, and equipment that offer challenges, but might lead to injuries if children act without thinking. Teach children the safe way to use potentially dangerous equipment and materials. Praise children for following safety rules.*
They poke, handle, and squeeze objects to discover what they are and what they can do.	*Cover exposed radiators. Remove toys and other items with jagged edges or splinters. Keep sharp items (knives, teacher's scissors) out of children's reach. Store cleaning materials and poisonous substances in locked cabinets.*

Glossary

Accident

Unplanned or unexpected situation which may result in minor or major injury to children or adults.

Emergency

Unplanned or unexpected event that calls for immediate action to keep children and adults safe.

Precaution

Step taken to prevent accidents or to ensure safety.

Safety

Freedom from danger, harm or loss.

Overview

> **Keeping children healthy involves:**
>
> - Maintaining indoor and outdoor environments that promote wellness and reduce the spread of disease
> - Helping children develop habits that promote good hygiene and nutrition
> - Recognizing and reporting child abuse and neglect

Good health is a state of well-being—physical, mental, and social—not simply the absence of disease. People who are healthy generally:

- are well-rested, energetic, and strong;

- eat the right foods;

- avoid (or use moderately) alcohol, cigarettes, and caffeine;

- exercise regularly; and

- get along well with others.

Healthy people feel good about themselves.

Each of us has certain daily routines that affect our health. Some of these routines may be good for us, and some may not. Because all of us want to become and remain healthy, we try to increase the number of good routines, such as snacking on fruits and vegetables, and decrease the number of bad ones, such as smoking or failing to get enough exercise.

As an early childhood educator, you play a key role in keeping children healthy. Children under the age of five have more illnesses related to infection than any other age group. Children in group care tend to be exposed to more diseases than those cared for in their own homes. Although preschool children can do many things for themselves, teachers need to maintain hygienic environments that promote wellness and reduce the spread of disease.

Hygienic environments promote wellness and reduce the spread of disease.

An important part of keeping preschool children healthy is providing many opportunities for them to get exercise by running, jumping, climbing, throwing, and catching. These types of play provide a safe release of energy as well as an opportunity to exercise developing muscles. Of course, most children need to rest after active play. A balanced program of active and quiet times, and indoor and outdoor activities, allows children to get both the physical activity and the rest they need. Most full-day programs allow time for children to nap or rest quietly in the afternoon.

Teachers can model healthy practices.

One way children learn about good health and nutrition is by following the lead of adults. When you wash your hands and encourage children to wash theirs, you model an effective way to prevent diseases from spreading. When you eat breakfast family-style with the children, you model a healthy nutrition practice—starting the day with a balanced meal. In addition, you teach about good health and nutrition in the course of daily life at the program. You offer nutritious snacks, clean soiled table tops, and encourage children to help you keep the room clean.

Preschool children can use self-help skills to keep themselves healthy. They put on their jackets before going out on a cold day, brush their teeth after meals, and wash their hands after using the toilet. Children can also learn to prepare, select, and eat nutritious foods. Cooking activities and eating family-style allow preschoolers to learn about good nutrition. When good health and nutrition habits are developed at an early age, they are more likely to continue throughout a person's life.

Teachers may be the only witnesses to the signs of abuse and neglect.

This module also addresses an important but disturbing aspect of keeping children healthy—recognizing the signs of abuse and neglect and reporting them to appropriate authorities. Other than a child's parents, teachers may be the only persons who have ongoing, daily contact with young children. Because you know the children well, you are likely to notice behavioral changes and physical signs that a child's emotional and physical health is in jeopardy. All teachers have the ethical and legal responsibility to report suspected child abuse and neglect.

Listed on the following pages are three sets of examples showing how teachers demonstrate their competence in keeping children healthy. Following each set of examples is a short reading and two questions to answer. When you have finished this section, compare your answers with those on the answer sheet at the end of the module. If your answers are different, discuss them with your trainer. There can be more than one good answer.

Maintaining Indoor and Outdoor Environments That Promote Wellness and Reduce the Spread of Disease

Check the room daily for adequate ventilation and lighting, comfortable temperature, and sanitary conditions.

Open windows or doors daily to let in fresh air.

Provide tissues, paper towels, soap, and plastic-lined, covered waste containers in places children can reach.

Complete daily health checks and be alert to symptoms of illness throughout the day.

Recognize symptoms of common childhood diseases and stay in regular contact with parents.

Wash your own hands and make sure children wash theirs frequently using the method recommended by the Centers for Disease Control.

Clean and disinfect table surfaces before and after preparing and serving food.

Follow a flexible daily schedule that offers a balance of relaxing and vigorous indoor and outdoor activities.

Ms. Williams enters the room and opens several windows. It is a cool day, so she raises them only a few inches. She checks the area around the children's sink and notices that the soap dispenser is full but the paper towel roll is running out. As she installs a new roll of towels, the children begin to arrive. She greets each child warmly, checking to see if anyone has signs of the cold that several children in the program had. "You have the sniffles today, David. Please blow your nose with a tissue from the box next to the sink," she says. David is having difficulty with this task, so Ms. Williams asks if she can help "It's hard," he says. "It goes through the tissue!!" She doubles the tissue and helps him blow his nose. After putting the used tissue into the waste can, she says, "Now let's both wash our hands to make sure all the germs are gone."

1. **What are three things Ms. Williams did to maintain a sanitary environment?**

   1. Opened windows- for fresh air
   2. Refilled paper towels
   3. Told David to blow his nose.

2. **What did Ms. Williams do to keep germs from spreading?**

   They both washed their hands.

Helping Children Develop Habits That Promote Good Hygiene and Nutrition

Encourage children to use self-help skills for toileting, handwashing, toothbrushing, and at snack and mealtimes.

"Rochelle, help yourself to some applesauce. Would you like to sprinkle cinnamon on top?"

Model healthy habits, such as handwashing, using tissues, eating nutritious foods, and sanitizing materials and surfaces.

"Uh-oh, here comes a big sneeze! I'd better get a tissue."

Introduce health and hygiene concepts through daily routines, conversations, books, cooking activities, and visiting health professionals.

"Chef Chavez, Hugo's dad, is going to help us make some healthy treats. Before we handle any food, we all need to wash our hands."

Plan and serve nutritious meals and snacks.

"Peaches are in season. Let's serve them for snack one day this week."

Sit with children, "family-style," during snack and meal times to encourage conversation and to model healthy eating habits.

"I've never had tofu before, but I'm going to try some. In Asian countries, people eat it all the time. Joel, would you like to try some?"

Help children recognize when their bodies need a change—rest, some food or water, or movement.

"Kegan, you've been painting all afternoon. How about playing catch with us?"

"What a delicious lunch we're having," says Mr. Lopez. "Nigel, will you please pass me the apples?" Nigel hands the bowl of apple slices to Mr. Lopez, and watches him eat his apple. "These crunchy juicy apples are good for us," Mr. Lopez says as Nigel reaches for his own apple slice. As the children finish lunch, they clear the dishes and wipe their placemats. Then they go to the sink to wash their hands and brush their teeth. Each child uses one squirt of soap, and vigorously washes his or her wrists, hands, and fingers. After drying their hands and tossing the used paper towels in the waste container, the children take their toothbrushes from an egg-carton holder. The brushes are labeled with the children's names and stored in the same slot each day. Mr. Lopez joins the children at the sink. "Remember to brush up and down," he says. Anna watches Mr. Lopez brush his teeth. "I'm brushing my teeth," she says proudly, with toothpaste in the corners of her broad smile. "Me too," says Mr. Lopez. "How do my teeth look?"

1. What did Mr. Lopez do to help the children develop healthy habits?

   1. Apples are good for us ✓
   2. Washed mats + hands
   3. Brushed their teeth

2. How did the children use their self-help skills to stay healthy?

   "Nigel, will you please pass me the apples"
   The children got their own toothbrushes.

Recognizing and Reporting Child Abuse and Neglect

Learn the definitions of physical abuse, sexual abuse, emotional abuse or maltreatment, and neglect.

Recognize the physical and behavioral signs that a child might be a victim of abuse or neglect.

Report suspected child abuse and neglect to authorities according to applicable laws and program policies.

Protect children by reporting suspected abuse or neglect without waiting for proof.

Maintain confidentiality after filing a report of suspected child maltreatment.

Support families and help them get the services they need.

When Carolyn spills juice down the front of her shirt, Ms. Kim quickly moves to help her find a clean shirt. As Carolyn takes off the wet shirt, Ms. Kim sees that the child's back is criss-crossed with loop-shaped bruises. Some look fresh; others seem older. When Ms. Kim asks what happened, Carolyn replies, "I was bad, so I got whipped." Ms. Kim tells Ms. Lee, the director, what she has seen and heard. They discuss the signs of possible child abuse. Ms. Kim decides she must report the incident to Child Protective Services (CPS), the local agency that responds to child abuse and neglect. She writes down her observations and concerns, so this information will be available when she calls CPS. Ms. Lee says, "We both need to keep this situation confidential. I will be here if you need someone to talk to." Ms. Kim calls CPS; she then calls Carolyn's parents to let them know she has filed a report. CPS sends someone to the program to investigate.

1. **What are the signs of possible child abuse in this situation?**

   Bruises, and the child tells the teacher what had happened.

2. **How did Ms. Lee support Ms. Kim?**

   * Reported it
   * Told her she was their if she needed someone to talk to.

Your Own Health and Nutrition

Staying healthy can improve your life.

Most of us know that good health and proper nutrition are important. The national focus on staying fit—which is stressed in the media and at the workplace—has provided much useful information and has led to an increased motivation to stay healthy. We have learned that staying healthy improves the quality of life and can actually prolong life.

Most of us know what to do to stay healthy. When we do what we know is best, we tend to feel better about ourselves. Perhaps you have done some of the following things to maintain wellness.

- Began walking or jogging more often.

- Joined an aerobics class or exercise program.

- Quit smoking or vowed never to start.

- Added more vegetables, fruits, and whole-grain products to your diet.

- Lost weight using a sensible diet.

- Began eating more starchy foods and less sugar, fats, and salt.

- Decreased the amount of unnecessary stress in your life.

- Discovered the positive effects of relaxation techniques.

Improve your health and nutrition one step at a time.

You may have found, though, that changing too much too quickly led to failure. Have you found yourself saying these things?

- "I tried to quit smoking but I felt like I was going crazy, and I couldn't stop eating!"

- "I don't have time to jog and still work, take care of my family, and do the gardening."

- "I'd like to serve healthier meals, but they take too long to plan and prepare."

Changing health and nutrition habits can be hard. We may know what to do; but don't actually do it. Blaming ourselves only makes us feel worse. It may help to think in terms of **more** and **less.** Try to do **more** of good things, such as:

- exercising

- eating foods low in fats, salt, and sugar

- getting enough sleep

- spending time with family and friends

Try to do **less** of or **stop** doing unhealthy things, such as:

- smoking

- eating foods high in fat or salt

- drinking alcohol

- letting stress build up

Consider your whole state of well-being—physical, mental, and social—as you answer the questions below. Your answers are personal and don't have to be shared with anyone.

What healthy habits do you want to maintain or improve?

eating foods that are good for me.
stop smoking + drinking
get in shape.

What unhealthy habits do you want to decrease or stop?

smoking/drinking

How do you think your overall health affects your work?

it affects how you interact w/ the children, and how can you teach them health if you don't maintain yours.

List three specific steps you will take to stay healthy or change unhealthy habits.

1. eat foods that are good for me

2. try & cut down on smoking

3. cut down on drinking

Give yourself the positive support and appreciation you would give your best friend, and you are very likely to succeed!

As a reference, we have included a summary of the Dietary Guidelines for Americans from the U.S. Department of Agriculture and the U.S. Department of Health and Human Services and a copy of the "food pyramid." You will find these resources on the following pages.

When you have finished this overview section, you should complete the pre-training assessment. Refer to the glossary at the end of this module if you need definitions of the terms used.

Summary of Dietary Guidelines for Americans[1]

Eat a selection of foods daily in adequate amounts.

"Good for you" foods include:

> fruits and vegetables
>
> whole-grain and enriched breads, cereals, and other foods made from grains
>
> milk, cheese, yogurt, and other products made from milk
>
> meats, poultry, fish, eggs, and dried beans and peas

Women and adolescent girls should eat calcium-rich foods, such as milk and milk products, for strong bones. Young children and women should eat iron-rich foods, such as beans, cereals, and grain products.

Maintain healthy weight by eating foods low in calories and high in nutrients.

Eat foods high in fiber and starch, such as whole-grain breads and cereals, dry beans and peas

Have at least three servings of vegetables and two fruits daily.

Have six or more servings of grain products (breads, cereals, pasta, and rice) daily.

Choose a diet low in fat, saturated fat, and cholesterol.

Eat lean meat, fish, poultry, and dried beans and peas as protein sources.

Use skim or low-fat milk and milk products.

Moderate your intake of egg yolks and organ meats.

Limit fats and oils, especially those high in saturated fat, such as butter, cream, lard, heavily hydrogenated fats (some margarine), shortening, and foods with palm and coconut oils.

Trim fat off meats.

Broil, bake, or boil rather than fry.

Read labels carefully to determine both the amount and type of fat present in foods.

---

[1] Based on the U.S. Department of Agriculture and U.S. Department of Health and Human Services, *Dietary Guidelines for Americans, 3rd Edition* (Washington, DC: U.S. Government Printing Office, 1990).

Use sugar in moderation.

Substitute starchy foods for those with large amounts of fats and sugars.

Use less of all sugars and foods containing large amounts of sugars, including white sugar, brown sugar, raw sugar, honey, and syrups (soft drinks, candies, cakes, and cookies).

Avoid eating sweets between meals. How often you eat sugar and sugar-containing food is even more important to dental health than how much sugar you eat.

Read food labels for clues on sugar content. When the word *sugar, sucrose, glucose, maltose, dextrose, lactose, fructose,* or *syrup* appears first in the listing, sugar is the main ingredient.

Eat fresh fruits, fruits processed without syrup, or fruits processed with light syrup.

Use salt in moderation.

Limit your intake of salty foods such as potato chips, pretzels, salted nuts, popcorn, condiments (soy sauce, steak sauce, garlic salt), pickled foods, cured meats, some cheeses, and some canned vegetables and soups.

Cook without salt or with only small amounts of added salt.

Flavor foods with herbs, spices, and lemon juice.

Add little or no salt to food at the table.

Read food labels carefully to determine the amounts of sodium they contain. Use lower-sodium products when available.

Practice these habits, too.

Increase your physical activity.

Eat slowly.

Take smaller portions.

Say "no" to second helpings.

Drink fewer alcoholic beverages and fewer caffeinated beverages.

Brush with fluoride toothpaste and floss daily.

The Food Guide Pyramid

A Guide to Daily Food Choices

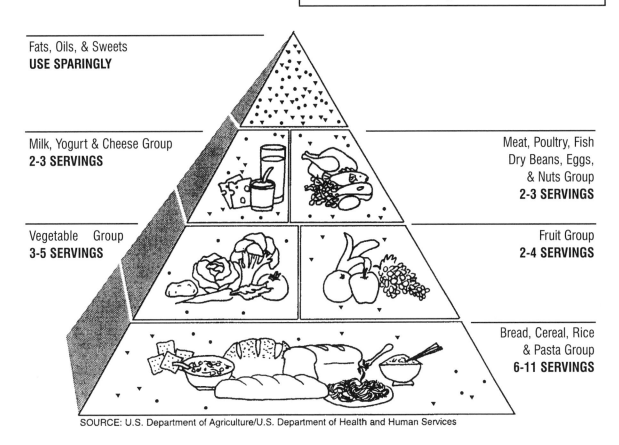

KEY
- •Fat (naturally occurring and added)
- ▾ Sugars (naturally occurring and added)

These symbols show that fat and added sugars come mostly from the fats, oils, and sweets group. However, foods in other groups, such as ice cream from the milk group or french fries from the vegetable group, can also be a source of fat and added sugars.

Fats, Oils, & Sweets
USE SPARINGLY

Milk, Yogurt & Cheese Group
2-3 SERVINGS

Meat, Poultry, Fish
Dry Beans, Eggs,
& Nuts Group
2-3 SERVINGS

Vegetable   Group
3-5 SERVINGS

Fruit Group
2-4 SERVINGS

Bread, Cereal, Rice
& Pasta Group
6-11 SERVINGS

SOURCE: U.S. Department of Agriculture/U.S. Department of Health and Human Services

Pre-Training Assessment

Listed below are the skills that teachers use to make sure children are healthy. Think about whether you do these things regularly, sometimes, or not enough. Place a check in one of the boxes on the right for each skill listed. Then discuss your answers with your trainer.

Maintaining Indoor and Outdoor Environments That Promote Wellness and Reduce the Spread of Disease

	I Do This:	Regularly	Sometimes	Not Enough
1. Check the room daily for adequate ventilation and lighting, comfortable temperature, and sanitary conditions.		☒	☐	☐
2. Open windows or doors daily to let in fresh air.		☒	☐	☐
3. Provide tissues, paper towels, soap, and plastic-lined, covered waste containers in places children can reach.		☒	☐	☐
4. Complete daily health checks and be alert to symptoms of illness throughout the day.		☒	☐	☐
5. Recognize symptoms of common childhood diseases and stay in regular contact with parents.		☒	☐	☐
6. Wash your own hands and make sure children wash theirs frequently using the method recommended by the Centers for Disease Control.		☒	☐	☐
7. Clean and disinfect table surfaces before and after preparing and serving food.		☒	☐	☐
8. Follow a flexible daily schedule that offers a balance of relaxing and vigorous indoor and outdoor activities.		☒	☐	☐

Helping Children Develop Habits That Promote Good Hygiene and Nutrition

	I Do This:	**Regularly**	**Sometimes**	**Not Enough**
9. Encourage children to use self-help skills for toileting, handwashing, toothbrushing, and at snack and mealtimes.		☒	☐	☐
10. Model healthy habits, such as handwashing, using tissues, eating nutritious foods, and sanitizing materials and surfaces.		☒	☐	☐
11. Introduce health and hygiene concepts through daily routines, conversations, books, cooking activities, and visiting health professionals.		☒	☐	☐
12. Plan and serve nutritious meals and snacks.		☒	☐	☐
13. Sit with children, "family-style," during snack and meal times to encourage conversation and to model healthy eating habits.		☒	☐	☐
14. Help children recognize when their bodies need a change—rest, some food or water, or movement.		☒	☐	☐

Recognizing and Reporting Child Abuse and Neglect

	Regularly	**Sometimes**	**Not Enough**
15. Learn the definitions of physical abuse, sexual abuse, emotional abuse or maltreatment, and neglect.	☒	☐	☐
16. Recognize the physical and behavioral signs that a child might be a victim of abuse or neglect.	☒	☐	☐

Recognizing and Reporting Child Abuse and Neglect
(continued)

	I Do This:	Regularly	Sometimes	Not Enough
17. Report suspected child abuse and neglect to authorities according to applicable laws and program policies.		☒	☐	☐
18. Protect children by reporting suspected abuse or neglect without waiting for proof.		☒	☐	☐
19. Maintain confidentiality after filing a report of suspected child maltreatment.		☒	☐	☐
20. Support families and help them get the services they need.		☒	☐	☐

Review your responses, then list three to five skills you would like to improve or topics you would like to learn more about. When you finish this module, you can list examples of your new or improved knowledge and skills.

① know more about
child abuse - and neglect!

Excellent

Begin the learning activities for Module 2, Healthy.

Learning Activities

I. Maintaining a Hygienic Environment

In this activity you will learn to:

- Keep the environment sanitary throughout the day
- Use and teach children to use the Centers for Disease Control handwashing procedures

---

What can you do to maintain a hygienic environment? First, you can check your classroom daily to make sure it is clean and uncluttered. Even when custodial staff clean your facility, you should do a daily check. Report any problems to your supervisor. It is your job to make sure that your room promotes wellness and minimizes the incidence of illness and disease.

It's important to keep the room clean and sanitary throughout the day. You do this by cleaning spills as they happen, disinfecting tables before and after eating or after the classroom pet has been for a walk; storing food in covered containers and at temperatures that reduce spoilage; and throwing away garbage promptly. You can invite children to assist with these chores and keep tissues, sponges, and paper towels within their reach. In addition, you must ensure that your room is sanitary.

Sanitary Procedures

Sick children can leave bacteria, parasites, and viruses on tables, materials, and equipment or these sources of germs can grow on perishable foods. Most diseases contracted by children are highly contagious; when one child is sick, the germs will very likely be passed on to the others. Diseases can be spread through bodily secretions (when a child sneezes), by direct contact (when children share food), and even when a child seems perfectly healthy (when a child is coming down with chicken pox). Therefore, everyone at the program must follow sanitary procedures to protect children's health.

To disinfect toys and equipment, begin by thoroughly washing surfaces with soap and water. Next, rinse with water to remove the soap solution. Then apply the appropriate bleach solution as described in the chart that follows, made fresh daily. Wait for one minute, then rinse. Finally, allow the surface of objects to air dry or wipe them with a clean towel. Wash and disinfect toys, equipment, furniture, and surfaces touched by children (floors, doorknobs, shelves) at least weekly. Some programs put washable toys in the dishwasher instead of applying the bleach solution. When using this method, use the complete dishwashing cycle and wash the toys separately from dishes.

Use a bleach solution to disinfect surfaces and materials.

Use This Bleach Solution	To Clean These Items

1/4 cup of bleach to 1 gallon of water
 	
or
 	
1 tablespoon of bleach to 1 quart of water
	All surfaces except play materials, including:
	    tabletops and counters;
	    bathroom;
	    walls;
	    door frames; and
	    mops, brooms, and dustpans used to wipe up body
	      fluid spills.

1 tablespoon of bleach to 1 gallon of water or 1 teaspoon of bleach to 1 quart of water	All play materials and objects children have put in their mouths.

Sanitize cots and bedding regularly.

To prevent the spread of disease, children should have their own bedding for napping. Individual sheets, pillows and pillowcases, and blankets, should be labeled with the child's name, and stored separately so they aren't touching another child's bedding. Sheets and pillowcases should be laundered at least once a week by parents or at the program and blankets should be laundered monthly. When bedding items get soiled or wet, place them in plastic bags or other closed containers until they can be washed at the program or sent home with parents. Washable mats or cots children use each day should be sanitized at least weekly and whenever soiled or wet. If mats or cots are used by different children each day they must be disinfected daily. You can further reduce the spread of respiratory infections by setting up cots at least three feet apart. Sleeping mats and cots should be stored so that the sleeping surfaces do not touch each other.

Keep bathrooms well-stocked with soap and paper towels.

Bathrooms and classroom sinks are major sources of germs. Check them daily to make sure they are clean and well-stocked with soap and paper supplies. It is easier and more sanitary for preschool children to use liquid soap in a dispenser than to use bar soap, which is slippery and can harbor germs. Hang dispensers for paper towels, tissues, and toilet paper within children's reach. Refill the soap dispensers, paper towels, tissues, and toilet paper if these items are stored in or near the bathroom. After use by a child or teacher, throw all paper products into washable trash containers lined with plastic bags. Trash containers with lids operated by food pedals are ideal, because children don't have to touch any germ-ridden surfaces.

Never use the same sink for toothbrushing and cleaning up body fluids.

Typically, children use classroom sinks for brushing teeth and for handwashing. Store toothbrushes in sanitary containers that allow for air drying. You can make a suitable container by cutting slots in a Styrofoam egg carton turned upside down or in a plastic milk container. Paper egg cartons are not appropriate because they cannot be washed. Sinks used by children should never be used to clean anything toxic or for any items that have been contaminated by bodily fluids such as urine, blood, or vomitus. If your program enrolls more than 30 children, you should have a large sink for rinsing soiled mops, clothing, and toys.

Many early childhood classrooms have a fish-filled aquarium or a small pet such as a gerbil or hamster. Children learn important health, nutrition, and other concepts by observing and helping to care for pets. Classroom pets should be in good health and have necessary shots on regular basis. Cages should have removable bottoms that can be cleaned and sanitized. Store food for animals in closed containers, out of children's reach. Invite children to help feed pets and give them fresh water daily. Children and adults should wash their hands immediately after handling pets, cages, food bowls, water bottles, and wastes.

Caring for pets is an excellent way to learn about healthy practices.

Handwashing Procedures[2]

Health professionals state that the most effective way to reduce illness is for teachers and children to wash their hands frequently and properly throughout the day. Good handwashing techniques reduce the spread of disease in child care by 50 percent and protect adults and children from serious illnesses.

Wash your own hands:

- before the first child arrives

- before preparing or serving food

- before and after handling body secretions (for example, wiping your nose or a child's, helping a child who is vomiting, helping stop a nose bleed)

- before and after administering medication

- before and after helping a child use the toilet

- after using the bathroom yourself

- after helping a child who may have a contagious condition

- after handling and caring for pets

Make sure children wash their hands:

- when they arrive

- before and after cooking activities

[2] Based on Centers for Disease Control, *What You Should Know About Contagious Diseases in the Day Care Setting* (Atlanta, GA: Centers for Disease Control, 1984).

- before and after eating

- after using the toilet

- after wiping their noses

- after a nose bleed

- after vomiting

- after handling and caring for pets

- after touching a child who may have a contagious condition

- before participating in water play

- after outdoor play

The Centers for Disease Control recommends using the following procedures for handwashing.   Teach them to children and have children follow them each time they wash their hands.

- Use soap and running water.

- Rub your hands vigorously as you wash them.

- Wash all surfaces: backs of hands, wrists, between fingers, under fingernails.

- Rinse your hands well. Leave the water running.

- Dry your hands with a paper towel. Throw away the towel.

- Turn off the water using a paper towel instead of bare hands.

Applying Your Knowledge

In this learning activity you use a checklist to determine which of your program's hygiene routines are satisfactory and which need improvement. Next, you plan ways to improve routines to make sure the program environment promotes wellness and reduces the spread of disease.

Health and Hygiene Checklist

Date: _____

Routines to Maintain a Healthy Environment	Satisfactory	Needs Improvement
1. Let in fresh air daily by opening windows or doors.	☒	☐
2. Check the room daily to make sure it is clean.	☒	☐
3. Store toothbrushes so they don't touch each other and can air dry.	☒	☐
4. Have children brush their teeth after eating meals and snacks.	☒	☒
5. Wipe off tables after eating and messy activities.	☒	☐
6. Date, label, and store food so it does not spoil.	☒	☐
7. Put garbage in metal or plastic pails—with lids—lined with plastic bags. Empty the pails at least daily.	☒	☐
8. Keep tissues, paper towels, and soap where children can reach them.	☒	☐
9. Check the bathroom daily to make sure it is clean and well-stocked with toilet paper, soap, and paper towels.	☒	☐
10. Follow a flexible daily schedule to meet children's needs for activity and rest.	☒	☐
11. Call parents to come and pick up a sick child, and separate the child from others.	☒	☐
12. Ensure children's linens are laundered weekly and blankets are laundered monthly.	☒	☐
13. Prepare fresh bleach solution daily.	☒	☐
14. Wash and disinfect play materials at least weekly and more often if needed.	☒	☒
15. Rinse brooms, dustpans, mops, and rags in a bleach solution after cleaning body fluid spills.	☒	☐

Routines to Maintain a Healthy Environment	Satisfactory	Needs Improvement

16. Wash your own hands:

- before the first child arrives
- before preparing or serving food
- before and after handling bodily secretions (for example, wiping your nose or a child's, helping a child who is vomiting, helping stop a nose bleed)
- before and after administering medication
- before and after helping a child use the toilet
- after using the bathroom yourself
- after caring for a child who may have a contagious condition
- after handling and caring for pets

17. Make sure children wash their hands:

- when they arrive
- before and after cooking activities
- before and after eating
- before participating in water play
- after using the toilet
- after wiping their noses
- after a nose bleed
- after vomiting
- after handling and caring for pets
- after touching a child who may have a contagious condition
- after outdoor play

Good

List the items you found in need of improvement on the chart that follows. Then describe the improvement strategies you plan to use.

Items Needing Improvement	Improvement Strategies
The Daycare I'm at doesn't brush their teeth	maybe try and start it!
I have never seen the teachers wash the toys at all.	ask them if they do!

Discuss these improvement strategies with your colleagues and your trainer. Make the needed changes in your routines, and check them off when they have been completed.

II. Responding When Children Are Sick

> **In this activity you will learn to:**
>
> - Recognize symptoms of common childhood illness
> - Follow your program's policies regarding sick children

Conduct daily health checks to look for signs of illness.

Children may come to the program with mild illnesses and may be contagious before they develop symptoms. A daily health check upon arrival will help you assess children's health status and determine who may be ill. Depending on your program's policies, children with certain symptoms may have to go home. As you greet children and parents, be alert for the following signs of illness:

- difficulty breathing

- yellowish skin or eyes

- unusual spots or rashes

- feverish appearance

- severe coughing (red or blue in the face, high-pitched croup or whooping sound)

- pinkeye (tears, redness of eyelid lining, irritation, swelling, discharge of pus)

- infected skin patches or crusty, bright-yellow, dry, or gummy skin areas

- unusual behavior (child is cranky, less active or more irritable than usual; child feels general discomfort or just seems unwell)

Children may become sick while at the program.

During the day, be alert for signs a child might be ill:

- frequent trips to the bathroom

- uncontrolled diarrhea

- complaints about difficulties going to the bathroom

- oral temperature of 101 degrees or higher

- sore throat or trouble swallowing

- headache or stiff neck

- nausea and vomiting

- loss of appetite

- frequent scratching of the body or scalp (may be a sign of lice or scabies)

Some of these symptoms are indicators of contagious illness, as summarized in the chart on contagious diseases[3]. The chart describes the symptoms and incubation periods for common childhood illness. If a child exhibits any of these symptoms, separate him or her from the other children. Inform your supervisor and contact the child's parents. It is a good idea to designate an area where sick children can rest and be cared for until taken home.

When a child has a severe cold, uncontrolled diarrhea, or a contagious illness as noted in the chart, he or she should not attend the program. Ask parents to inform you if their child or any family member has recently been exposed to or diagnosed with a contagious illness. Explain that you need this information to take necessary precautions to prevent the illness from spreading. Also, you may need this information to report certain communicable diseases to your local and state health authorities.

Diseases spread through the intestinal tract	Symptoms	When child can return to the program
Diarrheal diseases	Excess of liquid in stools and five or more stools in an 8-hour period	The child no longer has diarrhea, or, if due to infection, 24 hours after treatment has begun
Vomiting	Abdominal pain, digested/undigested stomach contents, refusal to eat, headache, fever	When vomiting has stopped
Hepatitis A	Fever, loss of appetite, nausea, yellowish skin and whites of the eyes, dark brown urine, light-colored stool	One week after illness begins, if fever is gone
Hepatitis B	Fever, yellowing of skin and whites of eyes, loss of appetite, nausea, joint pains, rash, weakness	When fever is gone, skin lesions are dry or covered, and child can participate in program

[3] Based on Centers for Disease Control, *What You Should Know About Contagious Diseases in the Day Care Setting* (Atlanta, GA: Centers for Disease Control, December 1984), and Pennsylvania Chapter, American Academy of Pediatrics, *Model Child Care Health Policies* (Washington, DC: National Association for the Education of Young Children, December 1993).

Diseases spread through the respiratory system	Symptoms	When child can return to the program
Bacterial meningitis	For younger children: fever, vomiting, unusual irritability, excessive crying with inability to be comforted, high-pitched crying, poor feeding, and activity levels below normal

For older children: fever, headache, neck pain or stiffness, vomiting (often without abdominal complaints), decrease in activity, and complaints of not feeling well | After fever has gone and a closely supervised program of antibiotics has been completed

Health Department may recommend preventive medicine for exposed children and staff |
| **Colds and flu** | Colds: stuffy or runny nose, sore throat, sneezing, coughing, watery eyes, and perhaps a fever
Flu: sore throat, fever, muscular aches, and chills | When coughing has subsided, fever is gone, and child can participate in daily activities |
| **Strep throat** | Red and painful throat, often accompanied by fever | Generally when fever has subsided and child has been on antibiotics for at least 24 hours |

Diseases spread by direct contact (touching)	Symptoms	When child can return to the program
Chicken pox	Fever, runny nose, cough, rash (pink/red blisters)	Six days after onset of rash or when lesions are crusted and dry
Head lice	Whitish-gray dots attached to hair shafts	After treatment and child's clothes and bedding have been washed in hot water (140° F) to destroy lice and eggs
Impetigo	Red oozing erosion capped with a golden yellow crust that appears stuck on	Twenty-four hours after treatment has begun
Scabies	Crusty wavy ridges and tunnels in the webs of fingers, hand, wrist, and trunk	Twenty-four hours after treatment has begun
Measles	Fever, runny nose, cough, and red-brown blotchy rash on the face and	Six days after the rash appears

Diseases spread by direct contact (touching)	Symptoms	When child can return to the program
Mumps	Swelling of the glands at the jaw angle accompanied by cold-like symptoms	After swelling subsides or nine days after swelling begins
Pertussis (Whooping Cough)	Cold-like symptoms that develop into severe respiratory disease with repeated attacks of violent coughing	Three weeks after intense coughing begins or five days after antibiotic treatment has begun
Ring worm	Skin: reddish scaling, circular patches with raised edges and central clearing or light and dark patches on face and upper trunk or cracking peeling of skin between toes Scalp: redness, scaling of scalp with broken hairs or patches of hair loss.	Twenty-four hours after treatment is begun
Pinkeye, Conjunctivitis	Eyes are pink/red, watery, itchy, lid swollen, sometimes painful	Twenty-four hours after treatment is begun

Administering Medication

Children may need to take medication during the day as treatment for an illness or an ongoing condition. *The National Health and Safety Performance Standards, Guidelines for Out of Home Child Care Programs* recommends that early childhood programs administer only those prescribed or ordered by a health care provider for a specific child. For non-prescription medications, parents must provide written permission referencing the health care provider's written or phone instructions. All medications should be in the original dated container with a child-protective cap. They must include instructions for use and disposal and be labeled with the child's name and that of the health care provider. Refrigerate medications when appropriate, storing them away from food and out of children's reach.

When administering medications, follow your program's policies and procedures. Be sure to read carefully the instructions so you are clear about the required dosage. Never administer one child's medication to another. Keep accurate records noting the child's name, the date and time, and the name and amount of medication administered.

What Teachers Need to Know About HIV

HIV (Human Immunodeficiency Virus) is the virus that causes AIDS (Acquired Immune Deficiency Syndrome). HIV attacks the white blood cells in the immune system that normally protect the body from viruses and bacteria. This makes it difficult and gradually impossible for the body to fight off infection.

HIV is not transmitted through casual contact or from being around someone who is infected. It cannot be transmitted by mosquitoes or pets. The virus does not live by itself in the air. You cannot get it by:

- being in the same room with someone;

- sharing drinks or food;

- being near when someone coughs or sneezes;

- hugging, shaking hands, or kissing as friends do;

- sharing a swimming pool, bath, or toilet; or

- sharing bed linens or towels.

HIV is transmitted in several ways.

HIV is transmitted through blood, semen, and vaginal secretions. A person **can** become infected in the following ways:

From mother to child (perinatal) during pregnancy or delivery. If the mother has HIV, her blood can transmit the virus to the baby during pregnancy or delivery. Most children under age 13 with HIV are infected in this way. Because HIV has been found in breast milk, mothers with HIV infection are discouraged from breast-feeding.

Through sexual intercourse with a man or woman who has HIV. Sexually abused children are at risk for HIV infection.

By sharing or getting stuck with intravenous needles that contain infected blood from a previous user.

From blood and blood product transfusions prior to 1985, before blood was tested for HIV infection. Many children were infected this way, including those with hemophilia.

Children with HIV infection may have special nutrition and therapy needs, but they can remain healthy for long periods of time. Because they are more susceptible to germs, good hygiene is very important. Since HIV is carried in the blood, you should **always** create a "barrier" between yourself and any person's blood when cleaning a cut or applying pressure to a bloody nose. A towel, rolled cloth, paper towel, or disposable gloves can be a barrier. If you are caring for a child with HIV infection, find out if training is available to help you learn how to meet the child's specific needs.

Lice Happen!

Even when you and your colleagues practice good hygiene, you may experience an outbreak of head lice—tiny brown parasites that make themselves at home on people's heads. Adult lice lay three to four eggs (nits) a day on human hair strands, about 3/4" from the scalp. Ten days later the eggs hatch, and nymphs emerge and begin to bite the scalp. These bites make a person's head itch. If you see a child scratching his or her head repeatedly (or if your own head itches), look for lice—either tiny white nits attached to strands of hair, or the adult lice moving around. Nits, unlike dandruff, do not move when the hair is moved.

Do not panic! Lice are quite common, do not carry diseases, and are not caused by unsanitary conditions. They are, however, extremely hardy. They have a 30-day life cycle and are easily transferred from one person to another—either from head to head or from pillows, rugs, seat backs, combs, bedding, hats, and so on. You need to respond immediately to rid the children and the environment from adults, eggs, and nymphs.

Your first step in lice removal is to send a letter to parents. Use a light-hearted tone for the letter to parents. Let them know that "lice happen," they are harmless, and there is nothing to be ashamed of. Include the following information in the letter.

A description of the life-cycle of lice: Parents need to know they must use a thorough and vigorous approach to ridding their child and home of lice.

How to identify lice: Ask parents to check the whole family immediately and continue checking over the next few weeks. Someone who is free of lice today could still get them after the eggs hatch. Ask parents to let you know if their child does have so lice so you can keep track of the seriousness of the incidence.

A joint home and program response is needed to get rid of lice.

What to do about lice on human heads: Tell parents to call their pediatrician for information on appropriate anti-lice shampoos for children and adults. They should follow the shampoo directions carefully, then use a fine-toothed comb to remove the dead adults and nits.

How to rid the home of lice: Explain that lice travel to bedding, clothing, stuffed animals, combs and brushes, carpets, and furniture. These items can be dry cleaned or washed in water that is at least 140° F. Items that are difficult to clean such as stuffed animals can be placed in sealed plastic bags for 35 days—5 days beyond the life cycle. Combs and brushes can be washed in anti-lice shampoo. Carpets, mattresses, and furniture should be thoroughly vacuumed and the vacuum bags tied in plastic and placed in outside trash cans.

You can use the lice outbreak as a "teachable moment."

An equally thorough response is needed at the program. Begin by checking all staff so they can use anti-lice shampoo and take steps to rid their homes of lice. Let the children know about the lice. Describe your lice removal plans. Explain that lice are harmless and not caused by anyone being dirty or careless. Remind children not to share combs, brushes, or hats.

Next, use the methods described above to clean all the items at the program to which lice may have attached. In addition to items listed already, you must clean dress-up clothes (especially hats), carpet squares, pillows, and mattresses. Send home children's bedding and special blankets and stuffed animals to be cleaned by parents.

Once you have survived your first outbreak of lice, you will be better prepared to tackle the next—and there will be one. As long as children are cared for in groups, lice are likely to follow. Lice have probably been around longer than humans, and may outlive us all.

Applying Your Knowledge

In this learning activity you review your program's policies regarding sick children and contagious illnesses. Next you read several brief vignettes and apply your program's policies in response to questions about how to handle the situations.

How Would Your Program Respond?

Rina's Chicken Pox

Rina returned to the program this morning after a brief bout with chicken pox. Her first spots came out seven days ago. Most of her sores have dried up, but a few are still oozing. Her father hands the teacher a bottle of calamine lotion and says, "Rina knows how to put this on, but we ran out of cotton balls. Can you give her some cotton balls to use?"

How would your program respond?

my program would explain to ~~ok~~ Rina's father that Rina could not return to school until all of her chicken pox are dried up!

If I was the teacher I would also explain to Rina's father that children should not be handling calamine lotion either.

Pam's Sore Throat

Pam and Kelly travel to and from the program together each day. Today Kelly's father drove the car pool. After Kelly's father had dropped off the girls and left for work, their teacher notices that Pam looks flushed and her eyes are watering. When asked how she's feeling, Pam says her throat hurts a lot.

How would your program respond?

my program would:
1. have the child rest for awhile in the book area
2. if she wasn't feeling well after awhile they would call her parents to come and pick her up.

Great

Marty's Head of Lice

When Marty's mother comes to pick him up Wednesday afternoon, his teacher tells her that Marty and several children have lice. The mother responds, "Well, I don't have time to deal with lice tonight. It will have to wait until the weekend. See you tomorrow."

How would your program respond?

My program would probably explain to Marty's mom that she would have to make time for Marty's head lice because by the weekend it could be worse, and more people would have it.

ok

Protecting a Family's Privacy

At a private meeting, a parent shares with the program director the news that her child has been diagnosed with HIV. She asks her to keep this information confidential.

How would your program respond?

My program would have to obey the mother's request, and not tell anyone.

Excellent

Discuss your responses with your trainer.

III. Encouraging Good Nutrition

In this activity you will learn to:

- Teach children that healthy bodies need a variety of foods every day
- Help children select and enjoy nutritious foods for snacks and meals

---

Teaching children good nutrition habits is a wise investment in their future. The foods children eat affect their well-being, physical growth, ability to learn, and overall behavior. Attitudes about food develop early in life and are difficult to change. Eating moderately, eating a variety foods, and eating in a pleasant, relaxed atmosphere are healthy habits for young children to form. Teachers can help children enjoy a variety of foods from their own and other cultures, and to learn what their bodies need to be strong, flexible, and healthy.

Some adults make the mistake of using food to reward or punish children. This is not a good practice because it may promote poor eating habits that continue into adulthood. When an adult tells a child, "You can't have dessert because you didn't eat your peas," the child learns that desserts are more desirable than peas. Children should be learning that it is best to eat a variety of nutritious foods.

Much of the health and nutrition education that takes place at an early childhood programs is indirect. It occurs when you serve a variety of healthy foods for snacks and meals, share relaxed, family-style meals, taste all the foods served and encourage children to do the same, and offer cooking as an interest area or activity. Children can also learn about healthy foods by talking with a visiting nutritionist or planting a vegetable garden.

The United States Department of Agriculture (USDA) Child and Adult Care Food Program (CACFP) provides funds which partially reimburse food costs to licensed public and nonprofit child care centers for nutritious meals and snacks served to children through age 12. For-profit child care centers can participate if they receive Title XX funding for at least 25 percent of the children enrolled. Meals and snacks served in programs enrolled in the CACFP must meet USDA guidelines for meal components and quantities.

To ensure that children receive nutritious snacks and meals, some foods may not be claimed for reimbursement. This requirement encourages programs to serve muffins rather than cakes, fresh vegetables rather than potato chips, and milk or juice rather than flavored drinks. The CACFP also provides training on topics such as nutrition, menu planing, family-style meals, sanitation, and using a variety of recipes. Ask the director if your program is enrolled in the CACFP. If not, suggest contacting your regional office of USDA to find out more about the benefits of enrolling in the CACFP.

Preschool children can learn about nutrition.

The USDA Child and Adult Care Food Program supports healthy nutrition.

Nutritious foods are good for both bodies and teeth.

An important topic related to nutrition is dental health. Almost everyone (98 percent of the population) gets cavities. Most children know sweet, sticky foods can cause cavities. However, children may not realize that, to prevent tooth decay, they must cut down on the number of times a day they eat sugary foods. It is always a good idea to have children brush their teeth after eating the foods listed below.

- peanut butter

- crackers

- bananas

- dried fruits (apricots, prunes, figs, raisins)

- bread (except 100% whole wheat)

- canned fruit packed in syrup

Although these foods are nutritious, they do stick to the teeth.

Serving and Eating Family-Style Meals

One way to make meal times relaxed and pleasant is to serve and eat meals family-style. This means that a teacher sits with a group of children at each table. Everyone eats the same foods, serves themselves, and enjoys pleasant conversation. During family-style dining, children are more likely to try new foods because they serve themselves. They can decide for themselves whether to put one pea or a spoonful on their plates. The following tips can help you begin or enhance family-style dining.[4]

Try these suggestions before the meal.

- Plan a menu including nutritious foods, including dessert fresh fruit, blueberry muffins, applesauce, fruit juice, or cornbread.

- Arrange the furniture so tables are far enough apart to walk between but close enough for quiet conversation.

- Plan to seat five or six children and one adult at each table.

- Ask children who are assisting to set the tables.

- Serve the food in serving bowls or on platters.

- Serve drinks in small pitchers so children can pour their own.

- Leave the salt and sugar off the table.

- Suggest that before eating, everyone take a deep breath, relax, and think about how the food will make them strong and healthy.

[4] Based on Elaine McLaughlin, Nancy Goldsmith, and Peter Pizzolongo, *Living and Teaching Nutrition* (College Park, MD: Head Start Resource and Training Center, 1983), p. 5-D.

- Invite children and teachers to begin serving as soon as everyone is seated.

- Maintain a leisurely pace so children don't feel hurried.

- Allow children to refuse food, but encourage them to taste a little of everything.

- Encourage children to serve themselves only as much as they can eat. If they can't finish what's on their plate, don't force them.

- Model good hygiene, safety practices, and manners.

- Ask children to clean up their own spills.

- Encourage conversation about the foods served, the day's events, or other topics of interest to the children.

- Respect cultural traditions and beliefs regarding mealtime rituals. For example, in some cultures, a respectful silence is appropriate before the meal begins and talking during meals is considered inappropriate.

- Keep a calm and relaxed manner.

- Allow children to leave the table when finished. They can clean their dishes, wash their hands, brush their teeth, then choose an activity.

- Ask the children who are assisting to help clean up and wash the tables.

Try these suggestions during the meal.

Try these suggestions after the meal.

Cooking With Children[5]

Cooking is one of the best ways to teach children about nutrition. Although the children may not know about vitamins or saturated fats, spreading a vegetable cottage cheese dip on whole wheat crackers, and mashing bananas for muffins gives much healthier messages than opening a package of chocolate cookies or a bag of corn chips.

Through cooking activities children develop self-help skills, improve fine-muscle coordination, increase cognitive skills, socialize with friends, and share in the responsibilities of daily living. They are proud to help with the real work of snapping the ends off beans, cracking eggs, and stirring raisins and cinnamon into yogurt to make a dip. Your job is to encourage each child to participate according to his or her interest and skill level.

Cooking provides many opportunities for learning.

5 Adapted with permission from Diane T. Dodge and Laura J. Colker, *The Creative Curriculum*® *for Family Child Care* (Washington, DC: Teaching Strategies, Inc., 1991), pp. 196, 198.

Here are some examples of the many learning opportunities that might take place during a cooking activity—making bread:

- learning what ingredients help make the bread nutritious (whole wheat flour, sunflower seeds, and nonfat dry milk);

- gaining a foundation in math (doubling the recipe so it will make two loaves);

- understanding scientific principles (observing how yeast makes the bread rise);

- expressing creativity (braiding loaves or making animal shapes);

- working cooperatively (taking turns sifting the flour);

- developing responsibility (remembering to punch down the dough when the timer goes off);

- showing consideration for others (making room at the table for another baker);

- learning self-help skills (washing the dishes while the bread is rising);

- strengthening hand muscles (kneading the dough);

- coordinating eye and hand movements (carefully measuring the ingredients);

- having fun (enjoying cooking and eating as a group); and

- showing pride (wrapping up several pieces of bread to take home to their families).

It is not necessary to plan special menus or use simplified versions of recipes to include children in cooking. The snacks and meals children cook can be part of the regular menu for the program. Here are some simple cooking activities preschool children might enjoy.

Children might enjoy making these simple foods.

Mashed potatoes. Children can peel potatoes, cut them into pieces, drop them into the cooking pot, and mash them after they cool.

Fresh vegetables and fruit—cooked or served raw with dips. Children can grate carrots, slice apples, shell peas, wash grapes, break the flowerettes off cauliflower or broccoli, and snap the ends off beans.

Fruit smoothies. Children can use a blender to mix milk and/or yogurt with fresh fruits such as bananas, strawberries, peaches, or whatever is in season.

French toast. It's fun to crack eggs, add the milk, and beat the mixture until it's smooth. Children can sprinkle in some cinnamon, then dip pieces of bread into the mixture. An electric fry pan will hold four to six pieces of bread.

Lemonade. Have children roll fresh lemons on the table top, then twist them on the juicer. Add some sugar and water to taste. Slice a lemon to put in the pitcher.

Pizzas. Spoon tomato sauce and sprinkle grated cheese and spices on crusts made from English muffins, French bread, pita bread, bagels, tortillas, or freshly made dough.

You might want to transfer some recipes to picture cards. On 5" x 8" pieces of cardboard, describe and illustrate each step in the recipe. Number each card so the steps in the recipe are easy to follow. Cover the cards with clear Contact paper to protect them from spills. Children can lay out the picture cards left to right on the table so they can follow the recipe one step at a time. This will make them feel more independent and confident about what they're doing.

Children can follow picture recipe cards.

You can also ask the children's parents to suggest cooking projects. By cooking their favorite foods, you show respect for children and their families. This also allows you to introduce the concept of family traditions into your program.

Here are some suggestions to help make cooking a success:

Try these suggestions.

- Use a work table that is no taller in height than the children's waists.

- Set up the table near a sink or have water on hand. If a blender or electric frying pan is used, make sure there is an electrical outlet that can be reached without an extension cord. An adult should plug and unplug appliances. Hang the cords behind the table so children don't trip.

- Use an electric frying pan or wok as a substitute for a stove. Children can use these appliances easily on a low table.

- Provide duplicates of favorite utensils so children won't be frustrated or lose interest while waiting for a turn. Parents might be willing to donate their duplicates of vegetable peelers, vegetable scrubbers, knives, spoons, graters, sifters, hand beaters, potato mashers, and so on.

- Provide knives with plastic serrated blades or blunt scissors if they will do the job. When steel knives are essential, supervise their use carefully.

- Make and display signs and posters on cooking safety. Remind children of safety guidelines before you start and during the activity. Comment when you see children following a safety rule.

- Provide aprons or smocks made of old shirts for all children. Much of the pleasure in cooking comes from rigorously stirring batter and enthusiastically beating eggs. Messes are inevitable.

- Keep cleaning supplies such as mops, sponges, and paper towels with in children's reach. Lock up cleansers.

Applying Your Knowledge

In this learning activity you plan and conduct a cooking activity. First, select a recipe, and make picture recipe cards. Then, gather ingredients and equipment, and invite interested children to prepare the food. After conducting this activity, complete the blank form that follows. Begin by reading the example that follows.

Cooking with Children

(Example)

Children: *Carlos, Deena, Troy*   **Ages:** *4 to 4 1/2*   **Date:** *April 23*

What you made: *Cheese burritos*

How did you involve the children in the cooking activity?

I set up the cheese burrito recipe cards on the table next to the electric fry pan. I laid out the ingredients—flour tortillas, cheese, oil for the pan, salsa—and utensils—cheese graters, spatulas, spoons, pot holders, knives, and so on. Carlos came over first. He wanted to grate some cheese. While I was showing him how to hold the grater so he wouldn't grate his fingers, Deena and Troy joined us. They wanted their own graters and cheese. I had plenty of equipment so the children didn't have to wait.

Deena and Troy followed the recipe cards. Carlos kept asking me what to do next.

What did the children learn from this activity?

Cheese melts when it is heated.

How to use the grater.

Deena and Troy tasted a new food—the salsa.

We talked about the ingredients in tortillas and how they are made, even though we used store-bought ones.

We talked about how eating cheese helps children develop strong bodies.

When you repeat this activity, what changes, if any, would you make?

I would put out some other ingredients in case children wanted to invent different kinds of burritos.

I would simplify the recipe cards—they were too detailed for Carlos to follow.

Cooking with Children

Children: _____ Ages: __3's__ Date: _____

What you made: __applesauce__

How did you involve the children in the cooking activity?

They peeled, cut and cored the apples + put them into the pan. ✓

What did the children learn from this activity?

That apples are good for them and you can eat them in all different ways. ✓

When you repeat this activity, what changes, if any, would you make?

Make sure the peeler, slicer, & corer machine works right before having the children try it. ✓

Good!

Discuss your answers with your trainer and the children's parents. Give the parents concrete suggestions for cooking with their children at home.

IV. Helping Children Learn Healthy Habits

In this activity you will learn to:

- Be a model for healthy habits during daily routines and activities
- Help children learn how to keep themselves healthy

The first step in teaching children good health habits is to practice them daily in your classroom. Through routines such as regular toothbrushing, frequent hand-washing, using and discarding tissues, and careful food handling, children can learn good health habits. Encourage children to do as much as possible for themselves—pumping soap in their hands, squeezing toothpaste on a toothbrush, setting the table, serving themselves, dressing for outdoor play. In addition, invite children to help you maintain a healthy environment. Although you don't want to expose children to toxic cleaning substances, they can wipe the table after you spray it with a bleach solution. They can shake out a new plastic bag for the waste can or help you empty and clean the tray at the bottom of the hamster's cage. After completing routines such as these, be sure that everyone washes their hands.

Children learn good health habits through routines.

During the day you can also help children learn good health habits as they play and participate in activities. Here are some suggestions.

Dramatic play. Provide props such as a cot, stethoscope, bandages and a white jacket so children can set up a hospital or dentist's office. This is particularly appropriate if one of the children or a friend or family member is ill or will be going to the hospital for an operation in the near future. Children might also rehearse upcoming visits to the doctor or dentist for check-ups and immunizations. Ask the children open-ended questions to help them recall what they know from their own experiences. In addition, stock the house corner with empty boxes or cans of healthy foods and pretend fruits and vegetables. Comment on the healthy meals children are preparing. "Your vegetable soup looks very tasty. I know it would help me stay strong and healthy."

Water play. Encourage children to bathe dolls and wash clothes. Talk about different parts of the body and how taking baths and showers helps kill germs.

Puppet shows. Suggest that puppets represent nurses, doctors, dentists, and so on. Invite children to make up stories about caring for someone who is sick or retell what happened when they visited the doctor or dentist.

Special events. Visit a farm to pick berries or learn about where food comes from. Take a behind-the-scenes tour of the supermarket. Invite a health professional to talk to the children about taking good care of themselves. Ask a parent and a new baby to visit the program and discuss what babies need to grow and develop.

Books. Read and plan follow-up activities for books such as *Stone Soup*, by M. Brown, *Morris Has a Cold*, by Bernard Wiseman, *Bread and Jam for Frances*, by Russell Hoban, and *Clean as a Whistle*, by Aileen Fisher. You and the children can make books about topics such as dressing for the weather or preparing a special meal.

Table toys. Make lotto or bingo games featuring pictures of food or healthy routines. Have children put together puzzles featuring body parts, health providers, farms, and supermarkets.

Art activities. Trace children's bodies on large pieces of newsprint and invite them to draw the features—such as hair, nails, and eyes—and clothing. Make collages about "healthy" topics such as exercising, healthy foods and junk foods, relaxing, or what makes each of us a unique individual.

Applying Your Knowledge

In this learning activity you describe a classroom routine you and your colleagues usually do without the children's help. It might be something you do before arrival or after most of the children have been picked up. Then you plan and implement a strategy for including children in completing the routine so they can learn about healthy habits. Read the example that follows, then begin the activity.

Including Children in Routines
(Example)

Date: *March 24*   **Routine:** *Preparing for Breakfast*

How do you carry out this routine now?

Before the children arrive, we wash and set the tables. Then, one of us goes to the kitchen to pick up our food trolley. Once the trolley is in the classroom we transfer the food to bowls and platters and pour the children's drinks. After all the children have arrived, we eat breakfast.

How will you change this routine to include the children?

We could add two jobs to our helper chart: helping to wash the tables at the end of the day so they'd be ready for the morning; and setting the tables for breakfast.

One of us could get the food trolley as we do now. Then, when all children have arrived, the "helpers" could set the table and assist with transferring the food to platters and bowls.

We could serve the juice in child-sized pitchers so children can pour their own drinks.

What happened when you implemented your plan for this routine?

The helpers all did their jobs eagerly. They were used to these tasks because they already do them for lunch.

Some of the children complained because they had to wait for breakfast.

Some of the children spilled their juice while trying to pour it into the cups.

What additional changes would you like to make to this routine?

Instead of transferring all of the food to bowls and platters, we will put out some as "finger food." This will accommodate the children who are very hungry.

We will provide more help to children who are learning to pour. Also, we will add some small pitchers to the water play props so children can practice pouring while they play.

Including Children in Routines

Date: 4/9/98   Routine: Andrea Nile/ Washing Tables after snack

How do you carry out this routine now?

When snack is over the children usually get up and go into the other room for circle. Then I clean the tables and sweep the floor. ✓

How will you change this routine to include the children?

I will ask the teachers if everyday we can pick two helpers and they can help me to do these two chores. ✓

What happened when you implemented your plan for this routine?

4/16/98 I tried this and the children really enjoyed it and the teacher thought it was a great idea! great✓

What additional changes would you like to make to this routine?

Maybe have a job board for it.

V. *Recognizing the Signs of Possible Child Abuse and Neglect*

In this activity you will learn to:

- Identify the four types of child abuse and neglect
- Recognize the signs of possible child abuse and neglect

Definitions of Child Abuse and Neglect

It is very likely that at some point in your career, you will care for a child who is abused or neglected. Children may be maltreated by relatives or nonrelatives, by people they know or by strangers, by males or females. Adults who abuse children come from every income level, race, and ethnic group. They can be of any age. The abuser may harm a child once, or repeatedly.

Teachers can play an important role in preventing or stopping child maltreatment. Because they care for children daily, they may identify the signs of possible mal-treatment that otherwise go unnoticed. Because they are professionals, they report their observations of the signs of possible abuse or neglect to the appropriate authorities. This learning activity addresses the first part of a teacher's role— recognizing child maltreatment. Learning Activity VI addresses the second part, reporting requirements.

Public Law 100-294 (reauthorized as the Child Abuse, Domestic Violence, Adoption and Family Service Act of 1992, Public Law 102-295) defines child abuse and neglect as:

physical or mental injury, sexual abuse or exploitation, negligent treatment, or maltreatment

- of a child under the age of 18, or except in the case of sexual abuse, the age specified by the child protection law of the State

- by a person (including any employee of a residential facility or any staff person providing out-of-home care) who is responsible for the child's welfare (or any other person known or unknown to the child)

- under circumstances which indicated that the child's health or welfare is harmed or threatened thereby . . . .

Child abuse and neglect is defined in Public Law 100-294.

Each state and many communities also have specific definitions of child maltreatment. Most definitions cover the following types of abuse:

- **physical abuse,** which includes burning, kicking, biting, punching, or hitting a child;

- **sexual abuse,** which includes using a child in any sexual context which includes fondling, rape, sodomy, and using a child in pornographic pictures or films;

- **emotional abuse or maltreatment**, which includes blaming, belittling, ridiculing, badgering, and constantly ignoring a child's needs;

- **neglect** which includes failing to provide a child with food, clothing, medical attention, or supervision.

Child abuse and neglect can result from **acts** (doing something to injure a child) or **omissions** (not doing or taking actions necessary to protect a child) on the part of a responsible person. Children who are being abused or neglected may exhibit physical and/or behavioral signs of their maltreatment. No single sign or clue proves abuse or neglect, but repeated signs or several signs together indicate the **possibility** that a child is being abused or neglected.

Signs of Physical Abuse

Physical signs, whether mild or severe, are those you can actually see, such as skin or bone injuries. Behavioral clues may exist alone or may accompany physical indicators. They range from subtle changes in a child's behavior to graphic statements by children describing their abuse. Clues to abuse may be found in they way a child looks and acts, what a parent or other responsible adult says or how he or she relates to the child, and how the adult and child behave when they are together.

Observe how a child looks and acts.

Physical abuse of children includes any nonaccidental physical injury caused by the responsible adult in single or repeated episodes. Sometimes, physical abuse is intentional, such as when an adult burns, bites, pokes, cuts, twists limbs, or otherwise harms a child. An injury might be the result of overdiscipline or inappropriate physical punishment, such as occurs when an angry or frustrated adult strikes, shakes, or throws a child. Although the injury is not exactly accidental, the adult may not have intended to hurt the child

Active preschoolers sometimes fall down and bump into things. These accidents may result in injuries to their elbows, chins, noses, foreheads, and other bony areas. Bruises and marks on the soft tissue of the face, back, neck, buttocks, upper arms, thighs, ankles, backs of legs, or genitals, however, are more likely to be caused by physical abuse. Another sign to look for is bruises that are at various stages of healing, as if they are the result of more than one incident.

Injuries to the abdomen or head, which are particularly vulnerable spots, often go undetected until there are internal injuries. Injuries to the abdomen can cause swelling, tenderness, and vomiting. Injuries to the head may cause swelling, dizziness, blackouts, retinal detachment, and even death.

When a child changes a soiled shirt, or rolls up his sleeves on a hot day, you might see bruises or burns that were covered by the clothing. Sometimes abusive parents dress their children in long sleeves or long pants to conceal the signs of abuse.

In addition to physical signs, a child **might** also exhibit behavioral signs of physical abuse. Children's remarks often provide clues. Therefore, it's important to listen carefully to what children say as well as what they do.

- When a teacher notices another big bruise on his leg, Troy tells her, "I fell down the stairs again."

- On most days, Daniel's mother picks him up. He finishes what he's doing, then gathers his belongings. Yesterday, Daniel saw his father at the door and said, "Uh oh, I'm not ready. My dad doesn't like to wait." Today, when a teacher asked about his painting, Daniel said, "This is a bad boy. He got a whipping because he acted like a baby."

Signs of Sexual Abuse

Sexual abuse includes a wide range of behavior: fondling a child's genitals, intercourse, rape, sodomy, exhibitionism, and commercial exploitation through prostitution or pornography. These behaviors are contacts or interactions in which the child is used for the sexual stimulation of an adult or older child.

Sexual abuse may be committed by a person under the age of 18 when that person is either significantly older than the victim or is in a position of power or control over the child. For example, if a 14-year-old babysitter forces a four-year-old child to look at his or her genitals, this would be considered exploitation, a form of sexual abuse. Although only 14 years old, this offender would be considered in a position of power over the child, and therefore his or her actions could be defined as sexual abuse.

The physical signs of sexual abuse include some that a teacher would notice while caring for young children. For example, while helping a child use the bathroom you might notice torn, stained, or bloody underclothing, or bruises or bleeding on the child's external genitalia, vaginal, or anal areas. If a child says that it hurts to walk or sit, or if he or she complains of pain or itching in the genital area, you should take note and watch to see if this is a recurring condition.

Children who have been sexually abused may also exhibit behavioral signs. They might act out their abuse using dolls or talk with other children about sexual acts. Their premature sexual knowledge is a sign that they have been exposed to sexual activity. They might show excessive curiosity about sexual activities or touch adults on the breast or genitals. Some children who have been sexually abused are very afraid of specific places, such as the bathroom or a bed. Older children who have been sexually abused may be very uncomfortable in situations where they have to undress. For example, such a child might refuse to put on a swimsuit so she could run through the sprinkler.

Some examples of signs that **might** indicate a child is being sexually maltreated include the following:

- The children and teachers are outside on the playground. Simone needs to go inside to the bathroom. Ms. Fox says, "I'll take her." The other teacher, Ms. Young, says, "But it's my turn." Ms. Fox insists that she will take the child. Simone says, "I don't have to go any more." Ten minutes later Simone comes up to Ms. Young and says, "I want you to take me. You don't hurt me."

- The children are sitting at the table eating breakfast. Nancy is wiggling around in her seat a lot. A teacher asks her if she needs to go to the bathroom. Nancy says, "No, it's not that." My bottom hurts where Gary poked me." Gary is her 12-year-old brother.

Signs of Emotional Abuse

Emotional maltreatment includes blaming, belittling, or rejecting a child; constantly treating siblings unequally; or exhibiting a persistent lack of concern for the child's welfare. This type of maltreatment is the most difficult to identify, as the signs are rarely physical. The effects of mental injury, such as lags in physical development or speech disorders, are not as obvious as bruises and lacerations. Some effects might not show up for many years. Also, the behaviors of emotionally maltreated and emotionally disturbed children are often similar.

Although emotional maltreatment does occur alone, it often accompanies physical and sexual abuse. Emotionally maltreated children are not always physically abused, but physically abused children are almost always emotionally maltreated.

The following are examples of signs that might indicate a child is being emotionally maltreated:

- Each time he picks up Nathan, Mr. Wheeler makes fun of his son's efforts. Typical comments include: "Can't you button that coat right? You never get the buttons lined up with the holes. You look like an idiot." "What's that a picture of? It looks like a five-legged horse." "Can't you climb to the top of the climber yet? All the other kids climbed to the top. What's the matter with you, are your legs too short?" Mr. Wheeler told a teacher, "I like to give Nathan a hard time. I don't want him to think he's better than anyone else. He needs to remember that he's got a lot to learn."

- The Jackson family has two children enrolled in the program. Five-year-old Neesie is an outgoing leader who excels at everything. Three-year-old Tiffany is a quiet child who plays alone or with one or two friends. Most days, when Mrs. Jackson picks up the girls she ignores Tiffany and lavishes praise and attention on Neesie. Today she says, "Neesie, let me see what you made today? Where's Tiffany? Sitting in the corner again?" Mrs. Jackson tells a teacher, "I know Neesie will do well in life—she's so smart. And Tiffany—I don't know what will happen to her!"

Signs of Neglect

Child neglect is characterized by a failure to provide for a child's basic needs. Neglect can be physical (for example, refusal to seek health care when a child clearly needs medical attention), educational (for example, failure to enroll a child of mandatory school age), or emotional (for example, chronic or extreme spouse abuse in the child's presence). Child neglect, like child abuse, may result in death. Neglectful families often appear to have many problems they are not able to handle.

When considering the possibility of neglect, it is important to look for consistencies. Do the signs of neglect occur rarely or frequently? Are they chronic (present almost every day), periodic (happening after weekends, vacations, or absences), or episodic (for example, seen twice during a period when the child's mother was in the hospital)?

Some examples of signs that **might** indicate a child is being neglected include the following:

- Sara falls down outside and badly scrapes her knee. A teacher cleans the knee with soap, puts on a bandage, and prepares an accident report for Sara's parents. Four days later, Sara complains her knee hurts. The teacher looks at her knee and notices the bandage has not been changed and the wound is becoming infected.

- Andrea tells a teacher she is tired today because her baby brother Max woke her up in the night. She says, "My mommy wasn't home yet, so I made Max a bottle and gave it to him. Then he finally went back to sleep."

Picking Up Clues from Families

Early childhood programs are family oriented, encouraging a great deal of formal and informal communication between teachers and parents. During daily drop-off and pick-up times and at scheduled conferences, parents provide details of family life, discuss discipline methods, or ask for help with problems. Some children enjoy talking about their families, so they too may provide information about the family's interactions and home life.

Conversations with parents can provide clues to how the parent feels about the child. Be alert to the possible signs of child abuse and neglect if the parent constantly:

- blames or belittles the child ("I told you not to drop that. Why weren't you paying attention?")

- sees the child as very different from his or her siblings ("His older sister Terry never caused me these problems. She always did exactly what she was told to do.")

- sees the child as "bad," "evil," or a "monster" ("He really seems to be out to get me. He's just like his father, and he was really an evil man.")

- finds nothing good or attractive in the child ("Oh well, some kids are just a pain in the neck. You can see this one doesn't have much going for her.")

- seems unconcerned about the child ("She was probably just having a bad day. I really don't have time to talk today.")

- fails to keep appointments or refuses to discuss problems the child is having in the program ("That's what I pay you for—it's your job to make her behave.")

- misuses alcohol or other drugs.

Isolation and extreme stress can lead to child abuse or neglect.

When you know a family well, you are in a better position to gauge whether a problem may be a chronic condition or a temporary situation; a typical childhood problem that the program can readily handle or a problem that requires outside intervention. Family circumstances may also provide clues regarding the possible presence of abuse or neglect. The risk of abuse or neglect increases when families are isolated from friends, neighbors, and other family members, or if there is no apparent "lifeline" to which a family can turn in times of crisis. Marital, economic, emotional, or social crises are among the causes of family stress that can lead to child abuse or neglect.

Abuse and Neglect in a Program

You may find it hard to imagine that child abuse and neglect could take place at an early childhood program, but it does happen. Thinking of this possibility may make you feel as though you are "snitching" on your colleagues or that your supervisors will be "spying" on teachers. It may help to remember that your primary responsibility is to keep children safe and healthy. One important way to do this is to be alert to the possibility of child abuse and neglect taking place right at the program site.

Much of the information provided already applies to both familial and institutional child abuse and neglect. There are, however, some specific signs that may indicate child abuse or neglect in a child care setting. Here are some examples:

- A child refuses to participate in activities supervised by a particular teacher.

- A child shows extreme fear of a teacher.

- A teacher notices that a colleague frequently spends time out of sight with one child.

- A teacher takes unscheduled breaks without telling his or her colleagues.

- A teacher says a child is "bad," "spoiled," or "needs to be taught some respect."

- A child states that he or she has been hurt by a teacher.

- A teacher shows favoritism to one child and gives that child special attention and treats.

- A teacher holds a child often, although the child seems tense and tries to get away.

If you see any of these signs, or others that cause you to suspect the possibility of child abuse or neglect, discuss your observations with your supervisor.

Applying Your Knowledge

In this activity you answer several questions about defining and recognizing child abuse and neglect. If you can't answer a question, review the information provided in this learning activity, then try again. An answer sheet is provided at the end of the module.

Defining and Recognizing Child Abuse and Neglect

1. A parent refuses to get medical care for a child who will die without treatment. Is this considered abuse or neglect?

   yes, because they (the parents) are neglecting to take care of the child ✓

2. What are the four types of child abuse and neglect?

   physical abuse
   sexual abuse
   emotional abuse or maltreatment ✓
   neglect

3. What are "acts and omissions?" Give an example of child abuse or neglect that is the result of an act and an example that is the result of an omission.

   Acts → doing something to injure a child.
   omissions → not doing or taking action necessary to protect a child

4. Does sexual maltreatment always include physical contact between an offender and child? Explain your answer.

   Not always / Can you think of examples?
   Yes, because they are touching them sexually.

5. Why is it difficult to identify emotional maltreatment?

   Because the signs are rarely physical. *yes!*

6. Why are teachers in an excellent position to identify signs of possible child abuse and neglect?

   Because they see the child all day, w/ out the parents or caregiver being around. *good*

Review the answer sheet at the end of this module. Discuss this learning activity with your trainer.

VI. Reporting Suspected Cases of Child Abuse and Neglect

> **In this activity you will learn to:**
>
> - Follow state and local requirements for reporting suspected cases of child abuse and neglect
> - Overcome emotional and other barriers to reporting

If you suspect or have reason to believe a child may have been abused or neglected, you are ethically and legally required to report that information so action can be taken to help the child and the family. In most states, early childhood teachers are, by law, required to report suspected child abuse and neglect. In addition, you have a professional responsibility to know and understand the reporting requirements of your state and local government, and your program. You must also follow established procedures for filing a report.

Teachers must follow established reporting requirements.

Each state law specifies one (or more) agencies to receive reports of suspected child abuse and neglect. Usually reports are made to the Department of Social Services, the Department of Human Resources, the Division of Family and Children's Services, or Child Protective Services of the local city, county, or state government. In some states the police department may also receive reports of child maltreatment. It is important to know who receives reports of suspected child abuse and neglect in your jurisdiction. State reporting statute includes this information.

State laws specify where to report suspected child abuse and neglect.

Some states require that either a written or an oral report be made to the responsible agency. In other states an oral report is required immediately, and a written report must follow in 24 to 48 hours. You will need to check your state law for the specific requirements.

Most states require reporters to provide the following information:

- the child's name, age, and address;

- the child's present location (for example, at the program);

- the parent's name and address;

- the nature and extent of the injury or condition observed; and

- the reporter's name and location (sometimes not required but very useful for the agency conducting the investigation).

Most programs have established policies defining the duties and responsibilities of all staff in reporting child abuse and neglect. If you don't have a copy of your program's child abuse and neglect reporting procedures, ask your director for one. Use it to complete the following chart.

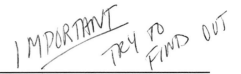

State and Local Policy on Child Abuse and Neglect

I report suspected child abuse and neglect to:

The phone number is:

I must give the following information:

I also must follow these state and local reporting requirements:

My report must be: Oral ☐   Written ☐   Both ☐

Make a copy of this keep it where you can easily find it.

Overcoming Barriers to Reporting

When you suspect a child is being abused or neglected, you may feel very reluctant to report your suspicions. It helps to remember that a report of child maltreatment is not an accusation; rather, it is a request to begin the helping process. But the reporting process does not always go smoothly. You may encounter difficulties that will discourage you from making future reports. If you are aware of these difficulties beforehand and plan ways to overcome them, you will be better able to fulfill your legal and ethical responsibilities.

Some teachers have personal feelings that are a barrier to reporting child abuse or neglect. They simply prefer not to get involved. They are afraid they have made a mistake and convince themselves that there is a perfectly good explanation for the child's injuries or behavior. They may fear other teachers or parents will think them incompetent or an alarmist. Teachers should realize that while they wait for positive proof of abuse or neglect, the child is vulnerable to continued maltreatment.

Another potential barrier to reporting is the special relationship between parents and a teacher (or two teachers). At times, when teachers observe signs of abuse or neglect, they may give parents or colleagues the benefit of the doubt. Even when they do suspect child maltreatment, they may fear that confronting the parent or colleague will result in a hostile, indignant, or distressed reaction or retaliation. It may help to remember that as a professional, your primary responsibilities are to protect children and to support their families. By reporting your suspicions to the appropriate authorities, you are protecting children. In addition, you are helping the whole family (or your colleague) get needed assistance.

Getting Ready to Report

Once you suspect a child is being maltreated, you must waste no time in reporting. Taking this action will probably make you feel at risk, confused, and generally uncomfortable. It is not a pleasant task. To alleviate some of your discomfort, you can use the following checklist to prepare for the report. (Note: some items may not be applicable to your situation.)

You do not have to prove your suspicions.

Your primary responsibility is to protect children.

Reporting Checklist

Done

1. Document your suspicions and review your observation notes and anecdotal records. ☐

2. Analyze your information to identify the things that cause you to suspect abuse or neglect. Make a list of the physical and behavioral signs you have observed. ☐

3. Describe the parent (or teacher) and child interactions you observed. Note instances when the adult indicated he or she finds the child difficult, worthless, or impossible to handle. Include examples of the adult's lack of interest in the child. ☐

4. Discuss with your colleagues the physical and behavioral signs you have documented. If they have reason to suspect abuse or neglect, discuss their reasons. ☐

5. Ask your supervisor what support he or she will provide once you file the report and what the program will do if the parent tries to remove the child. ☐

6. Set up a support system for yourself. After making the report, you may feel vulnerable and need to talk with others about your feelings and concerns, without breaching confidentiality. ☐

7. Review the program's reporting policy. ☐

8. Collect the information needed to file the initial report. ☐

9. Obtain the exact telephone number and address of the agency to which you should report. ☐

10. Obtain a reporting form, if required, or use a piece of paper. ☐

11. File your report. ☐

12. Notify the parents (or colleague) that you have filed a report. ☐

This checklist can help you organize your thoughts and secure the support you will need once the report is filed. You might not be able to wait until you have completed all the items on this checklist. In some cases, you may have to report your suspicions immediately.

Note that the last step on this checklist is to notify the child's parents (or your colleague) that you have filed a report. In most cases this will be a difficult conversation. You want to be supportive, while carrying out your primary responsibility—to keep the child safe and healthy. Try to maintain a professional tone. Describe **what** you reported ("repeated incidences of cigarette burns on Carl's arm"), **when** the report was filed ("this morning"), and **to whom** ("Child Protective Services"). Explain that you have carried out your legal, professional, and ethical responsibilities to file a report and are not involved in "proving" that abuse or neglect took place. In addition, express your willingness to support the family as they deal with this difficult situation. They may not respond to your offer immediately. However, it is important to let them know that you are not judging anyone's behavior. Instead, you have reported signs of possible abuse so their child and the family can get the help they need.

Offer support to the child and family.

After Filing the Report

In some states and local jurisdictions, authorities are so overwhelmed by reports of child abuse and neglect that staff cannot respond to every case. There may be internal policies that require the agency to respond first to cases that are life-threatening or extremely clear-cut. You may see no response to a report you have filed. If this happens, remember it is extremely important to continue supporting the child and family and advocating for them to receive needed services. In addition, you should continue to be alert to physical and behavioral signs of abuse or neglect. If necessary, file a second, or even third report. Some states have hotline numbers set up for filing reports. Find out if there is one in your state, and use it if necessary.

Applying Your Knowledge

In this activity you answer several questions about your responsibilities for reporting child abuse and neglect. If you can't answer a question, review the information provided in this learning activity, then try again. An answer sheet is provided at the end of the module.

Teacher Responsibilities for Reporting Child Abuse and Neglect

1. **Why do child maltreatment laws exist?**

   for the protection of chidren ✓
   and to help families

2. **How do maltreated children get assistance?**

   investigation by an agency ✓

3. **What happens to children if nobody reports child maltreatment?**

   it will continue, and
   probably get worse. ✓

4. **Under what circumstances do I have to file a report?**

   if you suspect something. ✓

5. **What will happen to me if I don't report?**

   fined or a jail sentence.
   (AND YOU WILL BE RESPONSIBLE)

6. **What if I'm wrong and the parents sue me?**

   They can't sue you,
   you had to do what you
   had to do. YOU'RE PROTECTED -
   THEY CAN'T SUE YOU FOR

   DOING YOUR JOB PROPERLY.

Summarizing Your Progress

You have now completed all of the learning activities for this module. Whether you are an experienced teacher or new to the profession, this module has probably helped you develop new skills for keeping children healthy. Before you go on, review your responses to the pre-training assessment for this module.

Complete

Write a summary of what you learned, and list the skills you developed or improved.

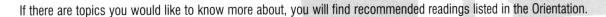

If there are topics you would like to know more about, you will find recommended readings listed in the Orientation.

Your final step in this module is to complete the knowledge and competency assessments. Let your trainer know when you are ready to schedule the assessments. After you have successfully completed these assessments, you will be ready to start a new module. Congratulations on your progress so far, and good luck with your next module.

Answer Sheets

Overview
(pp. 81-83)

Maintaining Indoor and Outdoor Environments That Promote Wellness and Reduce the Spread of Disease

1. **What are three things Ms. Williams did to maintain a sanitary environment?**

    a. *She opened several windows.*

    b. *She installed a new roll of paper towels.*

    c. *She conducted health checks as children arrived.*

2. **What did Ms. Williams do to keep germs from spreading?**

    a. *She helped a child blow his nose and discarded the used tissue.*

    b. *She washed her hands and made sure the child washed his.*

Helping Children Develop Habits That Promote Good Hygiene and Nutrition

1. **What did Mr. Lopez do to help the children develop healthy habits?**

    a. *He ate a family-style meal with the children?*

    b. *He modeled good nutrition by eating an apple slice and saying "Apples are good for us."*

    c. *He joined the children at the sink and brushed his teeth.*

    d. *He reminded the children to brush up and down.*

2. **How did the children use their self-help skills to stay healthy?**

    a. *They cleared the dishes and wiped the placements.*

    b. *They washed their hands.*

    c. *They got their own toothbrushes and brushed their teeth.*

Recognizing and Reporting Child Abuse and Neglect

1. **What are the signs of possible child abuse in this situation?**

   a. *Carolyn has loop-shaped bruises on large areas of her back.*

   b. *Some of the bruises seem old, some new.*

   c. *Carolyn says she was "whipped."*

2. **How did Ms. Lee support Ms. Kim?**

   a. *She discusses the signs of possible abuse with Ms. Kim.*

   b. *She reminds Ms. Kim to maintain confidentiality and says she will be available if Ms. Kim needs to talk about the situation.*

Defining and Recognizing Child Abuse and Neglect
(p. 128)

1. **A parent refuses to get medical care for a child who will die without treatment. Is this considered child abuse or neglect?**

   Yes. This is failing to provide health care, a form of neglect.

2. **What are the four types of child abuse and neglect?**

   Physical abuse, sexual abuse, emotional abuse or maltreatment, and neglect.

3. **What are "acts and omissions?" Give an example of child abuse or neglect that is the result of an act and an example that is the result of an omission.**

   An act refers to what a parent or other caretaker does that is child abuse or neglect; for example, burning a child's arm. An omission refers to what the person does not do; for example, failing to provide appropriate supervision.

4. **Does sexual maltreatment always include physical contact between an offender and child? Explain your answer.**

   No. The definition of sexual maltreatment includes exploitation, which might include forcing a child to look at pornography or the offender's genitals, or could include photographing a child for use in pornographic publications.

5. **Why is it difficult to identify emotional maltreatment?**

   The signs are rarely physical and some effects do not show up for years. Also, the behaviors of emotionally maltreated and emotionally disturbed children are often similar.

6. **Why are teachers in an excellent position to identify signs of possible child abuse and neglect?**

   Teachers see children almost every day. They might detect signs of possible child maltreatment that would otherwise go unnoticed.

Teacher Responsibilities for Reporting Child Abuse and Neglect

(p. 134)

1. **Why do child maltreatment laws exist?**

   To provide protection for children and to help families.

2. **How do maltreated children get assistance?**

   When possible maltreatment is identified and reported, an investigation by an agency will begin.

3. **What happens to children if nobody reports maltreatment?**

   If the maltreatment goes unnoticed and unreported, it is likely it will continue and perhaps escalate.

4. **Under what circumstances do I have to file a report?**

   If your knowledge of the child and his or her family and your professional training and experience lead you to suspect child maltreatment, then you must file a report.

5. **What will happen to me if I don't report?**

   If you fail to report, under your state's laws you might be subject to fines or even a jail sentence.

6. **What if I'm wrong and the parents sue me?**

   When you make a report in good faith, the law protects you. You cannot be sued for reporting child maltreatment because as a early childhood educator, you are mandated to do so.

Glossary

Body fluids

Liquids and semi-liquids eliminated by or present in the body, such as feces, urine, mucus, and saliva.

Diet

The kind and amount of food and drink regularly consumed.

Disinfectant

A cleaning solution that destroys the causes of infection.

Hygiene

Practices that preserve good health and eliminate disease-producing germs.

Infection

Invasion of the body by tiny organisms that cause disease.

Nutrient

A component of food that offers nourishment to the body.

Nutritious

Having large amounts of vitamins, minerals, complex carbohydrates, or protein, and being low in fats, salt, and sugar.

Sodium

A mineral normally found in seafood, poultry, and some vegetables; one of the components of table salt.

Starch

A carbohydrate food such as cereal, potatoes, pasta, and bread.

Module 3: *Learning Environment*

Overview

Establishing and maintaining a learning environment involves:

- Organizing indoor and outdoor areas that encourage play and exploration
- Selecting and attractively displaying materials and equipment
- Planning and implementing a schedule, routines, and transitions that meet children's needs

---

The learning environment is the physical space used by the children. It includes both the outdoor and indoor play spaces. The schedule and routines you follow each day are also part of a learning environment in which children can feel comfortable and competent.

You and the children will spend a considerable portion of the day together. If the physical environment is attractive and well-designed, you will find that children are more purposefully engaged in activities. As a result, you may discover that you enjoy your work with children much more. The quality of the learning environment affects how children and adults feel and act.

The quality of the physical environment affects how children and adults feel.

Features such as the size of the room, the colors of the walls, the type of flooring, the amount of light, and the number of windows all influence the quality of the indoor environment. While you may have limited control over many of these features, you have a great deal to say about how to organize furniture and materials and how to display children's work.

A well-organized classroom can support your goals for children and allow you more time to observe and interact with them in positive ways. You can arrange the furniture to define a variety of interest areas where children can play cooperatively in small groups. The selection of materials and how you display them convey powerful messages to children, encouraging them to choose activities on their own and to take care of materials.

Indoor and outdoor spaces should be well defined and offer a variety of choices.

The outdoors offers children a whole new range of experiences and textures. A good outdoor environment has soft and hard surfaces, shady and sunny areas, and protected and safe places for children to run and play. In a well-designed outdoor space children can run, jump, skip, throw and catch a ball, and use their "outside voices." These experiences provide a healthy release as children stretch their muscles, breathe in fresh air, take in the sunshine, and enjoy the freedom possible outdoors.

The daily schedule, routines, and transitions are part of the learning environment.

Your program's schedule, routines, and transitions also contribute to creating a comfortable atmosphere. When children know what to expect each day, it helps them feel secure. Each day will go more smoothly if the schedule, routines, and transitions are designed to meet children's needs.

Listed on the following pages are three sets of examples showing how teachers demonstrate their competence in establishing and maintaining a learning environment. Following each set of examples is a short reading and two questions to answer. When you have finished this section, compare your answers with those on the answer sheet at the end of the module. If your answers are different, discuss them with your trainer. There can be more than one good answer.

Organizing Indoor and Outdoor Areas That Encourage Play and Exploration

Establish a variety of well-defined and equipped indoor and outdoor interest areas that reflect children's current skills and interests.

Create soft, cozy areas where children can play alone, look at books, listen to music, or talk with a friend.

Define separate spaces indoors and outdoors for active and quiet play.

Adapt the environment, if necessary, to fully include children with special needs.

Provide sufficient storage for children's personal belongings, such as labeled cubbies or bins.

Arrange the outdoor area to support a variety of activities, such as climbing, swinging, building, running, and relaxing.

Mr. Lopez looks around the play yard. He sees several children acting frustrated. Sarah is in the shed pulling on a tire that is under a tangle of boards, riding toys, and rakes. Benjamin struggles to pull a tricycle out of the shed. Andy drops the watering can when a child chasing a ball races by the tomato plants he is watering. "This place needs some organizing," Mr. Lopez decides. Over the next week, he makes changes to encourage children's play and exploration. First, he arranges the tires and boards so that children can get them easily. He hangs the gardening tools within easy reach on the door of the storage shed. He moves the trikes to the path and the balls to the grass away from the garden. He tells the children about the different areas and reminds them where to ride their trikes and throw balls.

1. **What did Mr. Lopez know about the children?**

   a. children got aggrivated when they couldn't get things they wanted.

   b. other childrens play was getting interupted by the other children playing ball.

2. **How did Mr. Lopez organize the outdoor area so it would encourage play and exploration?**

   a. toys were in children's reach, and easy to find.

   b. designated certain area's to isolate quiet and loud.

Selecting and Attractively Displaying Materials and Equipment

Provide a variety of materials to encourage dramatic play, construction, small muscle development, and thinking skills.

Display learning materials related to current activities (for example, new materials might include firefighter hats, fire engines, and books on firefighters).

Use low open shelves and picture labels so children can easily select materials and return them independently.

Include dolls, picture books, photographs, and toys that positively portray different ethnic groups and people with disabilities.

Store materials and supplies that are used together in the same place.

Convey positive messages through the environment (e.g., this is a safe place; you belong here; you can find what you need).

It's rest time and Ms. Williams is using the time to make a list of the materials she wants to offer children the next day. During the morning, the children made get-well cards to send to a child who is in the hospital. There was a lot of interest in doctors and hospitals, so Ms. Williams brought out two story books about going to the hospital. She is now preparing a hospital prop box to add to the house corner. In it she puts two white lab coats, a stethoscope, ace bandages, and a pad and pencil. Next, she thinks about the fact that several children have seemed particularly anxious during the past few days. She decides to open the water table because she knows water play is a calming activity. She makes a note to add blue coloring to the water and to set out plastic squeeze bottles, eye droppers, measuring cups, and plastic tubes for the water table.

1. **What did Ms. Williams know about the children?**

2. **What activities and materials did Ms. Williams plan to offer for the children and why?**

Planning and Implementing a Schedule, Routines, and Transitions to Meet Children's Needs

Plan a schedule that includes large blocks of time when children choose what they want to do.

Offer a balance of activity choices including active and quiet; indoors and outdoors; and individual, small group, and large group activities.

Plan at least two periods a day for children to play outdoors.

Allow time for children to use their self-help skills in daily routines such as hand washing and dressing to go outside.

Use daily routines to teach new skills and concepts such as classification and sequencing.

Plan something for children to do during transitions between activities so they won't be restless.

It is clean-up time in the three-year-old room. Ms. Richards is helping a small group in the block area to clean up. It seems as if every block is out. "We have a big job in the block corner today," she says. "Let's start by finding all the blocks that look like this one. See how many triangles you can find." When all the triangle blocks are on the shelf, Ms. Richards says, "Jamie, what shape should we clean up next?" Jamie holds up a cylinder. "OK," says Ms. Richards, "let's find all the cylinders next." Ms. Kim realizes that the other children are going to be finished cleaning up before the block builders. She goes around to each interest area and tells the children to go to the meeting area when they are finished cleaning up and select a book to look at. "I'll be there to read our story in just a few minutes," she says. When the block builders finish their clean up, Ms. Kim is ready to read the story.

1. How did Ms. Richards use block clean up as an opportunity for learning?

2. What did Ms. Kim do to make sure that the children who were finished cleaning up had something to do?

How Your Environment Affects You

We are all affected by our environment. Whether sitting in the living room, shopping in a store, climbing a mountain, or sitting in a staff lounge, we react to the environment. Our surroundings affect our feelings, comfort levels, behavior, and ability to accomplish tasks. Consider how you behave in the following situations:

We are not always aware of how our environment is affecting us.

- Standing in a hot, crowded bus or subway when you are sandwiched in among strangers. (Perhaps you pull your shoulders in, try to avoid any contact with others, and count the minutes until you get off.)

- Eating in a special restaurant with a favorite friend. The lights are low, and the noise level is muffled. The smells are delicious, and attractive pictures hang on the walls. (You are probably relaxed, enjoying the conversation, and savoring each bite.)

- Preparing a meal in a strange kitchen when the owner is not there to help you. (You may be very frustrated, especially if you can't figure out how the kitchen is organized. You spend lots of time looking for the things you need. It's inefficient, and you may not cook as well as you usually do.)

It's easy to see in these examples how our environment can affect our actions and our feelings. But the influence of our surroundings is not always so clear. Sometimes we are not aware of how the environment is making us feel and act. To identify some less obvious factors in the environment that support you or work against you, take time to answer the following questions.

Think about a store where you like to shop. What makes it pleasant to shop in this store?

Now, think about a store you dislike. When you are there, you feel frustrated and angry. What makes it difficult to shop in this store?

Look over your answers to these two questions. Many of the factors you identified that make shopping enjoyable or difficult apply to the classroom environment as well. Your work environment should support you and work for you. If it is well-organized and appropriate for the children you teach, it can make your job easier and more enjoyable.

Next, think of your favorite place to be—indoors or outdoors. Close your eyes for a moment and imagine yourself in that space. How does it feel? Smell? Look? What do you hear? What are you doing? Are you alone, or are other people with you?

Describe your favorite place below.

Often when people describe their favorite place, they identify features such as the following:

- a quiet place to be alone;

- a soft and comfortable place to stretch out;

- a place where music is playing;

- a place where only the sounds of nature can be heard;

- a bright and sunny place where the air smells fresh and clean; or

- a colorful and attractive place.

Keep the features of your favorite place in mind as you consider the learning environment of your classroom and outdoor space. A comfortable environment for young children makes them want to be there. It also makes teaching more satisfying.

When you have finished this overview section, complete the pre-training assessment. Refer to the glossary at the end of this module if you need definitions of the terms that are used.

Pre-Training Assessment

Listed below are the skills that teachers use to establish and maintain an environment for learning. Think about whether you do these things regularly, sometimes, or not enough. Place a check in one of the boxes on the right for each skill listed. Then discuss your answers with your trainer.

Organizing Indoor and Outdoor Areas that Encourage Play and Exploration

	I Do This:	Regularly	Sometimes	Not Enough
1. Establish a variety of well-defined and equipped indoor and outdoor interest areas that reflect children's current skills and interests.		☒	☐	☐
2. Create soft, cozy areas where children can play alone, look at books, listen to music, or talk with a friend.		☒	☐	☐
3. Define separate spaces indoors and outdoors for active and quiet play.		☒	☐	☐
4. Adapt the environment, if necessary, to fully include children with special needs.		☒	☐	☐
5. Provide sufficient storage for children's personal belongings, such as labeled cubbies or bins.		☒	☐	☐
6. Arrange the outdoor area to support a variety of activities, such as climbing, swinging, building, running, and relaxing.		☐	☒	☐

Selecting and Attractively Displaying Materials and Equipment

	I Do This:	Regularly	Sometimes	Not Enough
7. Provide a variety of materials to encourage dramatic play, construction, small muscle development, and thinking skills.		☒	☐	☐
8. Display learning materials related to current activities (for example, firefighter hats, fire engines, and books on firefighters after a trip to the fire department).		☒	☐	☐
9. Use low, open shelves and picture labels so children can easily select materials and return them independently.		☒	☐	☐
10. Include dolls, picture books, photographs, and toys that positively portray different ethnic groups and people with disabilities.		☒	☐	☐
11. Store materials and supplies that are used together in the same place.		☒	☐	☐
12. Convey positive messages through the environment (e.g., this is a safe place; you belong here; you can find what you need.)		☒	☐	☐

Planning and Implementing a Schedule, Routines, and Transitions to Meet Children's Needs

	Regularly	Sometimes	Not Enough
13. Plan a schedule that includes large blocks of time when children choose what they want to do.	☒	☐	☐
14. Offer a balance of activity choices including active and quiet, indoors and outdoors, and individual, small group, and large group activities.	☒	☐	☐
15. Plan at least two periods a day for children to play outdoors.	☒	☐	☐

Planning and Implementing a Schedule, Routines, and Transitions to Meet Children's Needs

(continued)

	I Do This:	Regularly	Sometimes	Not Enough
16. Allow time for children to use their self-help skills in daily routines such as hand washing and dressing to go outside.		☒	☐	☐
17. Use daily routines to teach new skills and concepts such as classification and sequencing.		☒	☐	☐
18. Plan something for children to do during transitions between activities so they won't be restless.		☐	☒	☐

Review your responses, then list three to five skills you would like to improve or topics you would like to learn more about. When you finish this module, you will list examples of your new or improved knowledge and skills.

① outdoor space> the daycare I am at doesn't always allow the children to climb.

② Transition time is a confuessing time, and my daycare doesn't do anything during these times

Begin the learning activities for Module 3, Learning Environment.

Learning Activities

I. Using Your Knowledge of Child Development to Create a Learning Environment

---

In this activity you will learn to:

- Recognize some typical behaviors of preschool children
- Use what you know about child development to create a good environment for learning

---

Erik Erikson describes the preschool years as the stage of Initiative. This means that children are full of ideas about what to do and how to do it. They like having a variety of choices that respond to their varied interests. The more preschool children are encouraged to come up with ideas and try them out, the more confident they become in their own abilities.

A good learning environment for preschool children invites them to explore, makes it easier for them to work cooperatively with others, and encourages them to take responsibility for maintaining the environment. Preschool children have many skills and interests as well as needs that should be considered in planning the learning environment. They enjoy new challenges and will eagerly explore new, interesting materials you put out for their use.

Preschool children are active learners.

Preschool children can express their ideas and feelings in many ways. Using crayons, markers, and paints, they learn to represent these ideas in symbols. Playing with blocks or in the house corner, they recreate scenes from their own experiences. In the process they develop a deeper understanding of the world around them.

Preschool children are very social. They are learning how to share and to take turns, and they realize the advantages of working together. They learn these skills by having many opportunities to work with one or two other children. A good learning environment is therefore divided into six or more interest areas where small groups of children can work together undisturbed.

Preschool children enjoy being with others.

You have probably noticed that preschool children have lots of energy. They are continually refining large and small muscle skills, and they want to practice these skills, over and over again. A good learning environment offers children ample opportunities to acquire and practice new skills.

Planning a learning environment for preschool children means creating a setting and providing appropriate materials that enable them to expand their skills and understandings and to grow in all areas of development.

Applying Your Knowledge

The chart on the next page identifies some typical behaviors of preschool children. Included are behaviors relevant to creating and using an appropriate learning environment. The right column asks you to identify ways teachers can use this information to create a learning environment. As you work through the module you will learn new strategies and you can add them to the chart. You are not expected to think of all the examples at one time. If you need help getting started, turn to the completed chart at the end of this module. By the time you complete all the learning activities, you will find that you have learned many ways to create a good learning environment for preschool children.

Using Your Knowledge of Child
Development to Create a Learning Environment

What Preschool Children Are Like	How Teachers Can Use This Information to Create a Learning Environment
They enjoy large muscle activities such running, jumping, climbing, and riding tricycles.	*Set aside an indoor area for large play equipment. Plan some activities that use large muscles (for example, pounding clay or dough, woodworking). Make sure the outdoor area is safe for running and climbing.*
They are gaining increasing control of small muscles.	toys w/ small pieces, such as puzzles, playdough, pegs and peg boards.
They are learning to share and take turns.	Use clock and timers to show kids how long they have w/ that toy or activity! Have children ask their friends for toys.
They can play cooperatively with one or two others and often have "best friends."	have small group activities, and ALWAYS encourage the children to play w/ all their friends.
They sometimes need to get away from the group and be by themselves.	Quiet area is for this— which has maybe pillows and books and a tape player for tape/books.
They have a lot of energy but can easily tire.	Plan a balanced schedule.

Using Your Knowledge of Child Development to Create a Learning Environment

What Preschool Children Are Like	How Teachers Can Use This Information to Create a Learning Environment
They like to be helpful.	Job Boards come in handy here!
They can take responsibility for keeping the classroom orderly.	Organize material so the children know where everything goes, so they can take responsibility.
They love to play make-believe. Their dramatic play goes from family roles to people in the community and super-heroes.	Make this a house area, and then keep adding new and exciting props!
They have lots of interests.	Know the childrens interests, Give lots of choices!
They draw pictures and create objects that represent real things.	Leave lots of Art materials out - crayons, markers, paints, etc...

When you have completed as much as you can do on the chart, discuss your responses with your trainer. As you proceed with the rest of the learning activities, you can refer back to the chart and add more examples of how teachers create a learning environment for preschool children.

II. Conveying Positive Messages Through the Environment

In this activity you will learn to:

- Identify ways that the learning environment can promote independence, security, and a sense of belonging
- Arrange space and materials to give children positive and clear messages

---

All environments convey messages. Every room in your home says something different. Your living room may have soft furniture, low tables with magazines, lamps, and a soft carpet. The message is: "Come sit down. Read. Talk. Relax."

Fast-food restaurants are designed to get you in and out quickly. They are set up so you can select and order your food, get it immediately, pay, and be seated in a matter of minutes. The message is: "Hurry up."

Many schools have individual desks lined up facing the front of the room. In some older school buildings the desks are bolted to the floor. The message is: "No talking to other children. Listen to the teacher. The teacher conveys all information."

Your center's indoor and outdoor spaces also convey messages to children. If the environment is attractive, cheerful, orderly, and filled with interesting objects, the message is: "This is a good and interesting place. We care about you. You can have fun here."

The environment conveys powerful messages to children.

If a child entering your room sees a cubby with his picture and name on it, his art work displayed on the wall, and a place for his toothbrush, the message he receives is: "You belong here. We will help you take care of your things. This is your space, too."

A cozy corner of the room filled with large pillows, bright lights, and a shelf full of attractive books says: "Come sit here. Choose a book you like. Enjoy yourself."

Outdoors, hollow blocks and planks in a open space convey the message: "You can create your own structures and play in them."

What messages do you want children to receive when they come into your room? Listed on the following pages are positive messages and suggestions of how the environment can convey these messages to children.

"This is a cheerful and happy place."

- Walls are painted neutral colors (light gray, off-white, beige), and bright colors are used selectively (on shelves or containers).

- The outdoor space includes soft areas (e.g., grass or mats) where children can stretch out and relax.

- Furniture is clean and well-maintained. (Wood or plastic furniture is preferable to metal furniture.)

- Children's work is attractively displayed where they can easily see it.

- The room includes other decorative touches, including plants, displays of collections (such as shells, leaves, and stones), pretty fabrics to cover pillows or to use as tablecloths, and a well-lit fish tank.

- Areas of the room contain soft places for children (carpets, large pillows), soft materials (water, playdough), and soft pets (guinea pigs, rabbits).

"You belong here, and we like you."

- There is a cubby for each child, labeled with the child's name or picture.

- There is a place to keep a special blanket and a stuffed animal for nap time.

- There is a labeled place for each child's toothbrush.

- Each child's art work is displayed and protected.

- Pictures on the walls, in books, and in learning materials show people of different ethnic backgrounds.

- There are toys and materials that will interest specific children.

- There is child-sized furniture.

"This is a place you can trust."

- Equipment and materials are arranged consistently so children know where to find the things they need.

- Shelves are neat and uncluttered so children can make choices.

- A well-defined schedule is illustrated so children know what to expect.

- Routines follow a consistent order.

"You can do many things on your own and be independent."

- Storage shelves are low so children can reach materials. Toys with small parts are kept in boxes, plastic dish pans, or baskets.

- Materials are located in the areas where they will be used (crayons and markers near paper; blocks and block props in the block area).

- Picture labels on the shelves tell children where each toy or object belongs.

- A job chart shows how each child helps keep the room neat.

- Open spaces outdoors encourage children to run.

"You can get away and be by yourself when you need to."

- There are enclosed, quiet areas that accommodate one to two children.

- Outdoor materials and equipment allow children to play on different levels and create enclosed places.

- There is a large pillow or a stuffed chair off in a corner.

- There are headphones for a phonograph or tape recorder.

"This is a safe place to explore and try out your ideas."

- There are protected and defined quiet areas for small group activities.

- There is protected floor space to build with blocks without fear of traffic.

- The yard is fenced and soft cushioning is under climbing equipment.

- Attractive displays of materials invite children to use them.

- Toys are rotated so each week there is something new to explore.

Applying Your Knowledge

In this learning activity you identify ways in which your learning environment conveys positive messages to children. Then you decide what changes you can make in your indoor and outdoor space to reinforce these messages.

Message	How the Environment Conveys This Message	New Ideas to Try
"This is a cheerful and happy place."	Lots of choices, colorful area's, Lots of toys, everyones smiling; the teachers are happy - and want to be there	
"You belong here, and we like you."	friendly atmosphere; Things that are their size, and ready to be played with.	
"This is a place you can trust."	Whenever something goes wrong, the teachers are right there for the children.	

Message	How the Environment Conveys This Message	New Ideas to Try
"You can do many things on your own and be independent."	everything the childrens size; reachable; and easy to do - things they can't do teachers are willing to teach.	
"You can get away and be by yourself when you need to."	Their choice; Quiet area accessible to all children	
"This is a safe place to explore and try out your ideas."	Choices; No one telling them they can't do certain things	

After you have completed the charts, discuss your ideas with your colleagues. Use the chart below to note what changes you decide to make. Over the next few weeks, write down how children react to the changes you have made in your learning environment.

Changes to the Environment | **Children's Reactions**

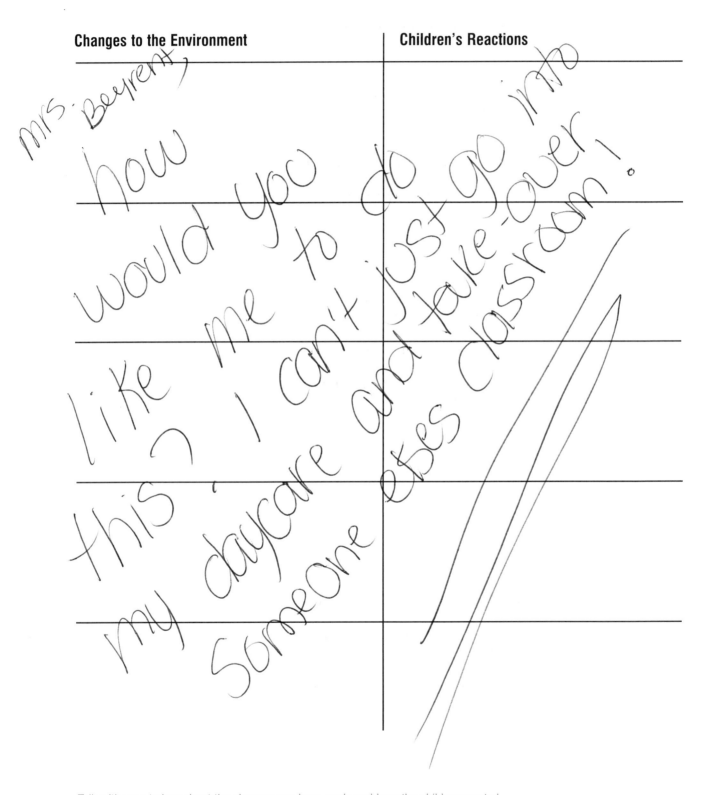

mrs. Beyrent,

how would you like me to do this? I can't just go into my daycare and take-over! Someone else's classroom!

Talk with your trainer about the changes you have made and how the children reacted.

III. Establishing Interest Areas in the Classroom

> **In this activity you will learn to:**
>
> - Identify the interest areas that are appropriate for your children
> - Locate interest areas so they are accessible and functional

An early childhood classroom includes a variety of clearly defined interest areas. This is done for two specific reasons. First, young children work best in small groups. It is easier for them to relate positively to only one or two other children than to a large group. By dividing your space into smaller areas, you can limit the number of children who can play together in any one area.

A second reason for creating interest areas in your classrooms is to offer children clear choices. Sometimes children want to work quietly alone or with one other child. An area set aside for books, art activities, or table toys allows several choices for quiet activities. Areas set aside for dramatic play, block building, woodworking, or large muscle activities offers children more active choices.

In most early childhood classrooms, you will find interest areas for dramatic play, block building, table toys, art, looking at books, and sand and water play. Other activity choices such as cooking, music and movement, and computers may be offered without creating an area if space is limited.

In setting up your indoor environment, keep in mind the following guidelines:

- Quiet areas (such as books, art, table toys, and private spaces) should be separated from noisier areas (such as blocks and house corner).

- Materials used together should be grouped together (e.g., crayons near drawing paper, block props near the blocks).

- Shelves, furniture, and carpets define areas.

- The art area should have a washable floor and be located near water.

- Blocks need clearly marked floor space and protection from traffic. Flat carpeting is best for this area.

- The library corner needs good light.

- An area large enough to accommodate the whole group should be designated for circle time. (This might be the library or block area.)

The chart that follows offers suggestions on how to arrange each interest area and describes what children are likely to do in each area.

Interest areas are especially appropriate for preschool children.

Several factors make interest areas work well.

Interest Area	Arrangement	What Children Do
Blocks	Away from line of traffic May be next to dramatic play area so activities can spill over Defined by low, open shelves Smooth, carpeted floor Wooden unit blocks stored on shelves by size and shape Props (people, animals, vehicles), small blocks, and construction materials in open containers	Learn about sizes and shapes Solve problems Cooperate to build group projects Engage in pretend play Grasp basic numerical concepts Use their creativity Lift and carry blocks
Art	Near the sink Washable floor Two-sided easels Table and chairs Materials stored in separate containers on low open shelf	Express ideas and feelings Develop small motor skills as they learn to use paint brushes, crayons, scissors Explore materials and make discoveries
Dramatic Play or House Corner	May be next to block area so activities can spill over Defined by shelves and furniture Child-size furniture and equipment (stove, table and chairs, stove, refrigerator) Dress-up clothes hung on low hooks Pots, pans, and other kitchen equipment stored on shelves or hung on peg board Props stored on low open shelf	Act out familiar adult roles (play house) Conquer fears (e.g., going to the dentist or being a scary monster) Learn to get along with other children Develop social skills—sharing, negotiating, compromising, appreciating other people Develop abstract thinking skills—creating mental images, relating one event to another Use small muscle skills
Sand and Water	Near a source of water Washable floor Smocks and a variety of props stored within children's reach	Release tension Learn about shape, size, and volume Use their creativity Make discoveries Cooperate with others Use small muscle skills

Interest Area	Arrangement	What Children Do
Library	In a quiet corner Carpeted floor Good light Comfortable places to sit Books reflecting children's culture and ethnicity, displayed on a stand with covers facing out A small table and chairs Materials for writing stored in open containers on low open shelves	Look at books Read books with an adult Look at pictures and letters Spend time alone Listen to books on tape Use small muscle skills Share a favorite story with a friend
Table Toys or Manipulatives	Away from noisy areas such as blocks and dramatic play Defined by low shelves Table and chairs Toys (e.g., beads and laces, bottle caps to sort, pegs and pegboards) stored in open containers on shelves Puzzles stored on racks	Notice the characteristics of things Group items by category Make patterns Use creativity Use small muscle skills Work independently or in a small group
Computers	Away from water, food, and paint Next to another quiet area such as the library Good lighting that does not cause glare on computer screens One or more computers and a printer set up against a wall or divider Two chairs at each computer Electrical cords out of children's reach Developmentally appropriate software stored within children's reach	Follow directions Use creativity Develop a sense of competence Spend time with an adult—as a teacher and a learner Learn by experimenting Cooperate with other children Share knowledge with another child

You may need to adapt the environment for children with special needs.

If you have children with physical disabilities in your program you will need to ensure that the space is safe and accessible. An expert consultant can help you to evaluate your classroom and outdoor areas to determine what changes, if any, are needed to encourage each child's full participation. You may take steps such as the following:

- Ensure that traffic patterns between interest areas are wide enough for a child using a wheel chair or a walker.

- Adjust tables so wheelchairs will fit underneath or equip them with trays. Provide tall stools so other children can sit comfortably at a raised table.

- Provide bolsters or other supports so children with mobility impairments can do activities on the floor.

- Provide adaptive equipment for standing.

- Use puzzles with knobs for children with visual impairments.

Applying Your Knowledge

In this learning activity, you identify strengths and weaknesses of two different floor plans of a preschool classroom. Then you draw a plan of your own classroom and decide what changes you want to make to improve the learning environment.

Classroom Arrangements[1]

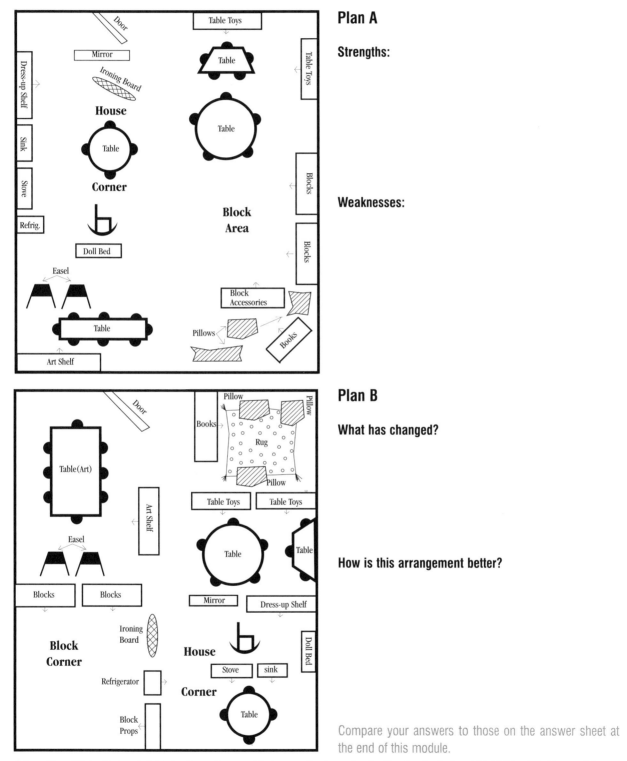

Plan A

Strengths:

Weaknesses:

Plan B

What has changed?

How is this arrangement better?

Compare your answers to those on the answer sheet at the end of this module.

[1] From Diane Trister Dodge, *A Guide for Supervisors and Trainers on Implementing the Creative Curriculum, Third Edition* (Washington, DC: Teaching Strategies, Inc., 1993), p. 81.

167

Use the space below to draw a plan of your classroom as it is now arranged.

On the basis of what you have learned in this module, what changes/additions do you want to make? Redraw your floor plan to show this new arrangement.

Discuss the new floor plan with your colleagues. Decide what changes you will make. Use the space below to record how children respond to these changes. Then discuss this learning activity with your trainer.

IV. Selecting and Displaying Materials

In this activity you will learn to:

- Select materials that reflect the abilities and interests of your current group of children
- Display and label materials so children can find what they need and clean up

For interest areas to work, teachers have to select materials that are appropriate. This means the children have the skills to use materials well. Equally important is how teachers organize and display materials so that children can find what they need and take responsibility for returning materials when they are finished. When interest areas are thoughtfully stocked and organized, children are more likely to make good use of them and to learn from their play.

Selecting the right materials for each interest area depends partly on what materials are available in your center. In an established center, each room already has a supply of materials and toys appropriate for the age group of the children. However, there are ways to expand this supply. You can rotate toys, using them for a few weeks and then putting them away for a while. Children will find matching games or props for the block area just as interesting in January as they were in September if they have been out of sight for several months in between. Some teachers trade toys with another classroom to give each group of children a greater variety of interesting materials.

Many excellent materials for preschool children can be collected and brought from home. For example, you can bring in dress-up clothes, props for the house corner, plastic bottles and measuring cups for the water table, bottle caps to sort and match, and collections for the science table. Finally, you can add to your supply of materials by making games to challenge children's growing interests.

In selecting materials, ask yourself these questions.

- Will it interest the children? Your daily observations of the children will help you identify children's interests.

- Do the children have the skills to handle it? For example, are they ready for ten-piece puzzles or only for puzzles with five pieces?

- Will it challenge children to think and explore? Assorted buttons or bottle caps will be just as interesting as colored shapes for sorting.

Well stocked interest areas invite children to play.

Teachers must continually evaluate the appropriateness of materials.

169

- Does it reflect the families and cultural backgrounds of the children? Pictures in children's books, wooden figures for the block area, and dolls in the house corner should reflect the diversity of our society and help children accept and respect these differences.

- Does it show people with handicapping conditions engaged in meaningful tasks?

- Does it promote equal use by boys and girls? Be sure, for example, to include male dress-up clothes in the house corner, and pictures that show men and women in different types of roles.

- Is it durable and in good condition? This means no broken parts and no missing pieces. Materials should be clean and free of splinters or any jagged edges.

- Are there sufficient open-ended materials that encourage children's creativity? Blocks, art materials, and many table toys can be used in a variety of ways.

- Does it help achieve your goals for children? For example, will it help children develop creativity? Learn to think? Develop language skills? Develop small and large muscle control?

(In Modules 4 through 10 you will find many ideas for selecting materials that will promote children's physical, cognitive, social, and language development.)

Take time to organize materials logically and display them attractively.

The organization and display of materials in the classroom is as important as what you put out. Interest areas will work much better if the materials are well-organized and inviting to children.

- Identify a specific place for each of the materials in the room.

- Group materials used together (e.g., crayons and markers with paper, utensils with playdough, small cars and figures with blocks).

- Make picture labels tapes for the shelves so that children can find and return the materials they use. Cover them with clear Contact paper or laminate them to make them last.

- Store toys with small parts or pieces in open, labeled containers, such as boxes or dish pans.

Applying Your Knowledge

In this learning activity you use a checklist to identify the materials and equipment typically found in nine interest areas. Read over the list and make a check beside each item you now have in your room. There are spaces for you to add items to the list.

House Corner

This area for dramatic play begins with a home setting but can be adapted as children's play themes expand to the larger community.

Equipment and Furniture

- ✓ Stove
- ✓ Sink
- ✓ Cabinet
- ✓ Refrigerator
- ✓ Small table and two to three chairs

- ___ Sturdy bed that holds a child
- ✓ High chair
- ✓ Full length mirror
- ___ A place to hang dress-up clothes

Props and Materials

- ✓ Dishes and silverware
- ✓ Pots and pans
- ✓ Cooking utensils
- ___ Aprons
- ___ Pot holders
- ___ Toasters
- ✓ Dolls (reflecting children's ethnicity)
- ✓ Prop boxes on varied themes

- ___ Tablecloth
- ✓ Dress-up clothes for men and women
- ✓ Telephones (at least two)
- ___ Magazines, paper, pens
- ✓ Suitcases and pocketbooks
- ✓ Hats
- ✓ Shoes

- ___ _____
- ___ _____

- ___ _____
- ___ _____

Table Toys

Good table toys help children distinguish likenesses and differences and promote small muscle control and eye-hand coordination.

- ✓ A low shelf to display toys
- ✓ A low table with four to five chairs
- ✓ A puzzle rack
- ✓ A selection of puzzles (about five)
- ✓ Pegs and pegboards
- ✓ Beads and laces
- ✓ Parquetry blocks
- ✓ Colored inch cube blocks
- ✓ Collections for sorting and classifying

- ✓ Attribute blocks
- ___ Nesting cups or rings
- ___ Cuisenaire Rods
- ___ Homemade games
- ✓ Bristle Blocks
- ✓ Tinker Toys
- ___ Stacking rings
- ✓ Sewing cards

- ___ _____
- ___ _____

- ___ _____
- ___ _____

Block Area

Unit blocks help children learn about sizes and shapes and develop a concrete understanding of math concepts. Through dramatic play with blocks and props, children deepen their understanding about the world around them.

- ✓ Low shelves for storage (preferably two)
- __ Colored inch cubes for decorating buildings
- ✓ Unit blocks in a variety of sizes and shapes
- __ Wood or rubber animals (zoo and farm)
- __ _____
- __ _____

- ✓ Small cars and trucks
- __ Traffic signs
- __ Wood or rubber people
- __ Paper, markers, and tape
- __ _____
- __ _____

Art Area

Stock the art area with a rich selection of materials that will encourage children to explore, create, and express themselves.

- __ A two-sided easel
- __ Paint brushes with long and short handles
- __ Paint holders
- ✓ Crayons—large and of good quality
- __ Water-based paint in a variety of colors
- ✓ Assorted water-based markers
- ✓ Large school pencils
- __ Sponges for clean up
- ✓ Collage items (fabric, buttons, feathers, yarn, ribbon)
- __ _____
- __ _____

- ✓ Glue
- __ Fingerpaint paper
- __ Easel paper
- ✓ Drawing paper
- __ Construction paper
- __ Playdough and utensils
- ✓ Scissors
- ✓ Smocks
- __ _____
- __ _____

Library

A selection of different types of books exposes children to the wonderful world of literature. Keep on hand children's favorites and regularly add new books to attract children's attention and interest.

- ✓ A display shelf for books (one that shows front cover)
- ✓ Several large pillows
- ✓ Books in good condition
- ✓ Books showing men and women in different roles
- ✓ Books appropriate for the children's ages
- __ A record player with headphones and records
- ✓ Puppets
- __ Paper and writing tools
- __ _____
- __ _____

- __ A small table with two or three chairs
- ✓ Soft carpeting
- ✓ Books on a variety of topics
- __ Books showing different ethnic groups
- ✓ Decorations (a plant, pictures on walls, a tablecloth)
- __ A tape recorder with headphones and cassettes
- __ A flannel board
- __ Rubber letter stamps and ink pads
- ✓ Coach w/pillows
- __ _____

Computers

___ Macintosh IILC, IBM, or IBM compatible with monitor
___ Keyboard
___ Surge protector
___ Diskettes and diskette holders or storage container

___ ——————————————————— No Computers!
___ ———————————————————

___ Printer and paper
___ Computer cables
___ Software

Large Muscle Area

___ A large indoor climber
___ A loft with a ladder
___ Cardboard cartons for children to crawl into

___ ——————————————————— nothing
___ ———————————————————

___ A set of large hollow blocks
___ Large-wheeled toys
___ A balance beam

Sand and Water

✓ A sand and water table
✓ Basins to hold sand and water
___ A shelf or box to hold equipment
___ Waterproof aprons
✓ A supply of empty plastic squeeze bottles
✓ Funnels

___ ————————————
___ ————————————

___ Plastic pitchers
___ Plastic basters or eye droppers
___ Plastic hoses
✓ Plastic boats
✓ Measuring cups
___ Sponges and mops for clean up

___ ————————————
___ ————————————

Science

___ A table or shelf for display
___ Animal(s) in a cage and food
___ Fish bowl
___ Balance scales
___ Magnifying lenses
___ Tape measure
___ Paper and writing tools

___ ——————————————————— nothing!
___ ———————————————————

___ Display table (for collections)
___ Books related to the displays
___ Old appliances to take apart
___ Magnets and an assortment of metal objects
___ Seeds growing
___ A Slinky

Woodworking

Real tools and soft wood are essential for a successful woodworking area.

___ A sturdy workbench (or homemade substitute)
___ Soft wood
___ A pegboard or shelf for storing tools
___ Hammers
___ Screwdriver and screws
___ Assorted objects: wooden wheels, leather scraps
___
___

___ A vise
___ Sandpaper
___ Saws
___ Nails with large heads
___ Hand drills

Nothing

After identifying the materials you have in your classroom, use the checklist below to assess how you have organized and displayed these materials in your classroom.

	Yes	No
There is a specific place for each type of material.	☒	☐
Materials used together are grouped together.	☒	☐
All materials have picture labels.	☐	☒
Toys with small parts are kept in labeled containers.	☐	☒

Review your responses with your trainer and colleagues and determine what changes you will make in your classroom. If you make any changes, use the space below to record how children react.

V. Organizing the Outdoor Environment

In this activity you will learn to:

- Organize the outdoor environment to offer children a variety of choices
- Determine what materials and equipment are needed to improve your outdoor space

The outdoor environment provides a whole new world for children to learn about and to explore. New scenery and a change of pace are good for children's emotional and physical health and well-being. Playing outdoors is also a good way for children to release pent-up energy. The outdoor space is as important as the classroom, and teachers need to plan outdoor activities as carefully as they plan indoor ones.

Whether your program operates in a rural, suburban, or city environment, the outdoors can provide a variety of new experiences to children. Probably no other area of an early childhood environment is as variable as the outdoor space. Some programs have only blacktop and a fence surrounding their outdoor space; others have natural surroundings that provide softness and invite exploration. Even in the most limited outdoor environments, there is much you can do to offer children a range of outdoor experiences.

The outdoor environment offers children a wide range of experiences.

If possible, the outdoor environment should include the following:

- easy access to and from the indoor space used by the program

- a drinking fountain and water spigot for attaching a hose

- nearby bathrooms

- a storage shed outdoors or indoors, near the door to the outdoor area

- soft materials such as sawdust, sand, or bark under swings, slides, and climbers

- a paved or hard-surfaced area for riding, skating, chalk drawings, and games

- a covered area for use in wet weather

- sunny areas

- shady areas

- places to be alone or with one or two friends (boxes, tents, logs, bushes)

- open, grassy spaces for tumbling, running, and sitting

- open fields for active or group play.

(See Module 1, Safe, for information on the characteristics of safe playgrounds.)

Children and staff need to dress for the weather.

You and the children will feel more comfortable outdoors if you are dressed appropriately for the weather. On cold days this includes dressing in layers (long sleeve shirt, sweater, and coat), and wearing a hat and gloves or mittens. On warm days, dress in loose clothing made from light fabrics, and perhaps wear a hat with a visor. You can keep on hand a box of extra clothes: loose T-shirts, shorts, and baseball caps in the summer; and scarves, hats, gloves, and sweaters in the winter.

The outdoor environment may need to be modified for children with special needs.

Children with special needs benefit from outdoor time, just as do all children. However, depending on the type and severity of the disability, the outdoors can be overwhelming and even frightening to a child who is unsure of how to get around an open space safely.

A good place to start in analyzing your outdoor space is to evaluate it from the child's point of view. A child with a visual disability will need help in navigating around the space. You will have to orient the child to the location of different play structures. Allow the child to touch the equipment as you describe its features and guide the child's first attempts. Stay close by to supervise and teach other children to assist those with visual impairments.

For children with hearing problems, point out possible hazards such as swings. Remind children to look carefully in all directions before running across the yard.

Special adaptations may be necessary for children with physical disabilities. Here are some suggestions:

- Provide bucket seats or straps on swings.

- Build ramps over uneven surfaces or on inclines for children in wheel chairs or who have poor balance.

- Place handholds and rails on climbing equipment and structures.

- Offer activities such as sand and water play and art on a table so children in wheelchairs can participate with others.

- Place straps on pedals of wheel toys.

Like the indoor space, the outdoor environment for preschool children should offer a range of choices. In addition to traditional outdoor activities such as swinging, sliding and climbing, using open spaces for running and riding, and space for construction and digging, many indoor activities can be brought outdoors and experienced in a whole new way.

Organize the outdoor environment to offer children choices.

Like the indoor environment, the outdoor space can be organized by interest areas that provide a variety of materials and experiences. Locate active play areas near each other and separate them from the quieter ones. Mark off clear pathways between areas to help avoid accidents. Store equipment and materials used outdoors in a storage shed or bring them outdoors from the classroom.

The chart that follows lists the types of activities you can offer children outdoors.[2] For each activity, it identifies materials and equipment needed, and what children are likely to do.

Activity	Materials and Equipment	What Children Do
Sand Play	Large covered sand box (wooden that folds back in sections or has a tarp cover) Pails, scoops, muffin tins, shovels, molds, funnels People and animals (small, inexpensive plastic or rubber) Old toy vehicles Pine cones, stones, twigs, leaves Access to water (faucet and hose or spray bottles or containers filled with water)	"Bake" pies and cakes Make roads Build castles Create houses and towns Dig, pour, sift, mold Solve problems Cooperate with others Pretend
Water Play	Water table or large tub Wading pool that meets safety requirements Buckets (small, plastic, with handles) Large brushes Painters' hats Squeeze bottles, sponges, pails, cups Hose Sprinkler Watering cans or plastic bottles with sprinkler tops Soap Bath, laundry, and cleaning props Bubble blowing props	Release tension Learn about shape, size, and volume Use their creativity Make discoveries Cooperate with others Use small muscle skills to pour, squirt, spray, scrub Paint with water (a fence, the building) Wash doll clothes Wash objects (the picnic table, a wagon, anything that "looks dirty") Blow bubbles Run through a sprinkler

[2] Based in part on Diane Trister Dodge and Laura J. Colker, *The Creative Curriculum for Early Childhood, Third Edition* (Washington, DC: Teaching Strategies, Inc., 1992), pp. 331-337.

Activity	Materials and Equipment	What Children Do
Wheeled Toys	Tricycles (institutional, in 2 sizes) Wagons Wheelbarrows Scooters Large set of traffic signs Set of cones (used to mark boundaries and safety zones) Hats (truck driver, firefighter, caps)	Ride bikes, pull wagons, and push wheelbarrows Pretend to drive trucks, fire engines, ambulances, and other vehicles Follow rules and stay within boundaries Learn to share and take turns
Games	Rubber balls (different sizes) Large bats (plastic, hollow) Bean bags Parachute Balance beam Hula hoops Ropes Tunnels	Throw, kick, catch, bounce, jump, and balance Explore new ways to move their bodies Crawl forward and backward Play with a friend or a small group Develop new skills
Construction	Boards Wooden boxes Saw horses Large blocks Tires Spools (donated by phone company) Large blocks Cartons and crates Roofing materials (cardboard, blankets, sheets)	List and carry Build hideaways Pretend Cooperate with others Take "safe" risks
Gardening	Sets of gardening tools (child-sized) Watering cans Hose with spray and sprinkler attachments Seeds or plants Containers Soil (for containers) Fertilizer (out of children's reach) Trellis for climbing plants (beans, peas, morning glories) String and sticks to mark rows	Dig, rake, and hoe Learn about what makes plants grow Measure and make graphs Work as a team with others Share products of the garden

Activity	Materials and Equipment	What Children Do
Snow Play	Tub or water table to hold snow Props (shovels, molds, buckets, dowels) Snow saucers Sleds Extra hats, mittens, scarves for children and adults	Take "safe" risks Dig and mold Experiment Create
Woodworking	Workbench and/or large tree stump placed on end Safety goggles Sets of child-size tools C-clamps Vises Wood scraps (splinter-free) Nails and screws with large heads Sandpaper Metal files Rulers and measuring tapes Paint Decorations (bottle caps, wooden spools, wire, cork, popsicle sticks, dowels)	Hammer, saw, drill, carry wood, sand, file, pull out nails, and fasten screws Use creativity Socialize with others Learn new words to describe their skills Measure, compare, learn about size and shape
Art	Easels Paints Paper Brushes Crayons Clothesline and clothes pins Collage items Glue Scissors Chalk Yarn String Any other items from indoors that children enjoy using	Paint Draw Express creativity Find new ways to use materials Participate in small group activities Cooperate and share Solve problems Experiment Draw on the sidewalk Weave

Activity	Materials and Equipment	What Children Do
Quiet Activities	Games Puzzles Legos Beads and laces Pegs and pegboards Books CD or tape player with CDs or tapes and headphones Table blocks Collections Any other items from indoors that children enjoy using	Spend time alone or with one or two others Solve problems Use creativity Sort and categorize Listen to music
Science and Nature	Pets Pet food, cages, water bottles Large and hand-held magnifying glasses Containers for collections Trowels Thermometers Rain and snow gauge	Care for and play with pets Dig in the dirt to see what lives there Examine natural items with hand lens Make collections Observe and categorize Learn new words Compare the temperatures in sunny and shady areas Graph rain and snowfall

Applying Your Knowledge

In this learning activity you identify the types of activities you now offer children outdoors. Then you select three new activities, or activities you want to improve, and list the materials and equipment you want to add to your outdoor environment. After introducing the materials to children, observe what they do and note your observations on the chart provided.

Improving the Outdoor Environment

Check the activities you now offer children outdoors:

✓ sand play   ___ wheeled toys   ___ construction

___ water play   ___ art   ___ gardening

___ snow play   ___ woodworking   ___ games

___ quiet activities   ___ science and nature

✓ tires to climb
✓ climbing structure

Select three activities to add or improve. Record what materials and equipment you add and what children do.

Activity	Materials and Equipment	What Children Do
	how?	

After completing this chart, discuss with your trainer the changes you made and how children responded.

VI. *Planning the Daily Schedule, Routines, and Transitions*

> **In this activity you will learn to:**
>
> • Plan a daily schedule and routines that meet children's developmental needs
> • Use transitions as learning times

The daily schedule should offer a balance of activities and be predictable.

The daily schedule states the sequence of the day's activities and tells when they will occur and for how long. When the schedule is consistent from day to day, children can predict what will happen. This predictability helps children feel more secure. The following are characteristics of a well-planned schedule.

- The day is **balanced** between active and quiet times; large group, small group, and individual activities; child-initiated and adult-led activities; and indoor and outdoor play periods.

- There is **sufficient time for transitions** so children don't have to hurry.

- There is **a long block of time for free play** when children can choose their own activities and pursue their own interests.

- **Outdoor play** is planned for at least 45 minutes. Programs operating for four or more hours have outdoor play twice a day.

- Children spend **very little time in large group activities.** Young children develop social skills by playing with one or two other children. After successfully playing in small groups, they are better able to participate in a large group activity.

A picture of the schedule helps children learn the order of the day.

A pictorial representation of the schedule helps children actually see the order of daily events. This can be done using drawings or photographs. For example, a series of photographs could show children arriving in the morning, playing at the interest centers, getting ready to go outdoors, playing outside, and so on. This can be particularly helpful for children who have very little consistency in their lives and do not have a sense of control over what takes place.

When they first enter the program in the morning, children might need reminders of what happens during the day. For example, "During free play we usually stay indoors. We'll go outside after snack." Children will feel empowered when they can state with accuracy what will take place next, "First I eat lunch. Then I brush my teeth."

While allowing for individual differences among children, the daily schedule should incorporate many opportunities for children to develop skills as they go about activities.

Language skills develop whenever children talk with each other and with adults, for example, during dramatic play, water and sand play, art experiences, block play, music and movement activities, and snack.

Physical skills develop as children use tools and art materials, climb to the top of the loft, jump in a pile of pillows, ride a tricycle, pull a wagon, build with blocks, and play catch with a friend or teacher.

Social skills grow as children learn to make friends, negotiate, handle disagreements, and feel and express empathy for others. Teachers can help children develop social skills by asking two children to help each other, inviting a child to enter a dramatic play theme, or modeling social skills by joining in children's play.

Cognitive skills develop as children explore the materials in the water table to see what floats or sinks, build a complex block structure, combine paint colors at the easel, and figure out a way to take turns carrying a favorite pocketbook.

Self-help skills are reinforced as children put on and take off dress-up clothes, set the table in the house corner, and select and put away toys.

Coping skills develop as children learn to deal with frustration when a puzzle piece won't fit or another child gets to the last empty swing first.

Routines are the events that take place ever day: arriving and leaving, eating, sleeping or resting, toileting, dressing and undressing, and cleaning up. They can take up significant portions of day, but it's a mistake to view them as "chores," to be quickly accomplished so children can move on to more meaningful activities. Instead, routines are opportunities to help children feel secure and to build their self-confidence. For example, children learn that each day after eating lunch, they go to the sink to brush their teeth and wash their hands, get their blankets from their cubbies, and go to their cots (ideally, children consistently use the same cot, set up in the same place in the room). Participating in routines allows children to develop:

- small muscle skills as they brush teeth, pour juice, serve themselves, and zip or button clothing;

- large muscle skills as they help set up cots or arrange chairs around a table;

- social and language skills as they talk with each other and adults during relaxed, family-style meals;

- self-help skills as they wash their own hands before and after eating;

- cognitive skills such as one-to-one correspondence as they set places at the table, putting utensils, plate, cup, and napkin at each place; and

- social skills as they work together to prepare for a meal.

The schedule should provide opportunities for children to develop important skills.

Routines can offer opportunities for learning.

In full-day programs, the daily schedule includes a block of time when children can nap or rest while doing quiet activities. Some children find it easy to fall asleep immediately; others need extra attention to help them relax enough to fall asleep. Many teachers find it helps to rub children's backs, play music at low volume, read stories, and sing songs softly to help children fall asleep. Those who can't sleep or who get up early can benefit from a restful period of looking at books, drawing, or playing with manipulatives such as beads and laces.

Transitions can be unsettling if children don't know what to do.

Transitions—the periods of time between one activity and the next—can be learning opportunities or problem times. If children have nothing to do while waiting, they may become restless. They sometimes act in ways that teachers don't like—wrestling with one another or running around the room. This is because they are bored.

During a transition, there are often some children who are still busy completing an activity and some just waiting for the next one. If one teacher is helping the children who are finishing an activity and the other teacher plans something for the rest of the group, transitions usually run more smoothly.

Here are some additional tips for making transitions go better:

Give children a warning. "In five minutes it will be time to clean up."

Involve children in transition activities. Children can help with activities such as setting the tables for meals, collecting the trash, washing the paint brushes.

Provide clear directions. State them clearly and simply. "Please find your mat and sit in the listening area. I'll be right there to read a story."

Be flexible whenever possible. Allow children extra time to complete special projects or activities when they seem very interested and involved. "We're going to let the block builders finish their building while the rest of us start to clean up. Then we can all hear about what happened in the block corner today."

Allow children to share their work. Children are often more willing to clean up if they have an opportunity to share and talk about their work. Gather the children in the meeting area after choice time and before clean up while their work is still evident. Invite children to talk about what they did, and then ask for volunteers to clean up each of the areas.

Keep children occupied. If children have something specific to do, they are less likely to act disruptively. For example, those who are finished eating or cleaning up could take a book to look at while they wait for the others, or get their coats on and go outside with one teacher.

Establish a signal for quiet. When the noise level gets too disruptive, use a signal such as a bell, an autoharp, raising hands, or blinking the lights to get children's attention.

Transition times can be used to teach new concepts, to practice skills, and to enhance creativity. Here are some suggestions for making transitions important learning times.

- Play a game of follow the leader. You can lead the children in picking up toys, going outdoors, making funny gestures, and so forth.

- Call out different categories as you move children from one activity time to another. ("If you're wearing red today, you can get your coat on." "Everyone wearing sneakers with laces can go quietly to the juice table.")

- Ask children to try out unusual ways to move. ("Let's go to our meeting place like big, slow, heavy elephants.")

- When you want children to be quiet so they can listen to you, play a clapping game—clap out different beats, loud and soft, and get children to follow.

- Learn finger plays that you can teach the children or special songs you can sing.

- Ask children to help each other. ("Kim, can you please help Sara find her mittens?")

Applying Your Knowledge

In this learning activity you review a sample daily schedule and identify what makes it appropriate for preschool children. Then you assess the appropriateness of your schedule and decide whether you want to make any changes.

Sample Daily Schedule

7:30 - 8:15	**Children Arrive:** Children participate in quiet activities and prepare for breakfast.	**Early Morning Schedule**
8:15 - 9:00	**Breakfast and Clean-Up:** As children finish breakfast, they may read books or listen to music until all are ready for the next activity.	

9:00 - 9:15	**Group Time:** A teacher leads one or more of the following activities:	**Morning Schedule**

- conversation
- stories
- sharing
- flannel board
- music and movement
- finger plays

9:15 - 10:30	**Choice Time:** Children choose activities in the following areas:

- art
- blocks
- books
- table toys
- house corner
- sand and water

10:30 - 10:45	**Clean Up:** Children put away toys and materials.
10:45 - 11:00	**Snack:** Children help set the tables and eat a snack together.
11:00 - 11:45	**Outdoor Play:** Children select from a variety of activities such as sand play; using balls, jump ropes, and large wheeled toys; gardening; painting; caring for pets; swinging; climbing; and so on.
11:45 - 12:00	**Story Time and Preparing to Go Home** (for morning programs): The group gathers for a story and to review the day. Then children prepare to go home.

12:00 - 1:00	**Prepare for Lunch, Eat, Clean Up** (for full-day programs): Assigned children help set the tables for lunch; others wash their hands and find their place mats. Children and teachers enjoy a family-style meal. As children finish lunch, they go to the bathroom in small groups and read books on their cots in preparation for nap time.	**Lunch**

1:00 - 1:10	**Quiet Activity Prior to Nap:** Children hear a story or song by a teacher, classical music, or a story record.	**Lunch** (continued)
1:10 - 3:00	**Rest Time:** Teachers help children settle down and relax. Children who do not sleep or who awaken are offered books, table toys, and other quiet activities.	

3:00 - 3:30	**Snack and Preparation to Go Outdoors:** Children help set the tables for snack and prepare for the next activity.	**Afternoon Schedule**
3:30 - 4:30	**Outdoor Play:** Children select from a variety of outdoor activities such as sand play; using balls, jump ropes, and large wheeled toys; gardening; painting; caring for pets; swinging; climbing; and so on.	
4:30 -6:00	**Choice Time and Going Home:** Children select from activities such as:	

- table toys
- stories
- board games

- songs, finger plays, or music
- coloring

Teachers talk informally with family members as children are picked up.

Why is this schedule appropriate for preschool children?

Compare your responses to those on the answer sheet at the end of the module.

Daily Schedule

How does your schedule measure up to the guidelines? Review the schedule you now follow and assess whether it meets the criteria you listed. Decide on any changes you want to make. Then, use the space below to record your daily schedule.

Time	Activity

Discuss your schedule with your colleagues and your trainer.

Summarizing Your Progress

You have now completed all of the learning activities for this module. Whether you are an experienced teacher or new to the profession, this module has probably helped you develop new skills in creating a learning environment for preschool children.

Before you go on to the next module, take a few minutes to summarize what you've learned.

- Turn back to Learning Activity I, Using Your Knowledge of Child Development to Create a Learning Environment, and add to the chart specific examples of what you learned about creating a good learning environment during the time you were working on this module. Compare your ideas to those in the completed chart at the end of the module.

- Next, review your responses to the pre-training assessment for this module. Write a summary of what you learned, and list the skills you developed or improved.

If there are areas you would like to know more about, you will find recommended readings listed in the Orientation.

Your final step in this module is to complete the knowledge and competency assessments. Let your trainer know when you are ready to schedule the assessments. After you have successfully completed these assessments, you will be ready to start a new module. Congratulations on your progress so far, and good luck with your next module.

Answer Sheets

Overview
(pp. 145-147)

Organizing Indoor and Outdoor Areas That Encourage Play and Exploration

1.   What did Mr. Lopez know about the children?
   a.   The children acted frustrated when they could not get equipment they wanted.

   b.   Some children's play and work was being interrupted by other children playing ball.

2.   How did Mr. Lopez organize the outdoor area so it would encourage play and exploration?
   a.   He made sure the toys and equipment were easy to find and within children's reach.

   b.   He designated certain areas for specific activities to protect quiet play and to give children space for active play.

Selecting and Attractively Displaying Materials and Equipment

1.   What did Ms. Williams know about the children?
   a.   They were concerned about the classmate who was in the hospital.

   b.   Some children appeared especially anxious.

   c.   The children would probably be very interested in the hospital prop box and water play.

2.   What activities and materials did Ms. Williams plan to offer for the children and why?
   a.   She prepared a hospital prop box and put out books about going to the hospital.

   b.   She planned a water-play activity because she knew it was a calming activity.

Planning and Implementing a Schedule, Routines, and Transitions to Meet Children's Needs

1.   How did Ms. Richards use block clean up as an opportunity for learning?
   a.   She demonstrated what it means to cooperate and help others by participating in clean up.

   b.   She made up a game of finding different shapes to clean up, thus teaching children the names of the block shapes and practicing classification.

   c.   She gave the children a chance to identify blocks they wanted to clean up, thus reinforcing classification skills.

2.   What did Ms. Kim do to make sure that the children who were finished cleaning up had something to do?
   a.   She spoke to each group of children and told them to select a book to look at in the meeting area.

   b.   She made sure that the children knew what to do and where to go when they were finished.

Using Your Knowledge of Child Development to Create a Learning Environment

(p. 155)

What Preschool Children Are Like	How Teachers Can Use This Information to Create a Learning Environment
They enjoy large muscle activities such running, jumping, climbing, and riding tricycles.	*Set aside an indoor area for large play equipment. Plan some activities that use large muscles (for example, pounding clay or dough, woodworking). Make sure the outdoor area is safe for running and climbing.*
They are gaining increasing control of small muscles.	*Set out toys with small pieces (for example, pegs and pegboards, laces and beads, Legos). Provide art materials such as markers, playdough, clay, and scissors.*
They are learning to share and take turns.	*Provide duplicates of some popular toys and materials. Show children how long they have to wait. Use a clock or a timer, or write their names on a list to help them learn to share.*
They can play cooperatively with one or two others and often have "best friends."	*Plan lots of small group activities. Define small areas for activities where several children can work together. Put out props for dramatic play and encourage children to play together.*
They sometimes need to get away from the group and be by themselves.	*Set up areas where children can be alone—a large stuffed chair, a loft, or a big cardboard box to hide in, and a listening area with headphones.*
They have a lot of energy but can easily tire.	*Plan a schedule that offers a balance of active and quiet activities and provides children with choices. Include soft places such as pillows and bean-bag chairs in which children can relax.*

Using Your Knowledge of Child Development to Create a Learning Environment
(p. 156)

What Preschool Children Are Like	How Teachers Can Use This Information to Create a Learning Environment
They like to be helpful.	*Decide on jobs that children can do alone or with adult help and make a job chart. Make name cards to show who has each job (for example, feeding pets, watering plants, setting tables, passing out snacks).*
They can take responsibility for keeping the classroom orderly.	*Carefully organize materials. Put things together that are used together (for example, put crayons and markers near drawing paper). Make picture labels to put on shelves to show where items belong, to help children see that everything has a place.*
They love to play make-believe. Their dramatic play goes from family roles to people in the community and super-heroes.	*Set up a dramatic play area that looks like a home. Put out dress-up clothes, kitchen utensils, and so on. Gradually add different kinds of props—for example, for playing hospital, fire-fighter, grocery store, or shoe store—to encourage dramatic play.*
They have lots of interests.	*Find out about children's interests through observations and conversations with parents. Give lots of choices. Add new materials and new toys so children often find something new to do.*
They draw pictures and create objects that represent real things.	*Keep crayons, markers, and large pencils on low shelves for use every day. Give children a good supply of unit blocks and props (for example, farm and zoo animals, people, cars). Talk with children about what they do.*

Classroom Arrangements
(p. 167)

Floor Plan A

Strengths:

- *The table toys are stored on shelves near the tables where they will be used.*

- *The book area is in a protected corner.*

- *Materials for each area are grouped together.*

Weaknesses:

- *Shelves are not used to define areas—there are no enclosed areas.*

- *The open spaces invite children to run.*

- *The block area is too open—buildings will be knocked down.*

- *The book corner (a quiet area) is right near the block area so children will be disturbed.*

Floor Plan B

What has changed?

- *Shelves are used to define different interest areas.*

- *Tables are moved to interest areas.*

- *The table toy area is enclosed by shelves and away from the line of traffic.*

- *Easels are in a protected area.*

- *The block area is protected and near other active areas.*

- *The book area is far from noisy interest areas and looks secluded and cozy.*

Why is this arrangement better?

- *Children are less likely to run in this room.*

- *Children will feel more protected in each interest area.*

- *The block area is enclosed so structures are less likely to be knocked down.*

- *Quiet interest areas (art, table toys, and books) are grouped together.*

- *Locating the house corner and block corner together promotes dramatic play.*

- *Materials are stored on shelves in the areas where they are to be used.*

Daily Schedule Checklist
(p. 187)

An appropriate daily schedule should offer:

- *A balance of active and quiet activities.*

- *At least one hour for choice time.*

- *Sufficient time for routines.*

- *Time for children to work together in large and small group times.*

- *Time to read story books to the whole group.*

- *One or two periods of outdoor time.*

- *Sufficient time for transitions.*

Glossary

Daily schedule

How you anticipate and plan for the day's activities. The schedule includes the times of day and the order in which activities will occur.

Learning environment

The complete makeup of the classroom and outdoor space including how it is arranged and furnished, materials and equipment, planned and unplanned activities.

Routines

Scheduled activities that occur every day, including meals, naps, toileting, washing hands, and going outdoors. All of these can offer opportunities for children to learn.

Transitions

The in-between times in a daily schedule when children have completed an activity period and are moving to the next one.

Overview

Promoting physical development involves:

- Providing materials, equipment, and opportunities for gross motor development
- Providing materials and opportunities for fine motor development
- Reinforcing and encouraging children's physical fitness

We adults use a wide range of physical skills every day. We walk and run, often several miles a day. We open car doors, carry boxes, and climb stairs. We grasp pencils, forks, cups, and other small items and use tools such as scissors and computer keyboards. Because we use our large and small muscles so frequently, we rarely think about the skills involved. In fact, however, we developed these skills through many years of practice.

Physical development refers to the gradual gaining of control over large and small muscles. It includes acquiring gross motor skills—such as crawling, walking, running, and throwing—and fine motor skills—such as holding, pinching, and flexing fingers and toes. Coordinating movement is an important part of physical development. For example, most children refine eye-hand coordination—the ability to direct finger, hand, and wrist movements—during their preschool years. They use eye-hand coordination to accomplish fine motor tasks, such as fitting a piece in a puzzle or using a fork or spoon. Children use their senses—especially sight, sound, and touch—to coordinate the movements of their large and small muscles.

Physical development involves the use and coordination of fine and gross motor skills.

A tremendous amount of physical development takes place during the first five years of life. During this time, young children learn to control their muscles and practice the physical skills they will use for the rest of their lives. They use their large and small muscles, along with all their senses, to make discoveries about their world and the effects of their actions. Therefore, it is crucial for children to have many opportunities to move their bodies and use their physical skills.

Physical fitness is important for everyone. Most young children do not have to be reminded to move their bodies. Infants will gleefully kick their legs and reach for objects. Toddlers often push, pull, and turn over anything they can get their hands or feet on. And preschool children delight in running and climbing as well as in building and knocking down. When children have opportunities to eat healthy foods and exercise their bodies, their fitness increases. If physical fitness habits are introduced in the preschool years, children are more likely to become adults with healthy lifestyles.

Physical fitness is tied to self-esteem.

Physical fitness is related to a child's positive sense of self. Many children develop views of themselves and attitudes about attempting new tasks on the basis of how they feel about their bodies and what they think they can or cannot do physically. Young children who have had many successful experiences using their fine and gross motor skills tend to feel competent. This sense of competence carries over into other activities. They are likely to continue exploring materials and attempting new challenges without worrying about failure.

Adults reinforce physical development and fitness in a variety of ways.

Early childhood programs and teachers play important roles in promoting children's physical skills. Quality programs provide ample, safe spaces indoors and outdoors where children can move their bodies, use their gross motor skills, have fun, and keep fit. The daily schedule includes time for active play in an environment that allows children to use their bodies as well as all their senses while they play. Teachers offer a variety of materials and equipment so children at different skill levels can use their fine and gross motor skills safely and without frustration. For example, one child can tear paper while another uses scissors; one can pull a loaded wagon while another needs to remove some of the cargo. And perhaps most importantly, teachers reinforce fine and gross motor skills by sharing their interest and pleasure in children's growing physical accomplishments.

Listed on the following pages are three sets of examples showing how teachers demonstrate their competence in promoting children's physical development. Following each set of examples is a short reading and two questions to answer. When you have finished this section, compare your answers with those on the answer sheet at the end of this module. If your answers are different, discuss them with your trainer. There can be more than one good answer.

Providing Materials, Equipment, and Opportunities for Gross Motor Development

Encourage children to use their large muscles throughout the day.

"Gabrielle and Michael, will you please help me move aside the large hollow blocks so we'll have more room for daning?"

Play indoor and outdoor noncompetitive games.

"In this game we'll all take turns going from here to the tree in different ways. Crystal, how will you go to the tree?"

Encourage the development of self-help skills that involve the use of large muscles.

"Jan, that was a good idea. You used the hollow block as a step stool to reach the sink."

Offer indoor and outdoor activities that challenge children to improve their gross motor skills.

"Now that the children have mastered the obstacle course, they're losing interest. Let's invite them to rearrange the items to offer new challenges."

Provide a variety of materials and equipment that encourages all children to use their large muscles.

"You can walk up the ramp to get to the slide or climb up the rope ladder."

"It must be something about the rain!" Ms. Williams says to Ms. Frilles. Choice time had been very noisy as the children tested limits by crashing blocks and banging pots and pans. "I think we need to move our bodies," she tells the children. "But we can't go outside," Mark moans. "It's raining!" "You're right. It's too wet to go out. Let's clean up, then we can try some new ways to move our bodies," Ms. Williams suggests. As the last blocks are put away, Ms. Williams asks several children to help her push the shelves against the wall. "We'll need this space for moving," she tells them. Ms. Frilles uses a long rope to make a large circle in the program of the area. "I need three children to move inside this circle. Dora, Sam, and Joe, show us how many different ways you can move without bumping into each other." Ms. Frilles describes the children's movements, "Dora is jumping! Sam is galloping! Joe looks like he's floating!" Meanwhile, Ms. Williams makes several other rope circles around the room and invites the other children to join in. The children walk, hop, leap, skip, slide, and crawl. Ms. Williams exclaims, "What terrific movers!".

1. How did the children let Ms. Williams and Ms. Frilles know they were ready for gross motor activities?

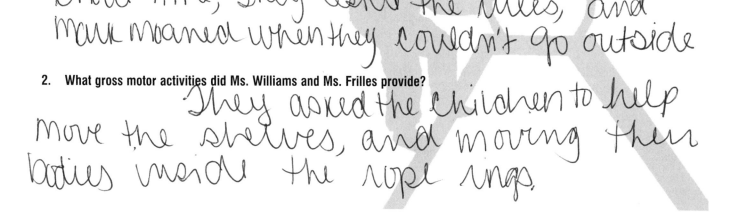

The children were noisey during choice time, they tested the rules, and Mark moaned when they couldn't go outside

2. What gross motor activities did Ms. Williams and Ms. Frilles provide?

They asked the children to help move the shelves, and moving their bodies inside the rope rings.

Providing Materials and Opportunities for Fine Motor Development

Encourage children to use their small muscles throughout the day.	"Hank, use your thumb and finger to give the fish a pinch of food."
Encourage the development of self-help skills that involve the use of small muscles.	"Theresa, you zipped your jacket today! Good for you!"
Offer activities that challenge children to improve their fine motor skills.	"This finger play is about catching a bee. I'll teach you the words and what to do with your fingers and hands."
Provide a variety of materials that fit together so children can practice their fine motor skills.	"Peter, you made an interesting house with the table blocks, yesterday. Would you like to use them again, or try building with Lincoln Logs?"
Provide materials and activities that accommodate different skill levels.	"Lloyd and Maddie, would you like to try weaving today? We have thick and thin yarn, and two kinds of looms."
Encourage children to participate in daily routines.	"Graham, you're doing a great job using your fork to pick up the peach slices. How do they taste?"

"Here's the pitcher," says Ms. Kim to Robert. "Hold your cup with one hand so the cup won't move." Robert holds his cup and pours the milk very quickly so that it overflows. "Oops, that milk came out too fast, didn't it?" smiles Ms. Kim. "There's a sponge on the sink you can use to clean it up." While Robert gets the sponge, Shannon picks up the pitcher. "I can make it go slow, Ms. Kim. Watch me." Shannon holds the pitcher and pours the milk very slowly, stopping before it gets to the top of her cup. "Good job, Shannon," says Ms. Kim. "Your hand and arm muscles were working well. I know that Robert is going to go slower next time too." Robert nods his head as he wipes up the spilled milk. "My peas keep falling off my fork," explains Patrick. "Use your spoon, silly," says Robert. "That would help, wouldn't it?" says Ms. Kim. "What else could you do?" Shannon looks up and says, "You could stick your peas on your fork like this," and spears four peas on her fork. Several other children at the table begin spearing their peas. "Well, we certainly did solve that problem," says Ms. Kim.

1. **How did Ms. Kim encourage the children to use their small muscles?**

   1. pour their own milk
   2. wipe up spilt milk
   3. asked them to think of ways to pick-up peas so they won't fall off.

2. **What did Ms. Kim say to encourage the children's efforts?**

   1. told Robert why the milk spilt.
   2. Reassured Robert he could still pour milk w/ out it spilling.
   3. asked Robert to clean-up spill - so he didn't feel bad

Reinforcing and Encouraging Children's Physical Fitness

Offer a variety of materials and activities that encourage children of different skill levels to be physically fit.	"We have balls of different sizes, Antonia. Pick one that feels comfortable to hold and I'll play catch with you."
Schedule time for active outdoor play every day.	"It looks like the rain has slowed to a drizzle, so let's get ready to go outdoors."
Provide opportunities for indoor active play during bad weather.	"During choice time today we'll use the hallway for trike-riding, bowling, and other activities."
Encourage children to coordinate use of their large and small muscles.	"Leroy, you worked hard to roll out the playdough. What are you making?"
Help children develop an awareness of rhythm so they can coordinate their body movements.	"Luis and Mary are hopping to the music. Marta and Pete are swaying. How else can we move to the New Shoes Dance?"
Introduce cooperative games and activities that build children's physical skills.	"You can use everything but your hands to keep the balloons in the air."
Help older children begin learning skills they can use to play sports and games.	"Yannick, put the wiffle ball on the tee. Pick up the bat with both hands near the bottom. Then, stand back and swing!"

When Ms. Díaz comes to pick up her daughter, Lindsay, she sees children steering tricycles around safety cones, pulling each other in wagons, crawling through cardboard boxes. She smiles when she finds Lindsay kicking a ball back and forth with Eula. Turning to Ms. Thomas, Ms. Díaz says, "Now that Lindsay's five, we'd like her to play soccer. Do you know of a neighborhood league for young players?" "Has Lindsay said she wants to play soccer?" asks Ms. Thomas. "No, not really," says Ms. Díaz, "but I want her to get plenty of exercise." "That's an important goal for all children," says Ms. Thomas. "We provide opportunities for children to move their bodies every day and we encourage families to exercise together. Most five-year-olds, however, aren't ready for competitive sports such as soccer. Can I tell you about the recreation center's family fun programs? I think you and Lindsay would enjoy the cooperative games they play." "Those sound interesting," says Ms. Díaz. "We could have fun and stay fit together."

1. **What outdoor activities encouraged children's physical fitness?**

   1 Riding tricycles around cones.
   2 pulling eachother in wagons.
   3. kicking a ball

2. **Why do you think Ms. Thomas suggested an alternative to soccer?**

   Because 5 yr. olds aren't ready for competitive games

Taking Care of Your Own Body[1]

Teachers need to take care of their own bodies.

As a teacher, you are concerned about children's physical development. However, it is essential that you take care of yourself, too. How many times a day do you:

- bend from the waist to pick up a child or an item on the floor?

- lean over a step-stool in front of a sink to wash your hands?

- sit on the floor and bend forward to play with a child?

- sit on a child-sized chair?

Try these suggestions.

The activities listed above are normal for teachers of young children. They are also activities that can produce sore backs and limbs. Here are some ways to maintain good posture and flexibility and to avoid physical pain as you care for children:

- Keep your lower back as straight as possible and avoid slouching when sitting or standing.

- Put one foot up on a stool or step when standing for a long time.

- Bend your knees, not your back, when you lean forward.

- Wear low-heeled, soft-soled, comfortable shoes to maintain proper posture.

- Bend your knees, tuck in your buttocks, and pull in your abdominal muscles when lifting a child or a heavy object.

- Avoid twisting when lifting or lowering a child or a heavy object. Hold the child or object close to you.

- Stretch your muscles before playing an active game with children. (It's a good idea for children to stretch their muscles, too.)

- Use adult-sized tables and chairs, if possible, when meeting with other adults or when participating in training.

- Talk with your supervisor and colleagues about staff coverage for short breaks. Do some stretching exercises and relax during these breaks!

Teaching is a physically demanding job. Think about your own fitness, daily movements on the job, and the work environment, and jot down brief answers to the questions that follow.

---

[1] Based on Susan S. Aronson, M.D., "Coping with the Physical Requirements of Caregiving," *Child Care Information Exchange* (Redmond, WA: Exchange Press, Inc., May 1987), pp. 39-40.

Do you follow a fitness program? For example, do you walk regularly or participate in an aerobic or sports program, eat foods that provide energy and are low in fat and sugar?

Yes, I do walk regularly and I try to eat foods that are good for me.

How can you improve your posture and movements throughout the day? How can you expand your fitness program?

Try not to be so lazy - Try and get involved in sports.

What changes to the environment or the schedule can you suggest so that you and your colleagues can avoid sore backs and limbs?

exercise daily.

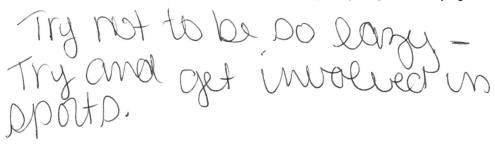

The suggestions you have just read and the ones you noted above, along with regular exercise and good health and nutrition practices, can help you promote your own physical development along with that of young children.

When you have finished this overview section, complete the pre-training assessment. Refer to the glossary at the end of this module if you need definitions of the terms that are used.

Pre-Training Assessment

Listed below are the skills that teachers use to promote children's physical development. Think about whether you do these things regularly, sometimes, or not enough. Place a check in one of the boxes on the right for each skill listed. Then discuss your answers with your trainer.

Providing Materials, Equipment, and Opportunities for Gross Motor Development

	I Do This:	Regularly	Sometimes	Not Enough
1.	Encourage children to use their large muscles throughout the day.	☒	☐	☐
2.	Play indoor and outdoor noncompetitive games.	☒	☐	☐
3.	Encourage the development of self-help skills that involve the use of large muscles.	☒	☐	☐
4.	Offer indoor and outdoor activities that challenge children to improve their gross motor skills.	☒	☐	☐
5.	Provide a variety of materials and equipment that encourages all children to use their large muscles.	☒	☐	☐

Providing Materials and Opportunities for Fine Motor Development

	I Do This:	Regularly	Sometimes	Not Enough
6.	Encourage children to use their small muscles throughout the day.	☒	☐	☐
7.	Encourage the development of self-help skills that involve the use of small muscles.	☒	☐	☐

Providing Materials and Opportunities for Fine Motor Development

(continued)

	I Do This:	Regularly	Sometimes	Not Enough
8. Offer activities that challenge children to improve their fine motor skills.		☒	☐	☐
9. Provide a variety of materials that fit together so children can practice their fine motor skills.		☒	☐	☐
10. Provide materials and activities that accommodate different skill levels.		☒	☐	☐
11. Encourage children to participate in daily routines.		☒	☐	☐

Reinforcing and Encouraging Children's Physical Fitness

	Regularly	Sometimes	Not Enough
12. Offer a variety of materials and activities that encourage children of different skill levels to be physically fit.	☒	☐	☐
13. Schedule time for active outdoor play every day.	☒	☐	☐
14. Provide opportunities for indoor active play during bad weather.	☒	☐	☐
15. Encourage children to coordinate use of their large and small muscles.	☒	☐	☐
16. Help children develop an awareness of rhythm so they can coordinate their body movements.	☒	☐	☐

Reinforcing and Encouraging Children's Physical Fitness

(continued)

	I Do This:	Regularly	Sometimes	Not Enough
17. Introduce cooperative games and activities that build children's physical skills.		☒	☐	☐
18. Help older children begin learning skills they can use to play sports and games.		☒	☐	☐

Review your responses, then list three to five skills you would like to improve or topics you would like to learn more about. When you finish this module, you can list examples of your new or improved knowledge and skills.

Begin the learning activities for Module 4, Physical.

Learning Activities

I. Using Your Knowledge of Child Development to Promote Gross Motor Skills

---

In this activity you will learn to:

- Recognize some typical gross motor skills of preschool children
- Use what you know about children to promote their gross motor skills

---

As with other areas of development, children's physical development follows an individual schedule for reaching milestones and mastering skills. In any group of preschoolers there is likely to be a wide range of physical abilities. For example, one three-year-old can skip with both feet, while another can skip on one foot only. Although the age when children accomplish a skill varies from child to child, the pattern rarely does. For example, children control their head movements first; then their torsos and arms, and finally their legs. Gross motor skills, such as rolling over, usually appear before those involving small muscles, such as picking up small objects. Movement normally begins with muscles close to the body center and moves outward as the child matures. To promote preschool children's gross motor skills, teachers need to observe individuals and understand the typical sequence of development.

Each child learns and uses gross motor skills according to an individual timetable.

The descriptions that follow present the sequence of gross motor development during the preschool years and the approximate ages at which children master certain skills. You will probably notice that the children in your class are developing several gross motor skills at the same time. As you work with children and observe their indoor and outdoor activities, you can learn which skills they have mastered and which ones they are developing.

Three-year-olds are usually sure and nimble on their feet. They can walk, run, and turn sharp corners with ease, often holding their arms out to their sides for balance or swinging them for sureness. They can walk up stairs using alternate feet. They will jump from the bottom stair and land on both feet. Three-year-olds have lots of energy. They like to run, gallop, and "dance" to music. They can hop several times in a row, balance on one foot for a few seconds, and walk along a line made with tape or a rope. They enjoy pushing and pedaling tricycles, using swings, and throwing, catching, and kicking large balls.

Three-year-olds have a lot of energy.

Four-year-olds can control how they use their large muscles.

Four-year-olds have all the energy of three-year-olds and greater control over their large muscles. Their running and walking movements may have sudden starts and stops. Hopping is a favorite activity; children can normally hop in a sequence of two or three hops. This leads to skipping. Children begin by skipping on one foot, then taking a walking step forward with the other. Balancing on a walking board, broad jumping, and throwing balls overhand are other favorite activities of four-year-olds. They can climb ladders and playground equipment with assurance and fearlessness. They skillfully pedal, steer, and turn corners on tricycles.

Five-year-olds can use their ball-handling skills to play games.

By age five, most children are refining their existing physical skills. They can run faster, ride tricycles with greater speed and skill, and climb higher and more freely. They can hop on one foot for a long distance and usually master skipping with alternating feet. They can also walk the full length of a balance beam without stepping off. Because five-year-olds can usually succeed in getting a ball where they want it to go, they enjoy ball games involving kicking, throwing, and catching. Some five-year-olds are learning to jump rope, do somersaults, and use an overhead ladder on a climber.

Applying Your Knowledge

The chart on the next two pages lists some typical behaviors of children in the preschool years, ages three to five. Included are behaviors relevant to physical development. The right-hand column asks you to identify ways teachers can use this information about child development to promote children's physical development. Try to think of as many examples as you can. As you work through the module you will learn new strategies and you can add them to the chart. You are not expected to think of all the examples at one time. If you need help getting started, turn to the completed chart at the end of the module. By the time you complete all the learning activities, you will find that you have learned many ways to promote children's physical development.

Using Your Knowledge of Child Development to Promote Gross Motor Skills

What Preschool Children Are Like	How Teachers Can Use This Information to Promote Gross Motor Skills
They walk easily and can balance themselves on one foot for several seconds at a time.	*Lay a wide strip of tape to the floor so children can practice balancing while walking forwards, sideways, backwards, with arms in front or behind, and over obstacles. Use tape or unit blocks to make a walking course with turns, curves, and obstacles.*
They run, jump, and hop.	Make environment ready for running, jumping, and hoping. Play non-competitive games
They move to music, imitate dance movements, and make up creative ways to move.	Offer children movement games, and play music for them to dance + move to.
They throw balls overhead and catch bounced balls.	Play catch w/ the children, have them play catch w/ eachother. Offer toys they can throw + catch
They climb.	Use indoor + outdoor play equipment. Encourage children to climb.
They ride tricycles.	Make sure tricycles are in good condition.
They use playground equipment such as slides, climbers, and swings.	Take children outdoors daily.

When you have completed as much as you can do on the chart, discuss your answers with your trainer. As you proceed with the rest of the learning activities, you can refer back to the chart and add examples of ways teachers promote children's physical development.

II. Observing and Planning for Children's Fine Motor Development

> **In this activity you will learn to:**
>
> - Identify children's developing fine motor skills
> - Plan activities that help children practice fine motor skills

Young children need to develop their small muscles for many tasks.

Young children use their small muscles for many tasks. They coordinate hands, fingers, and wrists to write and draw. They need strength in their small muscles to cut with scissors and use other tools. Control is required for buttoning, zipping, holding utensils, and other routine tasks. As children develop control and coordination of their fingers, hands, and wrists, they delight in stringing beads, completing puzzles, and placing pegs in pegboards. Fine motor skills are needed for these age-appropriate tasks and will be important later in life for writing, typing, driving, cooking, playing musical instruments, and so on.

Children learn to control and coordinate their finger, hand, and wrist movements at different rates. However, we can identify typical sequences of fine motor development and the approximate ages at which children master these skills.

Three-year-olds develop fine motor skills through routines and activities.

Although three-year-olds usually prefer large muscle activities, they are gaining greater control of their fingers, hands, and wrists. Their growing skills allow for active participation in family-style meals. They can spoon food from serving dishes, pass platters, and use spoons and forks to feed themselves. Most have learned to dress themselves. They can pull their pants up and down, put on shoes, and use large buttons and zippers. Fine motor skills allow three-year-olds to do many things for themselves. They can wash their own hands by turning the faucet on and off, pumping soap from a dispenser, and tearing paper towels off a roll. Three-year-olds enjoy using a variety of materials. They can string beads, place large pegs in pegboards, build towers and bridges with blocks, play with puzzles that have a few large pieces, use scissors to cut paper, turn the pages of a book one at a time, and explore the properties of playdough, clay, sand, and water. With practice, they progress from holding crayons with their fists to using their first two fingers and thumb. They scribble in a controlled fashion, using vertical, horizontal, and circular strokes. Three-year-olds may begin showing preference for the right or left hand.

Four-year-olds have greater control over finger, hand, and wrist movements.

Four-year-olds have more refined small muscle movements and eye-hand coordination than threes. They can cut easily with scissors and begin to draw pictures that represent real things. Some four-year-olds write recognizable letters and numbers. They can lace shoes; zip and snap most clothing; pour from small pitchers without spilling, serve and eat with a fork and spoon; and use knives for spreading and some cutting. Finger, hand, and wrist control allows them to build detailed structures with unit blocks and other construction materials. They can use tools in their hands to form shapes and objects with playdough and clay. As their coordination increases, they are able to use smaller versions of the materials they used when younger, such as Legos, beads and strings, pegs and pegboards, and construction toys.

Most five-year-olds have well-developed fine motor skills. Their drawings and paintings tend to represent real objects and include much detail. They can cut shapes with scissors. They usually use all utensils properly to serve food and eat. Five-year-olds have little difficulty dressing and undressing themselves. They can handle most buttons, snaps, zippers, and buckles, and are learning to tie shoes. Most five-year-olds can reproduce some letters and numerals and write "important" words such as their names.

Five-year-olds are refining their fine motor skills.

Daily routines in an early childhood classroom provide rich opportunities for children to develop fine motor skills. It may be tempting to hurry through chores such as dressing and grooming, toileting, and eating, but they deserve the same care and attention as other activities. Daily routines can offer new challenges and new ways to be independent and to make contributions to the group. For example, teachers can invite children to help prepare snacks and meals, set and clear the table, pass bowls and platters, and serve and feed themselves. Children might help mix paint, sweep or mop up a spill, wipe tables, or use the mini-vacuum to clean up some spilled fish food. All of these chores involve use of fine motor skills.

Children develop fine motor skills through routines and by playing with a variety of materials.

Most early childhood programs offer a variety of materials that help children develop their fine motor skills. Children can put together Legos and Unifix cubes, build roads with unit blocks, and push cars along toy highways. They might use tongs and egg beaters in the house corner, and paint brushes and playdough in the art area. Turning a jump rope outdoors allows children to coordinate wrist and hand motions. In an appropriate indoor and outdoor environment, the chances for children to use their small muscles are almost endless.

Sensory awareness—using sight, sound, touch, taste, and smell to get information—is a large part of fine motor development. Activities in which children use their senses as they manipulate objects help them coordinate movements. You can encourage children to:

Children rely on their senses to help them coordinate fine motor movements.

- serve food;

- tear, peel, slice, and scrape vegetables and fruits for snack;

- squeeze and identify objects hidden inside a bag;

- hold and pass around small canisters with various scents in them; and

- listen to small items rattle and bounce in "sound" canisters.

Children learn a variety of cognitive concepts through these types of activities, and develop fine motor skills by getting information from their senses.

Encourage children to use whichever hand they prefer.

As you observe children using their hands and fingers, you will see that most have developed a preference for using the right or left hand. Most children establish a preferred hand by age three. Some do not. It is important not to make a fuss over this preference. Encourage children to use whichever hand they prefer, by placing objects in their preferred hand. This helps children become more skilled in using the preferred hand. Most experts agree that it is inappropriate and often harmful to force a child to become right-handed if the child's preference is for the left hand.

Applying Your Knowledge

In this learning activity you conduct a series of observations of two children in your class. Over a five-day period, observe each child during routines and in different interest areas during indoor and outdoor choice times. Then use your observation recordings to summarize what you learned about the children's fine motor skills and plan strategies for encouraging the children to practice and refine their skills.

Observing and Planning for Children's Fine Motor Development

(Example)

Observation Dates: *April 24-29*

Observation Summary and Plan	Child #1: *Emma* Age: *3 years, 8 months*	Child #2: *Tomás* Age: *4 years, 6 months*
What fine motor activities are easy for the child?	*Tearing paper* *Cutting fringes in paper (usually with scissors in left hand)* *Stringing large beads* *Holding a paint brush* *Brushing teeth (usually with left hand)*	*Spreading peanut butter on crackers* *Cutting pictures out of magazines* *Painting and drawing recognizable people* *Hanging up cooking utensils on pegboard*
What fine motor activities are challenging?	*Cutting a straight line across a piece of paper* *Using tongs*	*Pasting pictures where he wants them to go* *Using a computer keyboard*
How can you use what you learned to encourage this child's fine motor development?	*I can help her to identify that she is left-handed and encourage her to use this hand for tasks.* *I can show her how to make a paper chain so she will have a reason to practice cutting straight lines.*	*Tomás seems a little leery of the computer so I can ask another child to show him how to use it.* *I can plan a cooking activity—making spreads with fresh fruit and cream cheese.*

Observing and Planning for Children's Fine Motor Development

Observation Dates: _____

Observation Summary and Plan	Child #1: Shannon Age: 4	Child #2: Heather Age: 3
What fine motor activities are easy for the child?	painting writing coloring glueing	painting glueing
What fine motor activities are challenging?	Beading	writting coloring
How can you use what you learned to encourage this child's fine motor development?	Encourage her to Bead and not to get so agrivated when she can't get the bead through the string	Encourage heather to go into the writting area.

Discuss your observation recordings and plans with your trainer and other teachers who work with these children.

III. Encouraging Physical Fitness

> **In this activity you will learn to:**
>
> • Provide indoor and outdoor environments and materials that encourage children's physical fitness
>
> • Plan activities that help children stay fit

Physical fitness is an important goal for all children and adults. Most preschool children are eager to exercise their bodies. They ride tricycles, move their bodies to music, crawl through cardboard boxes, and chase each other around the playground. Unfortunately, as children get older, opportunities for active play become more limited.[2] Although most elementary schools provide some physical education, only one state, Illinois, mandates daily physical education for all children from kindergarten through grade 12. A study by the Harvard School of Public Health found that from age six on, today's children weigh more and have more body fat than did children 20 years ago. This finding reinforces the need to begin physical fitness habits and activities early in life—during the preschool years.

It is important to encourage all children to be physically active.

Parents and teachers should encourage preschoolers to engage in vigorous aerobic play activities—running, playing tag, riding tricycles, walking, climbing, and jumping—that continue for 12 to 15 minutes without stopping. In addition, by providing necessary materials, equipment, and encouragement, adults can help preschoolers develop important skills. These skills can be divided into three categories:

Preschoolers are learning gross motor skills they may use later to play sports.

Object control skills such as kicking a ball, throwing overhand and underhand, catching, striking a ball with a bat or racket, and stopping a ball with the feet.

Locomotor skills such as running, hopping, skipping, balancing, and doing forward and backward somersaults.

Nonlocomotor skills such as pushing, pulling, and lifting.

Each of these skills provides a foundation for the more complex movements used by older children and adults to play games and sports. When children begin to learn these skills in the preschool years they are more likely to be interested in participating in sports and other physical fitness activities during the school-age years. This increases children's chances of becoming "fit" adults, who live longer and healthier lives.

[2] Cooper, Kenneth. *Kid Fitness: A Complete Shape-Up Program from Birth Through High School* (New York: Bantam Books, 1991).

Outdoor play promotes physical fitness.

In the outdoors, children are free to move and use their bodies in space. Spending all day inside in a large group can be stressful for everyone. Even when the weather is cold and damp, you and the children will benefit from a brief time outdoors. The outdoor environment is a world for children to explore and learn about, as well as a place where they can release pent-up energy.

In most early childhood programs, teachers are not responsible for the selection and placement of large fixed equipment. Typically, the outdoor area is equipped with stationary swings, slides, climbers, a sandbox, a path for wheeled toys, and a storage shed. To stimulate different types of physical activity, you can provide additional materials such as:

soft balls and soft bats	tunnels
jump ropes	cardboard boxes
bean bags and targets	woodworking tools
rocking boats	balance beams

(See Module 3: Learning Environment, for more on outdoor play environments.)

Try these suggestions.

When you take children outdoors, keep the following suggestions in mind to promote physical fitness.

Pay attention to what the children are doing and participate with them. Avoid chatting with teachers from other rooms or participating as the "coach" in large group activities only. Your interactions will support and reinforce children's physical activities.

Participate at the children's level as much as possible. Kneel or crouch, and roll balls or toss bean bags at a speed young children can handle.

Stress cooperation over competition. Encourage children to concentrate on enjoying the things they can do with their bodies, refining the skills they have, and learning new skills. They also can learn to value playing physical games with other individuals who have differing gross motor abilities.

Accept children's real fears of heights, moving fast on wheel toys, and so on. Offer to hold their hands, climb with them, or provide other types of physical assistance when appropriate. Try not to challenge them to go beyond what they think is safe.

Circulate around the outdoor area when not involved in an activity. Invite individual children to play with you, or encourage those who are wandering to play together. Often children become withdrawn outdoors when they think that their involvement will cause them embarrassment.

Move, stretch, or take a short run around the play area. You will probably have lots of company. Getting a little exercise during the day will help you feel refreshed, and lets children know that physical fitness is a part of your life, too.

Plan activities that allow children at different skill levels to feel successful and competent. Children feel frustrated when activities are too difficult, and they get no satisfaction from those that don't provide a challenge.

It is also important to provide indoor opportunities for physical fitness activities. Children and adults still need to move their bodies even when the weather is extremely inclement. Some suggestions follow.

When children can't go outdoors, provide for indoor physical activities.[3]

Hallways are perfect for riding tricycles, rolling balls, tossing bean bags into baskets, playing relay games, building with large blocks, marching to music, and bowling (use plastic milk containers as pins). To avoid overcrowding and confusion, coordinate with other classes to schedule use of the hallway and limit its use to several children at one time.

A classroom loft can provide many opportunities for physical play. Children can climb up and down stairs or a rope ladder, slide down a pole, swing (hang swings on hooks when not in use), or jump off a low platform into a pile of pillows.

Move aside furniture to create space in the room for vigorous activities. Put down mats for tumbling. Lead the children in aerobic exercises and cooperative games using props such as hula hoops, large balls, and parachutes.

Plan music and movement activities every day. Children enjoy music and movement activities such as dancing, marching, and creatively using their bodies in different ways, with and without musical accompaniment. You can plan music and movement activities during choice time, while children transition from one activity to another, and as part of group times. For example, you could ask children to:

- use their bodies to become animals, buildings, or vehicles;

- move from one place to another, crawling slowly like a snail, jumping like a kangaroo, or slithering like a snake;

- stretch high or make themselves big or small; and

- move their heads, arms, hips, and ribs in different ways;

(See Module 7, Creative, for additional suggestions about music and movement.)

Applying Your Knowledge

In this learning activity you plan and implement an activity to encourage children's physical fitness. This should be an open-ended activity that offers choices and can be enjoyed by children with differing interests and abilities. Read the example, then plan and implement your activity and respond to the questions.

[3] Adapted from Derry G. Koralek, *Responding to Children Under Stress* (Washington, DC: Head Start Bureau, 1994). pp. 99-100.

Encouraging Physical Fitness
(Example)

Activity Plan

Activity: *Making an obstacle course for practicing kicking skills*

Materials:

A tire, 2 hula hoops, 5-foot-long board, rope, saw horses, cardboard boxes, safety cones, and 5 large balls

Why are you planning this activity?

Several children have older siblings who play soccer, so there has been a lot of interest in kicking balls around the play yard.

How will the activity encourage children of different interests and abilities to use their physical skills?

The children can work together to design and build the obstacle course. Then, interested children can kick balls through the course. If appropriate, we can encourage children to rearrange the course to create new challenges.

Implement the activity, then complete the following.

Summary

Children: *Alex, Brianna, Drew, Marta, Inez*   **Ages:** *4 and 5 years*   **Date:** *April 30*

What did you and the children do?

I described the activity at group time. I explained that 5 children could participate today and we could repeat the activity tomorrow if more children are interested. The first 4 children joined me immediately; then Inez joined us after she saw what we were doing.

The children spent about 10 minutes setting up the course. They used the tire, hula hoops, saw horses, and safety cones. Then each child took a ball and kicked it around the course. Some kicked the ball next to the obstacles, others went through or around them. A few balls rolled down the hill.

How did this activity encourage physical fitness?

The children had to lift and carry the obstacles to make the course. They practiced kicking skills. They had to run down and back up the hill when they kicked their balls too hard.

Would you do this activity again? What changes would you make?

I would definitely do this again. The children had fun and used their large muscles. I might provide more safety cones and remove some of the other items that the children didn't use.

Encouraging Physical Fitness

Activity Plan

Activity: _parachute_

Materials: parachute + balls

Why are you planning this activity?

arms strength + fun

How will the activity encourage children of different interests and abilities to use their physical skills?

it is fun to watch the balls + the children work together to lift the parachute w/their arms.

Implement the activity, then complete the following.

Summary

Children: _Whole group_   Ages: _____   Date: _____

What did you and the children do?

we went outside and put the balls ontop of the parachute and started lifting it up & down

How did this activity encourage physical fitness?

It encouraged arm strength

Would you do this activity again? What changes would you make?

yes, I would do it again cuz the children enjoyed it.

Discuss this activity with your trainer and the parents of the children who participated. Encourage parents to include their children in family fitness activities.

IV. Creating an Environment That Supports Physical Development

---

In this activity you will learn to:

- Select materials and equipment that help children develop gross motor skills
- Select materials and equipment that help children develop fine motor skills

---

The environment should support children's development of physical skills.

When teachers know the range of physical skills that children can learn at a given age and stage of development, they can set up an environment that encourages further development of these skills.

An early childhood environment should be a safe place in which children feel confident and reassured as they climb, balance, draw, hop, dance, build, serve themselves, and clean up. A safe environment encourages children to practice skills they have mastered and try out new ones.

The types of materials and equipment you provide should reflect the range of skills, strengths, needs, and interests of the children in your class. Many open-ended materials such as blocks and art supplies are ideal for meeting diverse needs, because they can be used in different ways by children at different skill levels. Older preschool children who have had many opportunities to use their large and small muscles can usually have success with more challenging learning materials and equipment than can three-year-olds and children with limited experiences. It is crucial to provide a wide variety of items that offer children challenges without causing frustration.

Children can use their large and small muscles indoors in every interest area as well as outdoors. The chart that follows lists examples of materials that preschool children use which promote fine and gross motor skills. You can add your own ideas in the right-hand column.

Area	Opportunities for Using Gross and Fine Motor Skills	What We Can Add
Dramatic Play	Lifting dolls, utensils, and pots and pans Pushing and pulling carriages and wagons Setting the table and passing serving bowls. Using zippers, buttons, buckles, and snaps on dress-up clothes Writing an order in a restaurant Holding cups and pretending to drink	*Stepping Stones has a wide variety of all toys for these areas*
Table Toys	Taking out and putting in puzzle pieces Snapping together Bristle Blocks and Legos Stringing beads Picking up and dropping sorting items (buttons, bottle caps) into trays	
Blocks	Lifting unit blocks and hollow blocks Placing one block on top of another Moving wooden people, cars, and trucks Writing signs to label or protect structures	
Art	Fingerpainting Painting large strokes at the easel Drawing with crayons and markers Pasting and gluing paper, fabric, feathers, and other materials to make collages and assemblages Molding and stretching playdough and clay	
Library	Turning the pages of books Placing headsets on ears Moving felt pieces on a flannel board Pressing buttons on a tape recorder Writing and binding books	
Computer	Pressing keys on keyboard Using a mouse Inserting a disk into the drive Filling the printer with paper	

Area	Opportunities for Using Gross and Fine Motor Skills	What We Can Add
Music, Movement, and Large Muscle (indoors)	Climbing the rungs of an indoor climber Balancing in a rocking boat Crawling through a cardboard box Walking on a balance beam Tossing bean bags in a basket Moving to music Using rhythm instruments	
Sand and water	Pouring from a pitcher Squeezing sponges and turkey basters Directing the spray from a squeeze bottle Feeling the textures of wet and dry sand Rotating wrist or forearm to use eggbeaters or screw on jar lids	
Science and nature	Sprinkling food into a fish bowl Picking up rocks, shells, and other collections Looking at objects through a magnifying glass Carrying a pitcher to water plants Adjusting a microscope	
Woodworking	Holding a nail in one hand and using a hammer with the other Turning the rod on a vise Placing tools on pegboard hooks Making back-and-forth motions with a saw or sandpaper Picking up screws and nails	
Outdoors	Throwing, catching, and kicking balls Swinging from rungs on a climber Crawling through tunnels Pulling a wagon Digging in the sandbox or a garden Pulling weeds	

Applying Your Knowledge

In this learning activity you focus on two children in your class. For one child, identify a fine motor skill he or she is working on. For the other child, identify a gross motor skill he or she is working on. Then, list some toys, equipment, and/or materials that will promote development of the identified skill for each child. If possible, select children of different ages and abilities. First read the example, then complete the blank form that follows.

Creating an Environment that Supports Physical Development

(Example)

Date: *March 15*

Child/Age	Skill	Materials
Kara, 3 years	*Stringing small beads on strings. Kara can use the pegs and pegboard, but she has a hard time stringing beads.*	*Large beads and laces* *Paper plates and thick yarn for lacing* *Small interconnecting blocks*
Juan, 5 years	*Throwing and catching a small ball. Juan can catch a large ball, but he has a hard time catching smaller ones such as a tennis ball.*	*A large wiffle ball or other ball slightly larger than a tennis ball* *A Nerf ball (standard size)* *Beanbags and a container to throw them into*

Creating an Environment that Supports Physical Development

(Example)

Date: _____

Child/Age	Skill	Materials
Shannon age: 4	Shannon has a hard time beading	Beads, + macaroni yarn for the beading of beads + macaroni
Heather age 3	holding pens pencils, and markers, and crayons	have the writing area available for Heather,

Discuss this activity with your colleagues and your trainer. Conduct frequent observations of children's use of fine and gross motor skills so you will know when and how to change the environment in response to changing skills and interests.

V. Promoting Positive Self-Concepts Through Development of Physical Skills

In this activity you will learn to:

- Recognize how the development of physical skills can support children's socio-emotional growth
- Interact with children in ways that encourage a positive self-concept

Most early childhood teachers have observed first-hand the important role that physical development plays in helping children feel good about themselves. When a child learns to throw a ball, jump a distance, or cut with a pair of scissors, the sense of accomplishment is enormous. The pride that comes from mastering physical skills helps children feel good about themselves. This sense of confidence and competence leads to emotional security and a willingness to risk learning other tasks, social and cognitive, as well as physical. Thus, by addressing children's physical development, you are promoting their growth in all areas and contexts.

Most children will eventually develop physical skills on their own. However, they are more likely to feel proud of their accomplishments if they receive encouragement and support for their efforts. This is especially true if children are slower to develop than their peers or feel pressure from adults. Your encouragement is therefore crucial to ensuring a sense of success. Sometimes, however, the most supportive thing you can do is to give children an uninterrupted opportunity to work on a new skill. Rather than stepping in to help, stand back and allow the child to experience the pleasure of doing something on his or her own.

Here are some ways that teachers can provide encouragement.

Adult encouragement can help children feed proud of their physical accomplishments.

Try these suggestions.

Review or explain how to do an activity correctly before children try it. "John's ready to throw the ball to you. Follow the ball with your eyes, and keep your arms stretched out."

Suggest how a child can overcome an obstacle. "I'll give you a push on the swing. Then you can use your legs to keep going."

Verbally reassure a child who is reluctant or frightened. "I know this can be scary. Would you like me to hold your hand while you climb the ladder?"

Offer praise when a child tries something new. "I watched you go down the slide all by yourself. That was terrific, Renee."

Respect a child's progress, without making comparisons to other children. "You ran a lot faster today than you did last month, Lamont."

When you encourage children, be sure to let them know that you are praising them for their efforts—not how they stack up next to other children or standards. Children need to feel important in their own right, not because they meet someone else's measure of success. As always, it's important to offer sincere and specific praise. If praise comes too often and is vague, it loses its value. On the other hand, sincere and specific praise can make a child feel good and try harder.

It is important to provide materials and activities at appropriate skill levels.

Children acquire new skills when they play and learn in an environment that challenges them to try harder. If materials and activities are too easy, children can become bored and lose interest. At the same time, if they are too far beyond children's skill levels, children can become frustrated and give up.

The key to success is to create an environment and plan activities that interest the children and are appropriate to their capabilities. For example, a teacher might notice that Sharon, age three, loves to tear pieces of paper to make collages but needs practice in refining her small muscle skills. The teacher plans a collage activity where Sharon must use a scissors. However, Sharon does not have the skills needed to cut with a scissors. She becomes frustrated and refuses to participate in art activities at all. While the activity was a good one for developing fine motor skills, it was not appropriate for Sharon at this time, because it was beyond what she could do.

Sharon needs materials that lead to success rather than frustration. Her negative experience with the scissors needs to be offset with positive ones. To help Sharon practice the skills needed for using scissors (eye-hand coordination, finger agility and strength) her teacher might introduce materials she is able to use more successfully: finger puppets, clothespins to clip to the edge of a coffee tin, pegs and a pegboard.

Applying Your Knowledge

In this activity, you read several descriptions of children developing physical skills. Then you decide what activities you could plan and what you could say to help each child feel successful and competent.

Promoting Positive Self-Concepts Through
Development of Physical Skills

What the Child Is Doing	What Activities/Materials You Would Offer This Child	What You Could Say to Encourage the Child
Jason can kick objects forward with ease but is having difficulty kicking objects backward.	Outdoors have all sorts of balls available	Have him play kicking games.
All the children except Eduardo have fun walking on coffee can stilts. Eduardo can't seem to stay up on the "stilts."	Coffee can stilts	Keep trying Eduardo practice makes perfect
Every time the ball is thrown at Maria, she ducks or runs out of its path.	Ball games	Show her not to be scared + help her.
Lucy enjoys stringing large beads. One time she tried to make a necklace of smaller beads. She got frustrated and spilled the entire box of beads on the floor.	small beading games	tell her she can do the big ones so soon she'll be able to do the small ones.
Matthew likes to help pour juice for snacks. However, every time he takes a turn at helping, he spills a large amount of juice. Still, he loves to help out.	a pouring game in the water table	encourage him to keep pouring, and everyone spills things once and a while.

Review your responses with your trainer.

Summarizing Your Progress

You have now completed all of the learning activities for this module. Whether you are an experienced teacher or a new one, this module has probably helped you develop new skills for promoting the physical development of preschool children.

Before you go on to the next module, take a few minutes to summarize what you've learned.

- Turn back to Learning Activity I, Using Your Knowledge of Child Development to Promote Gross Motor Development, and add to the chart specific examples of what you learned while you were working on this module. Read the sample responses on the completed chart at the end of the module.

- Next, review your responses to the pre-training assessment for this module. Write a summary of what you learned and list the skills you developed or improved.

I've learned to encourage children that they can always succeed if they keep trying, and the teachers need to have these things always available for the children so they can learn to succeed in it.

If there are topics you would like to know more about, you will find recommended readings listed in the Orientation.

Your final step in this module is to complete the knowledge and competency assessments. Let your trainer know when you are ready to schedule the assessments. After you have successfully completed them, you will be ready to start a new module. Congratulations on your progress so far, and good luck with your next module.

Answer Sheets

Providing Materials, Equipment, and Opportunities for Gross Motor Development

1. **How did the children let Ms. Williams and Ms. Frilles know they were ready for gross motor activities?**

   a. *They tested the classroom rules and limits.*

   b. *They were very noisy during choice time.*

   c. *Mark "moaned" that they couldn't go outside.*

2. **What gross motor activities did Ms. Williams and Ms. Frilles provide?**

   a. *They asked the children to help move the shelves.*

   b. *They encouraged the children to move their bodies inside the rope rings.*

Providing Materials and Opportunities for Fine Motor Development

1. **How did Ms. Kim encourage the children to use their small muscles?**

   a. *She allowed the children to pour their own milk.*

   b. *She told Robert how to do hold the cup so it wouldn't move.*

   c. *She had Robert use a sponge to wipe up his spilled milk.*

   d. *She asked them to think of a way to pick up peas so the peas won't fall off a fork.*

   e. *She allowed them to spear peas with the fork.*

2. **What did Ms. Kim say to encourage the children's efforts?**

   a. *She told Robert why the milk spilled—because it came out too fast.*

   b. *She asked Robert to wipe up the milk instead of making him feel bad about the spill.*

   c. *She told Shannon that her hand and arm muscles were working well.*

   d. *She reassured Robert that he could pour more slowly the next time.*

   e. *She commented that the children had solved the problem.*

Reinforcing and Encouraging Children's Physical Fitness

1. **What outdoor activities encouraged children's physical fitness?**
    a. *riding tricycles around cones*

    b. *pulling each other in wagons*

    c. *crawling through cardboard boxes*

    d. *kicking a ball*

2. **Why do you think Ms. Thomas suggested an alternative to soccer?**
    a. *She knows that many five-year-olds are not ready for competitive sports.*

    b. *She thinks the family fun program will encourage Lindsay and her family to have fun and stay fit together.*

Using Your Knowledge of Child Development to Promote Gross Motor Skills

(p. 211)

What Preschool Children Are Like	How Teachers Can Use This Information to Promote Gross Motor Skills
They walk easily and can balance themselves on one foot for several seconds at a time.	*Lay a wide strip of tape to the floor so children can practice balancing while walking forwards, sideways, backwards, with arms in front or behind, and over obstacles. Use tape or unit blocks to make a walking course with turns, curves, and obstacles.*
They run, jump, and hop.	*Play noncompetitive games, such as cooperative musical chairs, so children can use their large muscle skills. Arrange the environment so children can jump, hop, and skip around and over objects.*
They move to music, imitate dance movements, and make up creative ways to move.	*Lead activities in which children can move their bodies to music with different rhythms. Offer experiences in which you direct children's movement and some in which children create their own movements.*
They throw balls overhead and catch bounced balls.	*Provide bean bags and balls of various sizes for children to throw and catch. Play catch with children and encourage children to play with each other. Teach older preschoolers simple ball games.*
They climb.	*Allow adequate time for children to use indoor and outdoor climbing equipment. Encourage children who are learning to climb so they feel competent and are not frustrated or fearful.*
They ride tricycles.	*Make sure tricycles are in good repair and the right size. If necessary, let the director know you need repairs or new trikes. Allow beginners to drag their feet on the ground at first—explain and demonstrate pedaling when children are ready. Make sure children know how to stop safely! Offer safety cones and traffic signs children can steer around.*
They use playground equipment such as slides, climbers, and swings.	*Take children outdoors every day for vigorous play and to use outdoor equipment. Be aware of which children need special encouragement because they are afraid.*

Glossary

Aerobic

Vigorous activities and exercises that involve deep breathing for sustained periods of time.

Eye-hand coordination

The ability to direct finger, hand, and wrist movements to accomplish a fine motor task, such as fitting a peg in a hole or piling blocks.

Fine motor skills

Movements that involve the use of small muscles of the body, hands, and wrists—for example, picking up puzzle pieces or cutting with a pair of scissors.

Fitness

The state of an individual's health that reflects his/her quality of life—includes the individual's level of endurance, strength, flexibility, percentage of body fat, and degree of nutritional balance.

Gross motor skills

Movements that involve the use of large muscles of the body, the entire body, or large parts of the body—for example, running, hopping, or climbing.

Physical development

The gradual gaining of control over large and small muscles.

Sensory awareness

The gaining of information through sight, sound, touch, taste, and smell—for example, smelling spices or turning in the direction of a voice.

Module 5: *Cognitive*

Overview

Promoting children's cognitive development involves:
• Creating an environment that encourages children to explore and discover
• Interacting with children in ways that help them develop confidence in their ability to think and solve problems
• Providing opportunities for children to construct knowledge about their world

Cognitive development is the process of learning to think and to reason. Children develop thinking skills by actively exploring their world, trying out their ideas, and observing what happens. Teachers promote children's cognitive development most effectively when they base their practices on how children learn best. The field of education has learned a great deal about children's cognitive development from the work of researchers such as Jean Piaget and Lev Vygotsky.

Through his research, Piaget observed that children pass through different stages of thinking as they develop. For example, Piaget observed that young preschoolers think that a tall, thin glass can hold more water than a short, wide one—even when they see identical amounts of water poured into both glasses. At this stage of thinking, children tend to focus on one feature of an object at a time—in this case, the height of the glass and not its width. By about age six or seven, though, children come to understand that the amount of water in both glasses is the same no matter how it looks. This understanding comes when children are old enough to think more abstractly—to think about ideas and concepts in their heads—and when they have had many direct experiences exploring water and other liquids. According to Piaget, young children grow cognitively as they interact with real objects and materials.

Piaget taught us that children think differently from adults.

Vygotsky's theories show us that children learn best through social interactions with adults and other children; children need adults and "competent peers" to support their beginning learning. Competent peers are children who already know what is being learned. Vygotsky compares this support to the scaffolding placed around new buildings as they are erected. This mental scaffolding provides a framework within which children can use their cognitive skills on their own. According to Vygotsky, adults are facilitators and guides who help children develop their own understandings about the world, rather than people who "give" children knowledge.

Vygotsky explained how adults facilitate and guide children's learning.

Thus, the work of Piaget and Vygotsky shows us that children develop cognitive skills by continually exploring their world and being supported by people who help them make sense of their experiences. You have undoubtedly observed how young children notice all kinds of things and events in their world. They see the smallest caterpillar that you might overlook. And it's not enough for them to just see the caterpillar; they have to touch it, pick it up, examine it closely, even smell it. By using all their senses, young children develop a real understanding of caterpillars. When you say the word, "caterpillar," children learn a label for this object they have explored first hand. On another day, when they see a worm, the same children may say, "Look at the caterpillar!" This is because they have noticed that a worm and a caterpillar have many characteristics in common. Although they are not actually correct, they are applying their new knowledge to a similar situation and striving to understand. We call this "constructing knowledge."

Self-confidence is an important part of cognitive development.

Children's cognitive development is not measured by how much information a child has memorized. While learning concepts and acquiring knowledge is, of course, important during these early years, learning to learn is even more important. To grow cognitively, children need to have the self-confidence and skills to explore, try out ideas, make mistakes, solve problems, and take on new challenges. Helping children develop and use their cognitive skills is an important part of your work.

Preschool children are curious and eager to explore the world around them. As a teacher, you can build on this natural curiosity to guide children's cognitive development. First, you can create an environment that encourages children to explore and make discoveries. Second, you can ask questions and talk with children in ways that help them develop confidence in their own abilities to think and solve problems. Third, you can provide opportunities for children to construct knowledge about their world.

Listed on the following pages are three sets of examples showing how teachers demonstrate their competence in promoting children's cognitive development. Following each set of examples is a short reading and two questions to answer. When you have finished this section, compare your answers to those on the answer sheet at the end of this module. If your answers are different, discuss them with your trainer. There can be more than one good answer.

Creating an Environment That Encourages Children to Explore and Discover

Call attention to sensory experiences as children use materials and participate in routines.

"How does the finger paint feel when you spread it on the shiny paper?"

Organize and display toys and materials logically by categories and attributes.

"Angie is putting away all the triangles on the music shelf. Tyrone, can you collect all the zoo animals and put them in the basin with their picture on the front?"

Display materials that encourage children to make discoveries.

"What did you see when you used the magnifying glass to look at the seashell?"

Provide materials such as plastic bottle caps, beans, buttons, and shells that invite children to sort, classify, and order.

"I see you put the bottle caps in two different piles. How did you decide where to put each bottle cap?"

Provide materials that match children's skills and interests and challenge children to extend their learning.

"Marcus and Jedi, here's a scale, a stamp and pad, and a mailbox to use in your post office."

Offer open-ended materials that children with varied skills and interests can use in different ways.

"The children used the pieces of fabric we put in the dramatic play area as tablecloths, flags, and scarves."

Offer materials that encourage children to explore cause and effect and make predictions.

"Leyla, tell me what happened to the sand when you sprayed it with water."

Ms. Thomas overhears two children discussing the marigolds they planted last month. "The orange ones are taller than the yellow ones," says Rion. "No they aren't," says Tracey. "They just look that way." Ms. Thomas listens to the discussion, then gets some string and scissors from the storage shed. She hands them to Rion and says, "Can you use these to figure out who's right?" Rion says, "Yeah. We can measure how far it is from the sidewalk to the top of each marigold." Rion holds the string tight on the ground, while Tracey unrolls it. "Higher, no lower," says Rion. Soon the children realize their approach is not working. Ms. Thomas says, "That was a good idea to use the string as a measuring tool. Is there another way you could measure with the string?" "I know, I know," says Tracey. "We can measure from the top of the soil to the top of the plants." The children try Amy's idea and find out that the orange marigolds are taller—but just a little.

1. **Why did Ms. Thomas give the string and scissors to the children?**

   1. Encourage children to solve the problems themselves.
   2. She knew the children could work together

2. **What did the children learn from their experience?**

   The children are capable of solving their own problems.
   They can find new ways to use materials

Interacting with Children in Ways That Help Them Develop Confidence in Their Ability to Think and Solve Problems

Point out children's use of thinking skills.

"You thought of a special way to string these beads. It makes an interesting pattern."

Show children that you accept and respect their work and ideas.

"Thanh, I've never seen a triple-decker cracker sandwich! What a good idea to put different kinds of cream cheese in each layer!"

Comment on children's work in a way that introduces new words and builds on their ideas.

"You used rectangles and squares to make a long block train. Where will the passengers get on and off?"

Ask questions to help children understand how past events relate to what is happening now.

"Remember the last time we made playdough? How did we make it less sticky?"

Answer children's questions and help them find their own answers.

"Nina, you're right, the snow on the window sill isn't as high as it was yesterday. What do you think happened?"

Ask questions that encourage children to think of several possible answers or solutions.

"I'm afraid someone might get hurt on that crowded climber. What could we do to make it safer?"

Ask questions that help children think about cause and effect or make predictions.

"Why do you think our plants look so droopy on Monday mornings?"

Ms. Williams is watching three children building a tall tower in the block area. She can see that if they add any more blocks, the building is likely to fall. She knows that even if it falls, no one is going to get hurt. When the building comes crashing down, Ms. Williams goes quietly into the block area and kneels down near the children. "I see your building fell down," she says calmly. "What do you think happened?" Terry says, "We made the building too tall." Ms. Williams asks, "Do all tall buildings fall down?" "No," says Heather, "this one was too skinny." Ms. Williams then asks, "How could you build a tall building so it won't fall down?" After thinking a minute, Sam responds, "We could make it fatter so it would be stronger." "Why don't you try that," says Ms. Williams, "and see what happens?"

1. **Why did Ms. Williams not interfere with the block builders when she could see their building might fall down?**

She knew that no-one could get hurt when the blocks fell, and she wanted the children to see for themselves what would happen

2. **How did Ms. Williams encourage the children to think through and solve the problem on their own?**

She asked the children questions
She didn't give them solutions
She let them try out their ideas

Providing Opportunities for Children to Construct Knowledge About Their World

Set up activities that allow children to test out their ideas.

"Why do you think some things sink to the bottom of the water and others float on the top?"

Plan activities that follow up on books you and the children have read to extend their understanding.

"Today we're going to have a color dance like in the story we read yesterday. Here's a basket full of colored scarves."

Help children apply what they have learned to new situations.

"Last week you made purple by mixing red and blue paint together. What will happen if you mix blue and yellow?"

Extend children's dramatic play by providing new props or making suggestions.

"That was a good idea to use the stuffed animals and health prop box to set up a veterinary office."

Plan activities that allow children to use their senses to explore.

"The nature trail is very quiet, but if you listen carefully, you can hear many different sounds."

Model how to use books to learn new information.

"I don't know what kind of butterfly that is. Let's look it up in our butterfly book."

Help children learn about their community by taking neighborhood walks and inviting guests to visit the program.

"Ms. Petrovich is our children's librarian. Today she's going to tell you a story."

Ms. Richards is sitting with three children at the science table. She has just put out a simple balance scale. "Can you make your hands into a balance scale?" she asks, while demonstrating what she means. "What would happen to your scale if I put one of these blocks in your right hand?" She places a block in each child's right hand and they discuss how it pushes that hand down. "Now, let's see which is heavier, the block or these four marbles." Ms. Richards places four marbles in each child's left hand. The children "weigh" each hand and discuss which feels heavier. There are different opinions. "How could we find out for sure which is heavier?" she asks. "We could use the balance scale," suggests Emily. "Let's try it," says Ms. Richards. Emily places her block in one margarine tub and the four marbles in the other tub. The tub with the block sinks down. "I knew it!" says David. "The block is heavier."

1. **How did Ms. Richards introduce and generate interest in the balance scale?**

   The children used their hands to create a balance scale
   She let the children measure

2. **What skills and concepts were the children learning?**

   Compare the weights of 2 objects
   hands on learning

Your Own Experiences with Learning

Learning is a lifelong experience.

People don't stop learning when they leave school; they continue to refine their thinking and reasoning skills. Think of people you know whom you consider good learners and thinkers. People who have confidence in their ability to learn generally have some of the following characteristics:

- They are not afraid to accept a challenge.

- When they confront a problem, they don't give up if they can't resolve it right away. They try to figure out what to do.

- They are curious and interested in learning new things.

- They are creative thinkers—they can look at something and see several possibilities.

- They speak up and say what they think.

We all know different things.

We don't all know the same things, nor do we need to. An auto mechanic knows a lot about the parts of a car, what makes it go, and how to fix it. When there's a problem, the mechanic tries to identify the cause. If you know very little about how a car operates, this doesn't make you less smart. You know other things the mechanic doesn't know. What really matters is whether we have the knowledge and skills we need to function successfully in our own lives.

Many factors affect our ability to learn something new. Most important is whether the new information is useful to us. If we can see a way to use what we are learning, we are likely to be more interested in making the effort to learn. It helps if the new information is related to something we already know about, or know how to do— or to something we've wanted to know for some time.

Learning style affects how we learn best.

Each of us has our own style or way of learning that works best for us. Some of us need to read over directions and think about them for a while. Others prefer to watch someone else demonstrate a task, or need to hear directions explained a couple of times.

As an adult you are aware of what helps you learn a new skill or new idea. Think of a time recently when you were in a learning situation-for instance, learning to swim, taking an adult education course, or going through these modules.

What made it easy for you to learn in that situation?

**Many factors can affect
our ability to learn.**

Some factors that affect our ability to learn relate to the instructor or to the material itself: how the information is presented, how it is organized, and whether it is at an appropriate level—neither too simple nor too complex. Our readiness to learn is also affected by how we feel at the time. If we are tired, distracted, uncomfortable, or unsure of what is expected of us, we are less likely to learn.

This training program is designed to help you learn new concepts and skills and feel good about yourself as a learner. Several strategies make it a positive learning experience:

- The information is organized into short learning activities so you won't be overwhelmed with too much information at once.

- All the learning activities relate to your work so you can apply the infomation easily.

- There are many examples within each module to help you understand the content.

- Answer sheets, a colleague, or your trainer can give you feedback.

- You receive your own set of materials which become an ongoing reference on the job.

- You complete many of the learning activities while caring for children.

As you enhance your skills and knowledge in ways that make you feel confident, you will be able to do the same thing for children. Like you, young children learn best when they are interested in and ready to receive new information. They construct knowledge by trying out new ideas and discovering what works and what doesn't on their own. As you go through these modules, you will try out many ideas and discover for yourself what approaches work best for you and for the children in your care.

When you have finished this overview section, you should complete the pre-training assessment. Refer to the glossary at the end of this module if you need definitions of the terms that are used.

Pre-Training Assessment

Listed below are the skills teachers use to promote children's cognitive development. Think about whether you do these things regularly, sometimes, or not enough. Place a check in one of the boxes on the right for each skill listed. Then discuss your answers with your trainer.

Creating an Environment That Encourages Children to Explore and Discover

	I Do This:	Regularly	Sometimes	Not Enough
1.	Call attention to sensory experiences as children use materials and participate in routines.		☒	
2.	Organize and display toys and materials logically by categories and attributes.	☒		
3.	Display materials that encourage children to make discoveries.	☒		
4.	Provide materials such as plastic bottle caps, beans, buttons, and shells that invite children to sort, classify, and order.	☒		
5.	Provide materials that match children's skills and interests and challenge children to extend their learning.	☒		
6.	Offer open-ended materials that children with varied skills and interests can use in different ways.		☒	
7.	Offer materials that encourage children to explore cause and effect and make predictions.		☒	

Interacting with Children in Ways That Help Them Develop Confidence in Their Ability to Think and Solve Problems

I Do This:	Regularly	Sometimes	Not Enough
8. Point out children's use of thinking skills.	☒	☐	☐
9. Show children that you accept and respect their work and ideas.	☒	☐	☐
10. Comment on children's work in a way that introduces new words and builds on their ideas.	☒	☐	☐
11. Ask questions to help children recall understand how past events relate to what is happening now.	☒	☐	☐
12. Answer children's questions and help them find their own answers.	☒	☐	☐
13. Ask questions that encourage children to think of several possible answers or solutions.	☒	☐	☐
14. Ask questions that help children think about cause and effect or make predictions.	☒	☐	☐

Providing Opportunities for Children to Construct Knowledge About Their World

	Regularly	Sometimes	Not Enough
15. Set up activities that allow children to test out their ideas.	☒	☐	☐
16. Plan activities that follow up on books you and the children have read to extend their understanding.	☒	☐	☐
17. Help children apply what they have learned to new situations.	☒	☐	☐

Providing Opportunities for Children to Construct Knowledge About Their World

(Continued)

	I Do This:	Regularly	Sometimes	Not Enough
18. Extend children's dramatic play by providing new props or making suggestions.		☒	☐	☐
19. Plan activities that allow children to use their senses to explore.		☒	☐	☐
20. Model how to use books to learn new information.		☒	☐	☐
21. Help children learn about their community by taking neighborhood walks and inviting guests to visit the program.		☒	☐	☐

Review your responses, then list three to five skills you would like to improve or topics you would like to learn more about. When you finish this module, you will list examples of your new or improved knowledge and skills.

Now begin the learning activities for Module 5, Cognitive.

Learning Activities

I. Using Your Knowledge of Child Development to Promote Cognitive Development

---

In this activity you will learn to:

- Recognize how preschool children learn best
- Use what you know about preschool children to promote learning

---

At one time people believed a child's mind was like an empty slate and that it was the role of adults to fill the slate with knowledge. This led to the idea that teaching meant deciding what children should know, telling them the information, and having them memorize and practice until they learned it.

We now know that children are active participants in the learning process. They are like detectives, eagerly trying to make sense of experiences. The more actively they go about learning, the more their brains work to try to understand new experiences. And the more they use their brain power, the more capable children become as learners.

This idea that learning takes place inside the child—rather than something that is poured into the child—is called "constructivism." It means that children construct knowledge—they apply what they already know to what they observe and try to explain and make sense of new experiences. By actively exploring using all their senses—seeing, touching, tasting, hearing, smelling—children test out their ideas and make discoveries. In so doing, they re-examine their previous ideas. Sometimes their experiences reinforce what they already know, and sometimes they change their ideas. In the process, children are building a clearer and (usually) more accurate understanding of their world and how things work.

Children "construct" knowledge about their world.

> Four-year-old Jason watches Taylor at the sand table scooping up sand and pouring it to make a sand wheel spin around. Later that day, while playing at the sand table, he gets the same scoop and dumps the sand into the top of the sand wheel but nothing happens. He tries more sand but it just piles up in the opening and the wheel doesn't move. Then he notices that the sand he scooped up is wet and sticks together. He dumps the wet sand out, scoops up some dry sand, and grins as the wheel begins to spin.

Jason observed how another child was able to make the sand wheel turn. He remembered what he had seen when he approached the sand table and applied what he learned. When it didn't work, he had to figure out what was wrong and try

---

another approach. His first idea—adding more sand—didn't work. His next idea—trying dry sand—did work. Thus, Jason constructed his own understanding of how to make the sand wheel work. Because he figured it out himself, he will be more likely to remember what he learned. Even more importantly, he is learning how to be a learner.

Preschool children ask lots of questions.

Children can ask endless questions to learn about the world around them. They can exhaust even the most patient adult!

They ask **why** questions to learn the purpose of things.

- "Why does the alarm clock go off in the morning?"

- "Why does the car need gas?"

They ask **what** questions to learn the names of things.

- "What is the thing that covers the light bulb?"

- "What is that thing that's flying around?"

They ask **how** questions to understand processes and relationships.

- "How does the water get hard into ice cubes?"

- "How did he get home when the bus broke down?"

Answering the many questions young children ask can feel like a full-time job. Sometimes a simple answer is all that is required: "That's a butterfly." Other times you can use the question to help a child think: "Let's try to think of all the ways he could have gotten home when the bus broke down."

Children learn by interacting with others.

Children teach each other every day. Watch two or more children playing with water, building with blocks, finger painting, or engaging in dramatic play. They may talk about what they are doing, share information, give each other advice, and correct one another. All learning doesn't come from the teacher.

Children need many opportunities to work and play with others. They don't learn by sitting and listening. They learn by observing others, hearing what others have to say, and putting their own ideas into words.

Play engages children in active learning.

Young children learn through play. By recreating experiences—with blocks, paints, clay, boxes—and re-enacting what they have experienced—through dramatic play—children gain a deeper understanding and clarify their ideas.

Sara Smilansky[1] identified four different kinds of play. Each type of play contributes to children's development and learning.

---

[1] Smilansky, Sara and Leah Sheatya, *Facilitating Play: A Medium for Promoting Cognitive, Socio-Emotional and Academic Development in Young Children* (Gaithersburg, MD: Psychosocial and Educational Publications, 1990).

Functional play occurs when children actively explore and examine the physical properties of materials and objects. By handling, experimenting, observing, listening, and smelling, children learn about their environment.

Constructive play involves using materials to create a representation of something. Children might build a farm with blocks, paint a picture of a dog, or make a cardboard box into a ship. This type of play requires children to recall what they know and recreate it.

Socio-dramatic play entails pretending to be someone else and making believe about a situation. Children re-enact experiences they have had, observed, or imagined. Socio-dramatic play is a cognitive task that requires children to remember the actions of the person or thing they are playing, select details about an event to replay, use real or imaginary props, and display appropriate words and gestures. Socio-dramatic play teaches children to think abstractly. By role playing, they come to understand their experiences on a much deeper level.

Games with rules is the fourth type of play. Board games such as Lotto or more active games like "Red Light, Green Light" require children to learn the rules and follow them. This type of play helps children learn to concentrate, understand rules, and control their behavior to conform to the rules of the game.

Teachers promote children's cognitive development by basing their practices on an understanding of how children learn. They provide many opportunities for children to actively explore, seek answers to their questions, and recreate what they have experienced.

The chart on the next two pages identifies some typical behaviors of preschool children. Included are behaviors relevant to promoting children's cognitive development. The right-hand column asks you to identify ways that teachers can use this information to promote cognitive development. Try to think of as many examples as you can. As you work through the module, you will learn new strategies and you can add them to the chart. You are not expected to think of all the examples at once. If you need help getting started, turn to the completed chart at the end of the module. By the time you complete this module, you will find you know many ways to promote children's cognitive development.

Using Your Knowledge of Child Development to Promote Cognitive Development

What Preschool Children Are Like	How Teachers Can Use This Information to Promote Cognitive Development
They learn by using all their senses—smell, taste, touch, sight, and sound.	*Make a tape of familiar sounds and ask children to guess what each sound is. Offer various textured items for collage making. Talk about how foods smell and taste. Have children identify mystery objects in a bag by touch.*
They are interested in cause and effect—what makes things happen.	Provide objects to explore with.
They have rapidly expanding vocabularies—they can name many things and explain their ideas.	Introduce new words for their vocabulary
They are curious and want to explore many things.	set-up a safe environment, and let the children experience it for themselves
They learn by using their imaginations in dramatic play and other activities.	New prop boxes for dramatic play - change thing every so often.
They believe there is a purpose for everything and ask many questions: "Why?" "How?" "What?"	Answer their questions and help them to answer their own questions.

Using Your Knowledge of Child Development to Promote Cognitive Development

What Preschool Children Are Like	How Teachers Can Use This Information to Promote Cognitive Development
They construct knowledge by exploring and making connections between new experiences and what they know from past experiences.	Ask children questions to encourage children to think.
They are developing an understanding of numerical concepts but need many experiences with real objects.	Offer many materials for the children
They learn to match, classify, and identify shapes and colors by playing with toys and objects.	a variety of materials
They have many ideas and like to gather information about the world.	Do activities w/in the community.
They are beginning to understand that pictures, letters, words, and numbers represent real objects and ideas.	label things such as shelves, cubbies and materials.

When you have completed as much as you can do on the chart, discuss your answers with your trainer. As you proceed with the rest of the learning activities, you can refer back to the chart and add more examples of how teachers can promote children's cognitive development.

II. Understanding How Preschool Children Think

> **In this activity you will learn to:**
>
> - Recognize how children think and seek to make sense of their experiences
> - Respond to children in ways that promote thinking and understanding

As an adult, you can read and take meaning from the words on this page because you understand the concepts they represent. When you add this new information to what you already know, you deepen your understanding. You can also learn by listening to a speaker or watching a video about a subject of interest to you.

Preschool children think and learn differently from adults.

Preschool children learn differently from adults. Written words hold little or no meaning for most preschoolers. They are beginning to recognize some letters and words but they are certainly not ready to learn from printed pages. Nor do young children learn best by sitting and listening. They learn best by doing. They have to explore, try out their ideas, and see for themselves what happens. They construct knowledge from their own experiences.

You may have heard people say that young children have their own ways of thinking. As a teacher working with children every day, you have probably enjoyed the "funny" things they sometimes say. Knowing why children say and do these "funny" things will help you understand how preschool children think. It will also help you appreciate how hard they are working to understand the world around them.

Preschool children take words literally.

Most young children don't realize that the same word can have different meanings, depending on how it is used. Because preschool children are still learning these multiple meanings, they can get confused.

- A three-year-old told her mother: "We went on a walk at school today. We were looking for signs of winter, but all I saw was one STOP sign."

- A teacher put on a tape and told the children to "move to the music," meaning "move your bodies as the music makes you feel." The children got up and moved over to the tape player.

These children took the words they heard very literally. They had a different understanding of the adults' words than was intended, and they acted on what they thought was meant. While adults find such mistakes amusing, it is important to respond in ways that respect children's efforts to learn. "Sign is a word with several meanings. I think your teacher meant . . ." "You did just what I asked you to do. Now, try listening to the music and see how it makes you want to move your arms and legs and bodies."

Preschool children generalize—they make a connection between what they observe and what they have experienced in the past. Sometimes they put ideas together that are not related.

Preschool children generalize from one experience.

- "Today we are having fish for lunch because the teacher is late. Whenever the teacher is late, we have fish."

- A four-year-old noticed that a friend didn't want ice cream for dessert. Later that night, the friend got sick. The next day, when offered ice cream, the child said, "Yes, because if I don't have ice cream, I'll get sick too."

Even though these children were not correct in their conclusions, they were making connections to try to understand and predict events in their lives.

If something looks bigger, young children believe it must be bigger. If they were able to think logically, they would see that the amount can stay the same, no matter how it looks. Here are two examples:

Preschool children judge things by how they look.

- If you put some sand in a low, long tray and then let a child watch you put the same amount of sand into a flower pot, he or she might say there is more sand in the pot than in the tray because the sand seems "deeper."

- Young children often break up their crackers at snack time because to them, lots of small pieces seem like more than one large piece.

Young children also tend to be egocentric thinkers—they believe that what is in their mind is also in yours. This doesn't mean they are selfish or only focused on themselves. It means that cognitively, they have trouble understanding that each person is different and has different thoughts and ideas.

Preschool children are egocentric in their thinking.

- A three-year-old with a toothache was asked if it hurt. "Yes," he replied, "Can't you feel it?"

- "Don't you know that?" children will ask in surprise, as if everyone should know what they know!

Listening to what children say is an excellent way to learn how they think and attempt to make sense of their world. Children teach us a lot about what they understand and what they are ready to learn.

Applying Your Knowledge

In this learning activity you observe and listen to the children in your group over a one-week period. Look for examples of how they are trying to make sense of the world. Try to find examples of the following: taking words literally; cause-and-effect thinking; judging things by how they look; and egocentric thinking. First read the example that follows. Then use the chart on the following page to record your observations.

Learning About Children's Thinking

(Example)

What the Child Said or Did	What You Learned
Tim was sure his piece of clay was bigger than Vanessa's because his was taller and hers was flatter. (They were the same.)	*Tim judges the quantity of clay by how it looks.*
When I told Delores she had "sharp eyes," she put her hands to her eyes and said, "They're not sharp."	*Dolores takes words literally. She is a concrete thinker.*
After a storm, Susan announced, "Thunder makes the rain."	*This is cause-and-effect thinking. Susan linked two events and believes that one caused the other.*

Learning About Children's Thinking

What the Child Said or Did	What You Learned

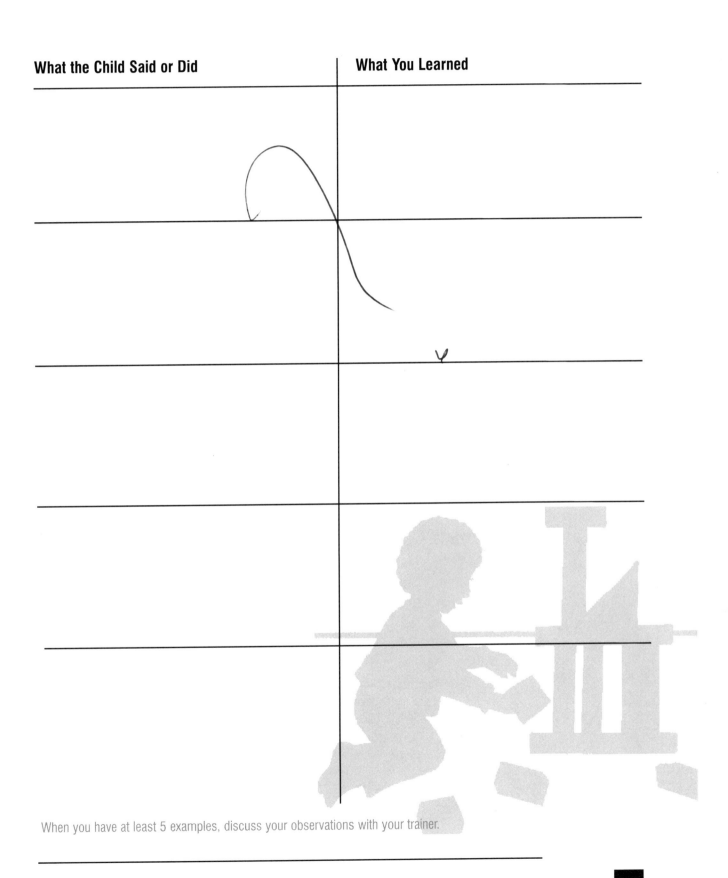

When you have at least 5 examples, discuss your observations with your trainer.

III. Encouraging Children to Explore and Discover

In this activity you will learn to:

- Recognize how children learn from their environment
- Ask questions that encourage children to explore and make discoveries

---

There is an endless amount of information that preschool children can learn. As important as what they learn, however, is whether they are learning how to learn. Children who are encouraged to explore and make discoveries on their own develop confidence in themselves as learners.

Creating an Interesting Environment

The indoor and outdoor environment is the setting you can use to help children develop cognitive skills. Many of the concepts and relationships you want children to learn are already present in the environment.

Many concepts are present in the environment.

Concepts such as colors, shapes, and sizes are evident in materials such as table toys, paints, and blocks. Relationships and principles of science and math, such as the graded sizes of unit blocks, what plants need to grow, and how many cups of juice are contained in a pitcher can be found or demonstrated in the environment. Children learn about cause and effect when they mix colors at the easel, add yeast to bread dough, and build a block tower that tumbles to the floor.

There are many fine materials you can purchase for your room. But don't overlook the wonderful "junk" you and children's parents can collect and use to promote cognitive development. Some examples of materials you can provide are given below.

Collections are found objects that invite children to sort, organize, and classify:

- keys
- buttons
- seeds and pits
- beans

- rocks
- shells
- leaves
- plastic bottle caps

Tools for exploring invite children to closely examine objects. When placed with the objects, children are more likely to use tools in their investigations. They may include the following:

- magnifying glasses near collections of sand, rocks, and leaves
- magnets and objects to test
- screwdrivers and an old clock to take apart
- a balance scale and objects to weigh
- measuring tools: rulers, cups, spoons, tapes, yardsticks

Table toys are ideal for encouraging children to explore and use their growing thinking skills. Every classroom should have manipulative materials such as the following:

- attribute blocks or beads
- parquetry blocks
- pegboards and pegs
- puzzles
- Cuisenaire rods
- matching games

- seriation games and toys (e.g., nesting cups, sound canisters, texture games, color chips)
- colored cubes
- shape-sorting boxes
- beads for stringing

The more varied the environment, the more opportunities children have to apply thinking skills as they explore and discover.

Skills Children Use to Explore and Discover

Children use a variety of skills to explore their world and make discoveries. As they strive to make sense of their experiences, children construct knowledge.

By using all their senses—touching, seeing, hearing, smelling, tasting—preschool children can identify the characteristics of things around them and seek answer to their own questions. Adults can help children learn the words used to describe different characteristics: hard/soft, red/green, loud/quiet, sour/sweet. You can encourage children to notice the characteristics of materials by asking questions such as the following:

Children use their senses to identify characteristics of things around them.

- "How does the sandpaper feel? How does the aluminum foil feel?"

- "When you sniff the bottle of vanilla, what does it remind you of?"

- "What did you hear when you placed the shell against your ear?"

Being able to identify how things are the same and how they are different is a skill that will help children when they learn to read. For example, to understand the symbols used in reading, children must be able to tell the differences between q and p, d and b. Before they can do this, they need many opportunities to compare, to match, and to identify how objects are the same and how they are different. Here are some questions you can ask to guide children in identifying similarities and differences:

Children can identify similarities and differences.

- "Can you find another block that looks like this one?"

- "How are these two buttons the same? How are they different?"

- "Which of these fruits have rough skins? Which have smooth ones?"

Preschool children are naturally quite interested in comparing themselves to others: how their hair is different, whether they have the same shoes. Encourage children to compare in a friendly, nonjudgmental way so that they learn to appreciate similarities and differences without forming prejudices. Recognizing how people are alike and different is an important step in learning to appreciate and value each other.

Children use classification skills to make sense of the world.

The ability to sort and classify helps children to make sense of the world. They sort objects, people, events, and ideas into groups according to a single trait they have in common. When a three-year-old says to his teacher, "You can't be a Mommy, you're a teacher," he is classifying. He has put this woman in a group of people called "teachers," and he thinks she can't also be a mother because that's another group. This is because preschool children tend to focus on only one trait at a time. Questions such as the following encourage children to use classifying skills:

- "What different groups could we make with these bottle caps?"

- "You sorted the beads by color. What other groups can you make?"

- "How are all the shapes in this group alike?"

Sequencing helps children understand number concepts.

Sequencing is the ability to put things in a certain order. A time sequence would be first, next, last; a sequence of sizes would be small, medium, and large. There can be sequences in sounds from loudest to quietest, and there can be sequences in color shades from darkest to lightest.

The ability to identify and order sequences is important for an understanding of number concepts. Children need to be able to count in order. You may have heard a child count proudly, "1, 2, 7, 5, 8, 9, 10." In addition to counting in the correct order, children need to understand that each number stands for a quantity of things. Five has real meaning only if a child understands that a group of five objects has one more than four and one less than six. Children need real-life opportunities to practice putting things in order and counting in sequence .

Here are some questions you can ask to help children develop sequencing skills:

- "What happened first in the story? Then what happened? What happened last?"

- "You made a pattern with your beads—red, yellow, blue, red, yellow, blue, and red again. What color bead will you string next to repeat this pattern?"

- "You made a long worm with the playdough. Can you make another one bigger than this one? Now can you make one that is smaller?"

Understanding cause and effect leads to predicting outcomes.

Preschool children seem to be constantly trying to figure out why things happen the way they do. For example, a five-year-old child noticed that the water level in the fish tank had gone down. He said to his teacher, "Look, the fish are drinking the water!" Rather than correcting the child or offering an explanation of evaporation, the teacher asked questions and suggested a way for the child to find out for himself what really caused the water to go down.

- "What makes you think the fish are drinking the water?"

- "You mean if we put out a bowl of water without any fish, the water wouldn't get lower? Let's try it and see what happens."

The children in this class soon discovered that even without fish the water level got lower. The teacher then planned some activities so children could learn more about the concept of evaporation, such as painting with water on a chalkboard and taking a walk after a rain shower when the sun was out.

Once children begin to grasp that things in their environment happen in certain way, they start making predictions—what might happen if . . . or what might happen next if . . . . They can apply what they have learned about cause and effect to a new situation.

The Value of Open-Ended Questions

Open-ended questions are ones that have many possible answers. Closed questions have only one right answer. For example, if you ask the children, "What kinds of food does our guinea pig like?"—an open-ended question—you will get a variety of responses. If you ask, "Does our guinea pig eat lettuce?"—a closed question— the children will answer either yes or no. They will not have to stretch their thinking to recall everything they know about the topic in order to respond.

Open-ended questions help children build on what they already know. Because there are many possible responses, these types of questions encourage thinking and imagination. With practice, teachers can become skilled at asking children questions that require them to do the following:

- Recall a past event: "What happened last time when . . .?"

- Explore cause and effect: "Why do you think . . .?"

- Make a prediction: "What do you think will happen when you . . .?"

- Think of several possibilities: "What other ways can you . . .?"

The more you practice asking open-ended questions, the more natural it will become for you.

Applying Your Knowledge

In this learning activity, you observe the children as they work and play indoors and outdoors and note examples of how they are using thinking skills. Next, record the open-ended questions you asked to extend their thinking. Review the example that follows, then conduct your observations and complete the blank chart.

Promoting Children's Thinking

(Example)

Thinking Skill	Interest Area	What the Children Did	What You Said to Promote Thinking and Learning
Identifying characteristics of things around them	*Science table*	*Emilio picked up and examined shells in a collection we put out.*	*"How does that shell feel?" "Which one is your favorite?" "What do you like about it?"*
Identifying similarities and differences	*Table toys*	*Kendra took out a Lotto game and spread out all the small cards of zoo and farm animals. She picked up a card with a zebra and matched it to a horse.*	*"How are these two animals the same?" "Can you see any ways in which they are different?" "Can you find another picture of an animal like the first one?"*
Classifying	*Dramatic play*	*Three children reorganized the dress-up items. They put all the clothes in one pile and all the accessories in another.*	*"How did you decide what to put in each pile?"*
Sequencing	*Outdoors*	*Deana and Jerome collected leaves from the playground. They spread them out on a table by size.*	*"You certainly found all sorts of leaves today. Some are big and some are little. How else could you organize your leaf collection?"*
Understanding cause and effect	*Blocks*	*Laeta built a road with a ramp for her car. She made the ramp so steep that the car went down too fast and fell off the road. She grew frustrated.*	*"Looks like that car is going too fast. What could you do to make it go slower?" When she couldn't think of an idea, I said, "What do you think would happen if this block were lower?"*

Promoting Children's Thinking

Thinking Skill	Interest Area	What the Children Did	What You Said to Promote Thinking and Learning
Identifying characteristics of things around them			
Identifying similarities and differences			
Classifying			
Sequencing			
Understanding cause and effect			

Discuss your observations and questions with your trainer.

IV. Planning Experiences with Sand and Water

> **In this activity you will learn to:**
>
> • Encourage children to construct their own knowledge exploring sand and water
>
> • Introduce a variety of props and suggest experiments that encourage children to learn about the properties of sand and water

Most children are naturally drawn to sand and water play. These activities let children be messy in a world that usually demands neatness and order. Think back to your own childhood. Can you remember how much fun it was to blow bubbles through a straw or bury your feet in cool, wet sand? These experiences were enjoyable and provided opportunities for learning. Sand and water play invite children to explore, experiment, and use their creativity. Children find these materials pleasing to look at and touch. For children, playing with sand and water can be a soothing and relaxing experience, or a challenging and exciting one.

Sand and water play encourage children to experiment and make discoveries.

As discussed throughout this module, preschool children like to experiment. They want to figure out what happens when sand gets wet or when they add food coloring to water. There are many ways to pour sand and water; many things to observe. Most importantly, there are no right or wrong ways to play with sand or water. While playing with these media, children can wonder and seek answers to their questions. They make many discoveries and construct knowledge about math and science, including concepts such as the following:

- When you add things to sand and water the properties may change.

- Sand and water look different when viewed through a magnifying glass or clear cup.

- Water changes when it freezes.

- Water evaporates and seems to disappear.

- Water changes other things (it makes sand soggy).

- Water is absorbed by different materials (blotters, cork, Styrofoam, paper towels) in different ways.

- Some objects float in water and others sink.

- You can see reflections and ripples in water.

- Water levels rise and fall.

- Some things dissolve in water (salt, food coloring) and others don't.

- Sand has a distinct texture (it can be fine or coarse, dry or wet).

- Containers of different shapes and sizes hold different amounts of sand and water.

For children to make the kinds of discoveries just described, you will need to offer a variety of props, many of which you can collect or ask parents to donate. Many of the props listed below can be used for both water and sand play.

Offer a variety of props to expand sand and water play experiences.

Props for Sand Play

Buckets and shovels
Cookie cutters
Funnels
Ladles
Measuring cups and spoons
Pebbles and rocks
Rake
Rubber animals and people
Seeds
Sifter
Straws
Toy cars/dump trucks
Whisk broom

Colander
Feathers
Gelatin molds
Magnifying glass
Muffin tin
Plastic dishes (regular and
    doll-sized)
Rolling pin
Seashells
Sieve
Sticks
String

Props for Water Play

Bubble-blowing materials
    (straws, soap flakes, glycerin)
Buckets
Corks
Food coloring/vegetable dye
Ladles
Measuring cups and spoons
Plastic or rubber bottles (with
    and without holes punched in them)
Soap (bar, liquid, flakes)
Whisks

Sponges
Squeeze bottles
Egg beater
Eye dropper
Funnels
Paintbrushes
Scale
Scoops
Strainer
Siphon

It's best to begin with just a few basic props. Then, observe children's play to see when new props are needed. For example, if you see children experimenting with different ways to fill a bottle, you might introduce a funnel.

Planned sand and water play experiences can lead children to make their own discoveries.

After children have had many opportunities to experiment with sand and water, you can plan experiences that encourage them to discover new skills and concepts on their own. Some examples follow.

- Present materials to children sequentially; for example, first dry sand and then wet, or first clear water and later colored or soapy water.

- Introduce different surfaces onto which children can pour water, such as wax paper, a blotter, a sponge, or plastic.

- Provide objects children can use to conduct sink or float experiments.

- Make a series of plastic containers with holes punched in them, so that children can see how long it takes for the different containers to empty.

- Offer materials that are proportional, such as measuring cups or nesting cups.

Applying Your Knowledge

In this learning activity you plan and implement an activity to promote children's learning through sand or water play. After you write your plan, introduce the activity to the children and record what happens. Review the example on the next page before you begin.

Sand or Water Activity Plan
(Example)

Setting: *Indoors at the water table during choice time*

Date: *November 9*

Purpose of activity:

To challenge children to construct knowledge about what makes some objects sink and others float in water.

Materials needed:

Water table with two inches of water. A box with objects: corks, piece of wood, plastic bottle with cap, a leaf, acorn, paper clips, a stone, modeling clay, chalk, wood and metal toys, plastic spoons, peach pits, sponges. (I will encourage children to find other objects in the room.) Two trays with illustrated signs: "Sinks" and "Floats."

How you introduced the activity:

At group time I asked the children: "What would happen if you put a stone in water?" We talked about things that float and things that sink. I told them they could experiment with the objects in the box and see what they could find out for themselves.

What happened?

Theresa, Paul, and Miguel went to the water table and began testing the items in the box. I explained the purpose of the trays. I challenged them to guess whether an object would sink or float before they tested it. They began looking around the room for other objects to try. During the morning, Sammy, LaShon, Toby, Tisha, and Tyrone joined the activity. I asked them what they noticed about the objects on each tray.

How did the activity promote cognitive development?

Children were making their own discoveries. They were learning to predict and getting better at guessing correctly. They were identifying different characteristics of objects that sink and float.

Would you do this activity again? If so, describe how you might change it.

Yes, it worked well. The next thing I will do is to suggest to children that some shapes of modeling clay will float and others sink. I will challenge them to make different shapes, test them out, and put the ones that sink on one tray, and the ones that float on another. Then we will talk at group time about what they discovered.

Sand or Water Activity Plan

Setting: _____ **Date:** _____

Purpose of activity:

Materials needed:

How you introduced the activity:

What happened?

How did the activity promote cognitive development?

Would you do this activity again? If so, describe how you might change it.

V. *Helping Children Develop Problem-Solving Skills*

In this activity you will learn to:

- Recognize why problem-solving is an important cognitive skill
- Help children to solve problems on their own

Problems are part of life. Every day children are confronted with problems that require solutions:

- The fingerpaint is too watery; it keeps covering up my design. What can I do?

- My block building keeps falling, but I want it to be tall like a skyscraper. How can I make it stronger?

- I want to play shoe store too. How can I join the group?

Because children get frustrated easily, it's tempting for adults to want to solve the problem quickly by offering a solution. Yet a quick solution from an adult doesn't teach children how to solve problems on their own. Learning how to solve problems is an important skill that will benefit children now and throughout their lives. Children who begin to see themselves as problem-solvers are more likely to tackle difficult problems when they get older. They will probably be successful in school, because they have confidence in their own abilities.

Teachers can encourage children to develop problem-solving skills by asking the kinds of questions that challenge children to think of their own solutions. The following situation shows how one teacher, Ms. Williams, used a series of open-ended questions to help Joey solve his own problem.[2]

Joey was playing with some cars on the floor when one of them rolled under the shelf. "Oh, no," said Joey as he heard it bang against the wall. "Ms. Williams," he said, "my car's under the shelf!" Ms. Williams came over to Joey. "Well, how can you get it out?" He stretched his arm under the shelf as far as it could go, but he couldn't feel the car. "You try," he said. Ms. Williams got down and felt around under the shelf. "You had a good idea, but I guess my arm isn't long enough either. Now what?" Joey had another idea. He would try with his foot. When his leg wouldn't fit in the space under the shelf, he tried the other leg, then gave the shelf an angry kick. "This is a frustrating

Problem-solving involves thinking of and trying out solutions to problems.

Teachers can help children solve problems themselves.

2 Adapted from Bess-Gene Holt et al., *Getting Involved: Your Child and Problem-Solving* (Washington, DC: Government Printing Office, 1981), p. 3.

problem, isn't it? But kicking the shelf won't help," Ms. Williams said. "Think about why it didn't work." Joey said, "My leg is too big." Ms. Williams smiled. "Yes, it is. So we know my leg won't work! What could we use that would fit?" Joey thought for a minute and said, "Hey, a stick." "Good idea, Joey." She went to the closet and came back with a broom. Joey poked the broom handle under the shelf and out rolled the car.

Together, Joey and Ms. Williams solved the problem. The next time his car or another toy goes under a piece of furniture, Joey will know that he can use a stick to get it out. He also learned that he is capable of solving his own problems.

Teachers can create an environment that encourages problem-solving.

One of the best ways for you to teach problem-solving is to create a classroom environment that values this skill. When a problem arises, let children know that almost all problems have solutions. Allow time for children to seek their own solutions with your support and guidance. Your attitude towards problems is very important. Here are some suggestions for encouraging problem-solving in your classroom.

Be patient. Children may need many opportunities to try and try again. You can help them by saying "I can see how hard you are trying," or by asking questions that may prompt a solution that will work. When Ms. Williams asked Joey, "What could we use that would fit?" she helped him try again rather than rushing in too quickly with an answer.

Accept and respect children's responses. Keep in mind that children think in different ways than adults do. They are more likely to continue to solve problems when they feel that all their ideas are accepted and valued.

Allow time for children to think. Young children may have trouble putting their thoughts into words. It may take some time for them to collect their thoughts and express their ideas. If adults are impatient, children will stop trying.

Offer help a little at a time. When the first solution to a problem doesn't work, help the child learn from the experience and think of other ideas. Observing what happens can help them think of a new solution. Mistakes are not failures; they are part of learning to solve problems.

Respond to children's questions by asking questions that stimulate thinking. "That's an interesting question. How could we find out how long the snowball will last indoors?"

Encourage multiple solutions. This will keep children thinking about new possibilities and options. "That was a good idea. Can you think of any other solutions that would work?"

Model problem-solving. For example, when repairing a wheel on a wagon, talk to children about what you are doing. "Now I see what happened. See how this wheel has a round washer and the broken one doesn't? It looks like all this wheel needs is a new washer." Children will learn that problem-solving is a normal part of daily living.

In addition to setting a tone that encourages problem-solving, you can teach children how to resolve problems by following specific steps. Often problems arise that affect the whole class. Involving children in discussing the problem, suggesting solutions, and deciding on a plan teaches children that it's possible to solve problems together. Here are the steps for problem-solving with a small group or with the whole class.

Discuss the situation. Present the problem in clear language and without making a judgment about what you think or what you feel is right. Invite children to give their ideas about the situation. Restate what each child says to clarify and make sure all ideas are validated. "So, you think that . . . ."

Generate possible solutions. The next step is to invite children to think of possible solutions. It's important to let children know that there is no one right answer; many solutions might work. Encourage everyone to contribute: "Does anyone have an idea?" You might offer to write down all the ideas on a chart so the group can discuss each one. Ask children to explain their ideas if they are not clear: "Can you say more about that?"

Make a plan. Review the list of solutions and ask children to think about which one they would like to try. Describe how it would work and make sure everyone has the same understanding. "OK, here's what I think we decided. See if you agree."

Implement the plan. The next step is to put the agreed upon solution into effect. Let children know that every solution to a problem doesn't always work. Explain that everyone will try out the plan and observe what happens. Agree on a time to come back and review the situation.

Assess the results. Evaluation is an important last step. Even in situations when it's obvious that a solution is working, it's a good idea to help children reflect on why it worked. Sometimes children are impatient and want to throw out an idea if it doesn't work out immediately. Encourage them to modify the idea and try again before abandoning the idea altogether.

The ability to solve problems, to think of a variety of solutions instead of giving up, is an important life skill. Teachers who are good problem-solvers themselves can inspire children to learn and practice this skill.

Applying Your Knowledge

In this learning activity you lead a group of children in solving a problem. First identify the problem. Using the steps outlined above, discuss the problem, help children generate solutions, and agree on a plan. Begin by reviewing the example that follows.

Helping Children Learn to Solve Problems
(Example)[3]

Children Involved: *The whole class*   **Date:** *October 11*

Identify the problem:

Superhero play is dominating the choice time. Several children take over the dramatic play area and the play often gets out of hand. Someone always ends up hurt. Also, it's having a negative impact on the classroom atmosphere and on children's work in other areas.

How did you discuss the situation with the children?

I talked about the problem at group time. I said, "I've been thinking about a problem and I need your help in solving it. Lately, I've been noticing a lot of Power Ranger play and it's worrying me. Someone is always getting hurt, and we've talked about how we want our classroom to be safe for everyone. I'm wondering what all of you think."

I invited the children to tell me their ideas. Tonya said, "They hit too much." Kevin said, "They have to hit to get the bad ones." Jerome said, "I hate it when everyone yells." Whatever anyone said, I restated it to validate the idea. For example, to Jerome I said, "It hurts your ears when there is so much noise." The children had a lot to say on the topic!

How did you lead the children to generate possible solutions?

I asked, "Since Power Rangers are strong, what other ways could they show they are powerful without hitting? Does anyone have an idea?" I listed the children's ideas which included things like getting people to the hospital, fixing things, making sure people don't litter, taking bad guys to jail.

How did you help the children make a plan?

I read back the list and asked the children which ones they wanted to try out. They decided tomorrow they would be "Power Fixers" in charge of anything that went wrong, including taking people to jail to be "fixed." They wanted me to keep a list of all the fixing they did.

After implementing the plan, how did you help the children assess the results?

At a meeting two days later, the children agreed that it was not as noisy in the room and no one had gotten hurt. Jerry, Michael, and Tyrone who especially like to play Power Rangers said they needed to be loud sometimes. Stacey suggested they do that outside on the playground. That was agreeable to the boys.

---

[3] Ideas from this example are drawn from Diane E. Levin, *Teaching Young Children in Violent Times: Building a Peaceable Classroom* (Cambridge, MA: Educators for Social Responsibility, 1994).

Helping Children Learn to Solve Problems

Children Involved: _____ **Date:** _____

Identify the problem:

How did you discuss the situation with the children?

How did you lead the children to generate possible solutions?

How did you help the children make a plan?

After implementing the plan, how did you help the children assess the results?

Discuss this activity with your trainer.

VI. *Engaging Children in Long-Term Studies*

In this activity you will learn to:

- Identify appropriate topics that children can explore over a period of time
- Develop a plan for engaging children in a long-term study

In this module we have discussed how children learn from their environment. In each of the interest areas of the classroom and outdoors, children can choose from a variety of activities that will help them construct knowledge about their world. Much of the learning is thus informal: teachers create a well-organized and exciting environment and children have daily opportunities to explore and try out their ideas.

Teachers can also promote children's cognitive development by engaging them in long-term studies[4]. A study enables teachers to focus planning around a topic that is of interest to children. Teachers can plan activities and experiences that invite children to raise questions, collect information, and demonstrate what they know.

Appropriate topics for a study are based on children's immediate interests.

The most appropriate topics grow out of the children's interests and what is happening in their own community. For example, children living in a fishing village in Alaska might be engaged in learning about different kinds of fish; children in a city might be investigating different stores in the neighborhood; and children in a rural area might be learning about the operations of a farm.

An appropriate topic matches the developmental abilities and interests of the children. Three-year-olds are primarily focused on themselves and their families. Fours want to know about other children and their neighborhood. And fives typically ask questions about how things are made, who does what jobs, and how things work.

In selecting an appropriate topic, consider the following questions:

- Does the topic address children's interests?

- Is the topic real, relevant to children's experiences, and age appropriate?

- Can children explore the topic first-hand?

- Are resources—such as people to talk to, places to visit, objects or living things to observe and explore, books—available?

- Can the topic be explored in a variety of ways over an extended period?

- Can children apply a variety of skills to exploring the topic?

---

[4] This discussion is based on *The Creative Curriculum for Early Childhood, 3rd Ed.*, Diane Trister Dodge & Laura J. Colker (Washington, DC: Teaching Strategies, Inc., 1992), pp. 54-56, and *Constructing Curriculum for the Primary Grades,* Diane Trister Dodge, Judy R. Jablon, & Toni S. Bickart (Washington, DC: Teaching Strategies, Inc. 1994), pp. 157-173.

Once you have identified an appropriate topic, gather all the information you can find. The children's librarian can identify a number of good books on most topics. Looking through these resources will inspire you to think of a wide range of "big ideas" and experiences you can offer children. For example, in a study about hats, some big ideas to explore with children might be the following: "We wear different kinds of hats for different purposes" and "Hats are made of different kinds of materials."

Identify and then visit any places you plan to take the children. This will give you many ideas for focusing children's attention when you do take the trip. Talk to people who work there about what you want children to see and about safety issues.

Gather pictures, books, and other items related to the topic that you can share with the children. Parents can be excellent resources and may, in fact, be experts on the topic. Involving family members in a study is a wonderful way to enrich children's experiences.

As previously discussed, children learn best when they can actively question, explore, and research a topic. Through investigation, children see, hear, touch, smell, and as a result, develop a personal understanding. Investigation experiences can take many forms. Children investigate when they:

pose questions	create experiments
take trips	handle objects
conduct interviews	look at pictures
have discussions	observe objects/events
explore materials	listen to experts

The kinds of experiences you plan will vary depending on the topic. Active investigation experiences related to a study on caterpillars and butterflies might involve collecting caterpillars, finding out what kind of environment they need, and what they eat; creating an appropriate caterpillar or butterfly home in the classroom; observing them closely over time; taking a trip to a nature center to see an exhibit; talking to experts; taking photos of how they change.

When we learn something new and then describe it in our own words, draw a picture of it, or act it out, we deepen our understanding. Children gain understanding when they recreate what they have learned. As children investigate and make discoveries, they relate this new information to what they already know. When they represent their ideas in drawings, block structures, or models, they demonstrate what they know.

Materials for constructing these representations may include the following:

blocks	collage materials
markers, crayons and paper	journals and colored pencils
tempera paint and water colors	cartons and boxes
clay and playdough	

Learn as much as you can about a topic.

Plan experiences that will enable children to be active investigators.

Provide opportunities for children to recreate what they are learning.

Children can also recreate what they have learned through dramatic play. In dramatic play, children take on different roles, create imaginary settings and situations, use appropriate props, dress up, interact with others, and recall the sequence of events. For example, children might want to set up a post office after visiting one and interviewing the people who work there. This would involve creating or obtaining the appropriate props, deciding on who will take different roles, and arranging for "customers" to come and mail letters. Dramatization experiences can also involve acting out a story, making up a play and presenting it, or putting on a puppet show.

When teachers plan studies that engage children's interest, surprising things can happen. Children come up with ideas and questions about the topic, and this often leads to new investigations and the need to recreate what children have discovered. Teachers have to be good observers and be willing to change plans, add new props and materials, and follow children in new directions. In many cases, children and teachers become co-constructors of knowledge.

A long-term study should have a closing activity.

Some studies last for more than a month, others might last just a few weeks. The length of a study depends on how involved children become and the variety of experiences and materials you can offer children as they explore a topic.

After spending considerable time on a study, it is important to give some thought to how it will end. Closing activities for a study might be a class book of drawings and photographs on the study; a display of projects and artwork children created; a play presented to family members. Closing activities give children a chance to share what they have learned and feel pride in their accomplishments.

Applying Your Knowledge

In this activity you plan a long-term study that will engage children in conducting first-hand research. First you identify an appropriate topic using the criteria described above. Then you identify ways you can learn about the topic, the investigation experiences you will offer children, and what opportunities you will plan for them to recreate what they have learned. Finally, you describe how you will conclude the study. Begin by reading the example on the next page.

Planning a Long-Term Study
(Example)

Topic you selected: *How Buildings Are Built*

Explain why this topic is appropriate for your children:

A building is under construction across the street from our program. The children have been talking about the large machinery brought in to dig the foundation. Antonio's uncle is the foreman on the job and Antonio talks about him with such pride that other children have become interested. Because it's so close, we can take trips regularly to observe what is happening. We can study the construction site over an extended period—probably all year.

What did you do to prepare for this study?

I talked to Antonio's uncle about the project, and he was very open to helping. He will let me know when something interesting is happening so we can visit at those times and take pictures. I made a list of the different jobs people do and who the children might interview. The children's librarian gave me some excellent books on construction projects, story books, and resource books. I've been reading through these resources for ideas. I also found some posters of construction workers and the machines they use which I will display in the classroom.

What are some "big ideas" children can investigate?

People have different kinds of jobs on a construction site. They use machines and equipment for different purposes. Buildings go up in a certain order.

What investigation experiences will you offer children?

We will visit the site regularly during the year and take photographs of what is happening. We will have discussions about what we saw after each trip. Antonio's uncle will be visiting our class to talk to the children. He will also give us a tour of the site. I plan to take pictures of each worker we interview and make a chart with the children's comments about what they learned from each person. Before each interview, we will discuss what we know about the job that person does and what questions we have.

What opportunities will you provide for children to recreate what they are learning?

I'll add bulldozers, tubes, backhoes, ramps, derricks, and construction workers to the block corner. In the house corner, I'll put hard hats, lunch boxes, carpenter aprons, work boots, and work shirts. The books will be added to the library. We will make a mural of the site and children can make a scrap book tracing the whole project.

How do you plan to conclude the study.

This study will go on all year, so I plan to do other studies as well. At the end of the year, we'll have a family night dinner so the children can share what they learned. We will have the scrapbook, the mural, and lots of photos and stories the children can talk about.

Planning a Long-Term Study

Topic you selected:

Explain why this topic is appropriate for your children:

What are some "big ideas" children can investigate?

What investigation experiences will you offer children?

What opportunities will you provide for children to recreate what they are learning?

How do you plan to conclude the study.

Discuss your plan with your colleagues and trainer.

Summarizing Your Progress

You have now completed all of the learning activities for this module. Whether you are an experienced teacher or a new one, this module has probably helped you develop new skills for promoting children's cognitive development.

Before you go on, take a few minutes to summarize what you've learned.

- Turn back to Learning Activity I, Using Your Knowledge of Child Development to Promote Cognitive Development, and add to the chart specific examples of what you learned about promoting children's cognitive development during the time you were working on this module. Compare your ideas to those in the completed chart at the end of the module.

- Next, review your responses to the pre-training assessment for this module. Write a summary of what you learned and list the skills you developed or improved.

If there are topics you would like to know more about, you will find recommended readings listed in the Orientation.

Your final step in this module is to complete the knowledge and competency assessments. Let your trainer know when you are ready to schedule the assessments. After you have successfully completed these assessments, you will be ready to start a new module. Congratulations on your progress so far, and good luck with your next module.

Answer Sheets

Overview
(pp. 239-241)

Creating an Environment That Encourages Children to Explore and Discover

1. **Why did Ms. Thomas give the string and scissors to the children?**
   a.   *She wanted to encourage the children to solve the problem themselves.*

   b.   *She knew the children could work together to find an answer to their question.*

2. **What did the children learn from their experience?**
   a.   *They are capable of thinking and solving their own problems.*

   b.   *They can find ways to use materials in new ways.*

   c.   *Sometimes how something looks can be deceiving.*

Interacting with Children in Ways That Help Them Confident in Their Ability to Think and Reason

1. **Why did Ms. Williams not interfere with the block builders when she could see that their building might fall down?**
   a.   *She knew that no one would get hurt when the blocks fell.*

   b.   *She wanted to let the children find out for themselves what would happen.*

2. **How did Ms. Williams encourage the children to think through and solve the problem on their own?**
   a.   *She asked questions that helped the children think about what made the building fall.*

   b.   *She didn't give them any solutions but helped them think of their own ideas.*

   c.   *She encouraged them to try out their ideas.*

Providing Opportunities for Children to Construct Knowledge About Their World

1. **How did Ms. Richards introduce and generate interest in the balance scale?**
   a.   *She had the children use their hands to create a balance scale.*

   b.   *She let the children measure two sets of objects in their hands and let them determine which felt heavier.*

2. **What skills and concepts were the children learning?**
   a.   *They were learning to compare the weight of two objects.*

   b.   *They were gaining first-hand experience with how balance scales work.*

   c.   *They were learning that four objects could be lighter than one.*

Using Your Knowledge of Child Development to Promote Cognitive Development

(p. 250)

What Preschool Children Are Like	How Teachers Can Use This Information to Promote Cognitive Development
They learn by using all their senses—smell, taste, touch, sight, and sound.	*Make a tape of familiar sounds and ask children to guess what each sound is. Offer various textured items for collage making. Talk about how foods smell and taste. Have children identify mystery objects in a bag by touch.*
They are interested in cause and effect—what makes things happen.	*Comment on children's discoveries. Provide objects to explore and plan activities that let children test ideas (e.g., what happens when a plant isn't watered). Talk about the effects and what might have been the cause.*
They have rapidly expanding vocabularies—they can name many things and explain their ideas.	*Introduce new words for vocabulary building. Provide names for objects, feelings, places, events, and so on. Talk with children and encourage them to describe their activities, feelings, and ideas.*
They are curious and want to explore many things.	*Set up a safe environment in which children can choose materials they want and carry out their plans. Put out new and interesting materials for children to investigate with their senses and with tools, such as a magnifying glass.*
They learn by using their imaginations in dramatic play and other activities.	*Offer new props and materials that build on children's play themes. Create prop boxes tied to themes of interest to the children. Step into a dramatic play role to comment or make suggestions that will lead the children to a higher level of play.*
They believe there is a purpose for everything and ask many questions: "Why?" "How?" "What?"	*Take children's questions seriously. Ask questions yourself to find out what they really want to know. Give answers they can understand and ask more questions to stretch their thinking. Admit when you don't know the answer. Model ways to use books and other resources to find answers.*

Using Your Knowledge of Child Development to Promote Cognitive Development
(p. 251)

What Preschool Children Are Like	How Teachers Can Use This Information to Promote Cognitive Development
They construct knowledge by exploring and making connections between new experiences and what they know from past experiences.	*Make comments and ask questions that encourage children to construct their own understandings. "It took two scoops of water to fill the cup. How many scoops of water will it take to fill the pitcher. Do they both hold the same amount of water?"*
They are developing an understanding of numerical concepts but need many experiences with real objects.	*Offer a variety of materials children can use to sort, group, match, count, and sequence. Help them practice counting and matching one to one while setting the table, counting the times they ride around the tricycle track, and sorting the blocks.*
They learn to match, classify, and identify shapes and colors by playing with toys and objects.	*Provide a variety of appealing table toys and interesting materials such as rocks, shells, buttons, and keys. Comment on what children are doing: "You made a row of red pegs." "You lined up the rocks by size, from large to small."*
They have many ideas and like to gather information about the world.	*Go on neighborhood trips. Collect leaves, rocks, and other items on a nature walk, then have children explore and organize the objects. Invite children to share their ideas with the group.*
They are beginning to understand that pictures, letters, words, and numbers represent real objects and ideas.	*Use word, picture, and number labels to identify materials, cubbies, and interest areas and to provide information such as how many children can use an area at one time. Write children's stories on charts and in home-made books so children can connect spoken words to print.*

Glossary

Abstract thinking

The ability to think about ideas and concepts in one's head without using concrete materials.

Classify

To put objects or events in groups on the basis of a common characteristic or attribute.

Closed question

A question for which there is only one right answer.

Cognitive development

Development of the ability to think and reason.

Concept

An idea that combines details or several other ideas in an organized way.

Concrete

Relating to real objects.

Construct knowledge

To actively seek to understand an event or idea by applying what one already knows to make a new experience meaningful.

Discriminate

To notice the differences among things.

Egocentric

The belief that everyone thinks the same thoughts and has the same feelings.

Long-term study

Planning opportunities for children to investigate a topic over time and recreate what they have learned.

Open-ended question

A question that can be answered in many ways.

Open-ended material

A toy or other item that children can use in different ways.

Problem-solving

The process of thinking through a problem and coming up with one or several possible solutions.

Representation

The act of creating a model of something such as a building built with blocks, a picture of a flower, or a clay dog.

Sequencing

Putting things or events in logical order.

Module 6: **Communication**

Overview

Promoting children's communication skills involves:

- Encouraging children to listen and speak
- Helping children use language in meaningful ways
- Providing materials and experiences that support emerging literacy skills

---

Communication is the ability to express and share ideas, desires, and feelings with other people using words or nonverbal methods. Children develop communication skills in five related areas: listening, comprehending, speaking, reading, writing. Each of these skills is an important part of children's emerging literacy—the gradual, ongoing process of learning to communicate through language.

The foundation for literacy is established in early childhood. Children construct their own knowledge about literacy through active exploration of their environment and through interactions with adults, peers, and older children. The drive to communicate is very strong and begins within the first few months of life. The cries of newborns are reflexive, but soon babies learn that crying will bring a trusted adult to meet their needs. Within a short time, infants communicate joy by smiling and cooing when they see a familiar face. As parents and caregivers respond, infants begin learning about the give and take of conversations.

Literacy skills emerge gradually over time.

By the end of their first year, babies are communicating intentionally, through verbal and nonverbal means. They make sounds while pointing at objects they want or while raising their arms to be picked up. Within a few years, a toddler develops the ability to understand and use language. Children learn to say thousands of words, to understand what the words mean, and the rules for using words simply by being around adults who listen to them, talk to them, and introduce them to reading and writing. When adults encourage and respond to children's efforts to communicate, children's emerging literacy skills develop naturally.

Understanding and using language is crucial to cognitive development. Learning depends on a child's ever-growing ability to make meaning out of words and eventually to read and write them. Social development, too, depends on language. The child with highly developed verbal skills may form friendships more easily than one who has difficulty expressing him or herself. And language is an important factor in emotional development. Children gain confidence when they can use words to communicate their feelings accurately to others.

The ability to communicate affects all areas of development.

Teachers promote children's communication skills in several ways. They listen and respond to children's thoughts and feelings, engage them in conversations, and encourage them to use words to tell others what they want. Teachers serve as language models for children. By using words to describe what a child is doing, they help the child become more aware of objects and actions. Teachers also create an

Teachers play a central role in helping children acquire communication skills.

environment that shows children the many uses for language. They label cubbies, makes signs for interest areas, write down children's dictated stories, and encourage children to play and talk with each other. Finally, teachers provide a variety of books and other written materials that respond to children's cultures, interests, experience, and skills. They include paper and writing tools in each interest area and help children discover the pleasures of words through storytelling, poems, finger plays, and songs.

Listed on the following pages are three sets of examples showing how teachers promote children's communication skills. Following each set of examples is a short reading and two questions to answer. When you have finished this section, compare your answers with those on the answer sheet at the end of the module. If your answers are different, discuss them with your trainer. There can be more than one good answer.

Encouraging Children to Listen and Speak

Accept a child's way of speaking while serving as a model for standard use of language.	If a child says "I throwed the ball," the teacher could say, "Yes, you threw the ball a long way."
Encourage children to talk to each other by making suggestions or planning activities that will accommodate just a few children.	"It looks like Sarah's baby is sick. Why don't you ask her what's the matter?
Pay close attention to children's words and actions and help them express their ideas clearly.	"Are you saying that you want to use the wagon?"
Make comments and ask questions that communicate interest and help children learn how to take turns in conversations.	"Your dad said you had fun at the street festival on Saturday. What did you like best?"
Stop while reading a story to talk about the characters and what they are doing.	"Why do you think Frances' mother keeps giving her bread and jam sandwiches for every meal?"
Be aware of signs of a possible speech disorder or hearing impairment and discuss these observations with the child's parents.	"A language development assessment could help us why Lars continues to use single words to communicate and what we can do to support him."
Learn words in children's home languages to reinforce their language development.	"¡Buen trabajo Selena! Good job! You certainly did a lot of planning to build that."

Jerry, who just turned three, taps Ms. Kim on her shoulder and points toward the block corner. "Do you want me to see something in the block corner?" asks Ms. Kim. Jerry nods and leads her there. He points at David, who is making an enclosure for the red truck. "Mine," says Jerry picking up the truck. "I need it," says David, grabbing it back. "Were you playing with the red truck, Jerry?" asks Ms. Kim. Jerry nods and holds the truck tightly. "Then say, 'David, I'm playing with the truck.'" Jerry says, "I play with truck." Ms. Kim asks David what he is making. "A garage," he answers. "Maybe you and Jerry could make it big enough for the truck and the cars. Do you want to do that, Jerry?" Jerry says, "Make my own." Ms. Kim says, "You could have two garages with a road in between. Then your cars and trucks can go back and forth. Is that okay?" The boys agree. "It's nice to see you can work together," says Ms. Kim. "Next time, Jerry, you can use your words to tell David what you want. I'll come back soon to see how you're doing."

1. How did Ms. Kim know what Jerry wanted?

2. How did Ms. Kim help Jerry use words to express his feelings and thoughts?

Helping Children Use Language in Meaningful Ways

Tape picture and word labels to containers and shelves where toys and materials are stored.

"Please put the truck on the shelf with the picture of the big dump truck."

Record children's words that describe their work.

"I'm going to write what you said. 'This is a bus bringing my mommy home.'"

Make and post at children's eye-level signs with words and pictures that provide information or ask children to make choices.

"Write your name under the apple or the pear so we'll know what we need for snack."

Help children make and display signs that communicate their own ideas.

"You can use the paper and markers on the shelf to make signs for your store."

Involve children in making books about topics or events that are important to them.

"This book is about all the new things you are learning to do for yourselves. Listen and you will hear all your names in the story."

Show children how adults use reading and writing to learn or to do a task.

"The book that came with our new computer program will tell me how to install it."

"Welcome back!" says Mr. Lopez to Kara, Avida, and Ms. Nolan, an intern from the community college. The children and Ms. Nolan have just returned from a walk to the park across the street from the program. "What did you see on your walk?" "We saw a big bird!" Grace tells him. "And a bird's nest," Kara adds. "The bird was flying around and then it sat on its nest," Avida explains. Mr. Lopez asks, "Would you two like to write a story about what you saw at the park?" Kara and Avida get some paper and markers from the shelf and begin scribbling on their paper. Ms. Nolan asks, "What does your story say?" "That's a picture of the bird," Kara says. "It says bird." "Tell me more about the bird you saw," says Ms. Nolan, "and I'll write down what you say." "We saw a big bird," Kara dictates. "It sat on its nest in a tree," Avida adds. Ms. Nolan writes their words and reads them aloud.

1. Why did Mr. Lopez suggest that the children write a story?

2. How did Ms. Nolan help the children use language in meaningful ways?

Providing Materials and Experiences That Support Emerging Literacy Skills

Create a well-lit, carpeted, library area with comfortable places to sit and books displayed so the covers face out.

"Carson, if want to read another 'Clifford' book, look for his picture on the cover."

Create a writing area, within or separate from the library area, stocked with reading and writing materials.

"Janine, the mailbox is very full. Would you like to deliver the letters?"

Provide props and dress-up clothes that support children's interests and emerging literacy skills.

Here are some prescription pads the doctor can use."

Teach children short poems and finger plays during transitions or activities.

"This is the way we clean the brushes, clean the brushes, clean the brushes!"

Display books, including some in children's home languages, that match children's abilities and reflect their cultures and families in positive ways.

"The librarian showed me an entire shelf of Spanish versions of the children's favorite books."

Read to children at story time and in response to requests; invite children to retell familiar stories.

"Who can tell us what happened in the story when the rainbow fish learned to share?"

Encourage family reading and writing times by lending books and sharing donated writing supplies.

"Ms. Vaughn, Carly would like to borrow this book so you two can read it at home."

Ms. Williams is about to read a story, *Caps for Sale*, to a small group of children. She begins by saying, "Today I'm going to read the story about a peddler who sells caps. He has a funny way to carry his caps. Does anyone remember where he carries them?" "On his head," shout the children. "Right, and here he is," says Ms. Williams, showing the children the cover of the book. "He also has a special order for wearing the caps. First his own checkered cap, then the . . ." Ms. Williams listens while the children tell which color comes first and then in what order the caps are arranged. She reads the story with lots of expression, pausing to let the children recite familiar phrases. After reading the story, Ms. Williams brings out some caps so the children can act out the story.

1. **What did Ms. Williams do to interest the children in hearing the story?**

tapping her shoulder, pointing to the block corner, nodding, and leading her there + asked questions about what had happened

2. **How did Ms. Williams use the group story time to support children's emerging literacy skills?**

she told him what to say to David she respected what he wanted + she repeated what he said in a complete sentence.

Your Own Experiences with Communication

Communication skills are central to our ability to relate to others. Effective communication involves receiving a message, interpreting it, and sending back an appropriate response.

Many factors affect communication.

Many factors influence how well we understand the communications we receive from others. These include how we are feeling at that moment, how well we know the person, and how carefully we listen. For example, suppose you've had a bad morning before coming to work. You are feeling overwhelmed. Your colleague greets you by saying: "This storeroom is a mess! I can't find anything in it!"

You may interpret this message as a criticism and respond defensively: "When am I supposed to find the time to deal with the storeroom? I can hardly keep up with everything else I have to do!" Your colleague may be surprised by your response and herself react defensively: "Don't you think I'm just as busy as you are?" Neither of you meant to cause angry feelings, but that's exactly what happened.

On another day, when you are feeling more on top of things, you might interpret the message very differently and respond, "You're absolutely right. We've been so busy with other things, we never seem to get to the storeroom. Maybe we can ask for a parent volunteer to help us out." This time you interpret the message as a simple statement about a problem that needs to be addressed.

Communication involves receiving and interpreting information clearly.

Effective communication skills allow us to accurately convey our thoughts and feelings to others. We send messages verbally (using words) and nonverbally (using gestures and body language).

Verbal messages can be clear if we say what we mean ("I'd like to go to a movie tonight. What time is best for you?"). But they can be unclear if we fail to express our true thoughts, hoping the other person will give us the answer we want ("What do you feel like doing tonight?").

In addition to sending clear messages, we need to receive them as they were intended. Sometimes this requires that the sender provide more information. To help clarify the message, use questions and statements such as the following:

- Are you saying that . . . ?

- Do you mean . . . ?

- Do I understand correctly that . . . ?

- It sounds like you want . . . .

How do you rate your ability to communicate effectively?

	I Do This:	Regularly	Sometimes	Not Enough
1. I state my ideas clearly.		☒	☐	☐
2. I express my feelings in words.		☒	☐	☐
3. If I'm not sure what someone means, I seek more information from the sender.		☒	☐	☐
4. I pay attention to gestures and body language when interpreting a sender's message.		☐	☒	☐

Review your answers to this brief checklist. Are there any areas you would like to improve? As you go through this module and learn ways of helping children communicate, you may discover some strategies for improving your own communication skills.

When you have finished this overview section, you should complete the pre-training assessment. Refer to the glossary at the end of the module if you need definitions of the terms that are used.

Pre-Training Assessment

Listed below are the skills that teachers use to promote children's communication skills. Think about whether you do these things regularly, sometimes, or not enough. Place a check in one of the boxes on the right of each skill listed. Then discuss your answers with your trainer.

Encouraging Children to Listen and Speak

	I Do This:	Regularly	Sometimes	Not Enough
1.	Accept a child's way of speaking while serving as a model for standard use of language.	☒	☐	☐
2.	Encourage children to talk to one another by making suggestions or planning activities that will accommodate just a few children.	☒	☐	☐
3.	Pay close attention to children's words and actions and help them express their ideas clearly.	☒	☐	☐
4.	Make comments and ask questions that communicate interest and help children learn how to take turns in conversations.	☒	☐	☐
5.	Stop while reading a story to talk about the characters and what they are doing.	☒	☐	☐
6.	Be aware of signs of a possible speech disorder, or hearing impairment and discuss these observations with the child's parents.	☒	☐	☐
7.	Learn words in children's home languages to reinforce their language development.	☒	☐	☐

Helping Children Use Language in Meaningful Ways

	I Do This: Regularly	Sometimes	Not Enough
8. Tape picture and word labels to containers and shelves where toys and materials are stored.	☑	☐	☐
9. Record children's words that describe their work.	☑	☐	☐
10. Make and post at children's eye-level signs with words.	☑	☐	☐
11. Involve children in making books about topics or events that are important to them.	☑	☐	☐
12. Show children how adults use reading and writing to learn to do a task.	☑	☐	☐

Providing Materials and Experiences That Support Emerging Literacy Skills

	I Do This: Regularly	Sometimes	Not Enough
13. Create a well-lit, carpeted, library area with comfortable places to sit and books displayed so the covers face out.	☑	☐	☐
14. Create a writing area, within or separate from the library area, stockedwith reading and writing materials.	☑	☐	☐
15. Provide props and dress-up clothes that support children's interests and emerging literacy skills.	☑	☐	☐
16. Teach children short poems and finger plays during transitions or activities.	☑	☐	☐

Providing Materials and Experiences That Support Emerging Literacy Skill
(continued)

	I Do This: Regularly	Sometimes	Not Enough
17. Display books, including some in children's home languages, that match children's abilities and reflect their cultures and families.	☒	☐	☐
18. Read to children at story times and in response to requests; invite children to retell familiar stories.	☒	☐	☐
19. Encourage family reading and writing times by lending books and sharing donated writing supplies.	☒	☐	☐

Review your responses, then list three to five skills you would like to improve or topics you would like to learn more about. When you finish this module, you can list examples of your new or improved knowledge and skills.

Begin the learning activities for Module 6, Communication.

Learning Activities

I. Using Your Knowledge of Child Development to Promote Language Skills

---

In this activity you will learn to:

- Recognize some typical behaviors of preschool children that are related to language development

- Use what you know about children to promote their language skills

---

The foundation for a child's ability to understand and use language is rooted in the loving relationships between infants and their parents and caregivers. Adults attempt to make sense of infants' cries, coos, and gestures and introduce the back and forth nature of human interactions. When adults convey positive feelings, infants soon express similar feelings of pleasure. As in all areas of development, children learn to understand and use language at their own pace. Some say their first words at age one; others hardly speak at all before age two.

Preschool children use language for many purposes—to gain information, understand concepts, express feelings, share ideas, make plans, and solve problems. Their interest in learning about the world around them is evident in the continual questions they ask. Preschool children tell stories to describe past events or express imaginative ideas. They use language in increasingly complex and involved forms of dramatic play. They talk about what they want to do, who will play what role, and what will happen.

Most preschool children like to talk—to each other, to teachers, and sometimes to themselves. When preschool children converse, they are learning subtle and complex cues about interaction. They find ways to enter a conversation or change its direction, and they learn how to give and get information. They also discover what kinds of talk are appropriate in specific situations.

It's not unusual to hear preschool children (especially younger ones) carry on lively solitary conversations as they play. This is one way they practice using language. Children may say words over and over until they can pronounce them without thinking. They might repeat a chant—"bop, bop, boppity, bop"—or describe what they are doing. For example, a child might talk to himself while recalling something he already knows how to do—make purple paint:

> "Red and blue makes purple. First, some red." Colin pours some red paint into an empty container. "Now I need some blue." He adds blue paint to the container. "Stir it all around." He stirs the paint with his brush, then makes a purple circle on his paper. "That's really purple."

Language is a powerful tool for preschool children.

Preschool children are learning about the art of conversation.

Some preschool children talk to themselves while they play.

Children enjoy the sounds of language and often use words creatively.

Preschool children enjoy making all kinds of sounds—words, nonsense syllables, rhythmic chants, and tapping feet. Many children love poems, chants, and songs with rhymes and repetitive words and phrases. Teachers can introduce traditional chants such as: "One potato, two potato, three potato, four . . ." and make up chants that describe children's activities: "We're putting on our coats and hats, coats and hats, . . ."

Children sometimes make up their own words, and they use words creatively. Adults who are good listeners can hear children using language imaginatively.

- "A hopicoper" describes a helicopter.

- "A doesn't-smell bush" describes an azalea bush that has no fragrance.

- "Mess-up paper" is scrap paper.

Children can learn to use words rather than fists to handle disagreements.

Every day children learn new words and discover different approaches to making themselves heard and understood by other people. They do this while negotiating how to take turns using a toy, describing something that happened to them, or directing each other's play. As their language skills grow, children become increasingly able to convey their feelings in words rather than through actions. The more accurately they can describe what is bothering them, the better able they are to resolve problems with words rather than aggression.

Applying Your Knowledge

The chart on the next two pages lists some typical behaviors of preschool children. Included are behaviors relevant to the development of communication skills. The right-hand column asks you to identify ways that teachers can use this information about child development to promote communication skills. Try to think of as many examples as you can. As you work through the module, you will learn new strategies for promoting communication skills and you can add them to the chart. You are not expected to think of all the examples at once. If you need help getting started, turn to the completed chart at the end of the module. By the time you complete all the learning activities, you will find that you have learned many ways to promote children's communication skills.

Using Your Knowledge of Child
Development to Promote Communication Skills

What Preschool Children Are Like	How Teachers Can Use This Information to Promote Communication Skills
They use language to think, learn, imagine, plan, make requests, direct others, and solve problems.	*Plan activities and provide materials in each interest area that allow children to use language for different purposes. Talk and listen to children and encourage them to talk and listen to each other. Expect that the classroom will be filled with children's voices.*
They tell stories about imaginary and real experiences that take place in the past as well as in the present.	write down childrens stories Have children illustrate their stories.
They participate and take turns in conversations with peers and adults.	Model the rules and showing children manners.
They make up and act out scenarios with plots and different characters who solve a problem or do something specific.	Have dramatic area available for play Provide many props.
They can retell favorite stories, sometimes in correct sequence.	Read favorite stories & plan activities that build off of them.
They ask many questions and can answer open-ended questions that have no right or wrong response.	Answer questions directly and have them help you answer questions (find the answers)

Using Your Knowledge of Child Development to Promote Communication Skills

What Preschool Children Are Like	How Teachers Can Use This Information to Promote Communication Skills
They learn most rules of grammar without direct instruction. They may make mistakes because there are exceptions to a rule.	Don't point out mistakes.
They may be learning one language at home and another at the program.	Become familiar w/ phrases of their language.
They are learning that printed words are symbols for spoken words and convey messages.	Label things such as: cubbies, containers and shelves.
They scribble and write invented letters and words.	Don't point out mistakes in writing.
They like a wide variety of books.	Have books available in different languages and cultures.
They can memorize songs, poems, rhymes, and books with repetition.	Read easy books w/ repeated phrases.

When you have completed as much as you can do on the chart, discuss your answers with your trainer. As you proceed with the rest of the learning activities, you can refer back to the chart and add examples of ways teachers can promote language development.

II. Observing Children's Listening and Speaking Skills

In this activity you will learn to:

- Observe how children use and respond to language
- Identify signs a child is gaining listening and speaking skills

---

As with other areas of development, the language skills of preschool children vary greatly. Some children talk constantly, while others speak mainly when spoken to. Some speak in long, complex sentences, while others make brief statements and need to be encouraged to expand their ideas. Some children pronounce sounds and words with great precision, while others are still learning to master vowels and consonant sounds. It can be difficult to know when a child is learning to listen and speak at a slower, but perfectly normal pace, and when a child needs special attention. You will know that a child is making progress in language development, if he or she:

- reacts with pleasure to sounds, poetry, dramatic play, stories, and music;

- uses the teacher's name in conversations or to get attention;

- understands, remembers, and responds to the speech of other;

- seeks answers to questions.

Children acquire sounds of speech in a predictable pattern. Before speaking in phrases and sentences, children learn the sounds of speech (consonants and vowels) in a language. As they learn to make speech sounds by shaping their mouths and coordinating their teeth and tongues, they will often make mistakes. In fact, most children do not master all speech sounds until about age eight. So, it is quite appropriate for a three- or four-year-old to have difficulty making the "th" or "ch" sound, while a six- or seven-year-old may have no trouble at all. It is important for teachers to understand the developmental stages of speech so that they know what is normal and what is appropriate for children at different ages.

It's also perfectly natural and normal for preschool children to make mistakes in using language. In fact, mistakes are signs that children are mastering standard rules of grammar, such as adding "s" to a noun to make it plural. They make mistakes because there are exceptions to many rules. It takes time to master all of these exceptions. Here are some typical mistakes a child might make:

"I have two feets."   "She's my goodest friend."
"I hurted my knee."   "I feeled happy."

Making mistakes is a normal part of speech and language development.

The best way for teachers to respond to such mistakes is simply to restate what the child has said using standard language. "Yes, you have two feet." Children are embarrassed when adults constantly point out their mistakes or ask them to say something correctly. These interruptions can cause children to lose their train of thought and may discourage future attempts to express ideas and feelings. For example, Harold has discovered that he can describe past events by adding "ed" to the end of a verb. He says, "I runned all the way around the playground." Instead of correcting his mistake, Ms. Richards responds, "That was a long way. You ran very far." Over time, as Harold listens to Ms. Richards and other people who model standard use of language, he will learn the exceptions to this and other grammatical rules.

Some children are learning two languages at the same time.

There may be children in your class who are learning a second language at the program, usually English, after having learned a first language at home. In such situations, it is perfectly normal for children to say very little for several months. Once children begin talking at the program, they are likely to use words from both languages in the same sentence, temporarily lose some skills in their home language, and make many grammatical errors. Children with strong skills in their first language, however, are more able to develop language skills in the second. Teachers can build on these skills by encouraging children to use their first language at the program, as well as at home. If possible, speak with the child in his or her first language. If this is not possible, learn a few important words in the home language, seek classroom volunteers who speak the language, and encourage children who speak the same first language to play together.

Some children may need greater exposure to words and language use.

Children who have little exposure to language in their home settings may appear to have language delays. Their language skills will grow if they have opportunities to explore the world beyond their homes, play and talk with other children, and interact with adults. Such children are more likely to talk if you show by your facial expression and undivided attention that you think they have something important to say. Listen patiently for as long as it takes a child to make a statement or ask a question. Make sure the classroom setting helps children feel comfortable and secure so they will be willing to talk.

These strategies can help children increase their vocabularies and make sense of grammatical rules.

Try these strategies to help children with limited language skills:

Restate children's words and introduce the names of objects, actions, and feelings. "You would like to use the pots and pans. Tell Nina, 'I want to use the pots and pans.'"

Introduce concepts by describing what children are doing. "You are rolling the truck on the carpet. Now you are rolling it up the ramp. Now you are rolling it down the ramp."

Repeat several examples of standard use of language at one time. When a child asks, "He goes out?" the teacher can respond, "Is he going out? Yes, he is going out. Ron is also going out. Are you going out?"

Talk more slowly than normal so children can hear your words and pay attention to how your sentence is organized.

Stuttering is common among preschoolers. Children may stutter because they have had little practice in speaking, or because they are trying to talk too fast. They might repeat words or have difficulty getting a word out. When a child is excited or frightened, he or she is even more likely to stutter. Stuttering often goes away as the child learns to speak more slowly and carefully. Be patient when listening and responding to a child who is stuttering. Your calm demeanor will help the child relax and speak more slowly. Also, look for possible reasons for stuttering. Is the child worried or scared? Is the child's speech corrected often or does the child have his words or sentences finished for him? Does the program environment help the child feel secure? Is there a predictable schedule to help the child feel comfortable?

There are several reasons why a child might stutter.

Some preschoolers have extremely limited language skills and show few signs of progress. In these instances, teachers need more information to effectively encourage the child's language development. If there is no other explanation for a child's limited language skills, he or she may have a language delay, a physical abnormality, such as with the teeth, palate, tongue, or vocal cords, a respiratory problem, a hearing problem, or a speech disorder such as lisping. The following are signs that a preschooler might have a speech and language disorder:

Be alert to signs of a possible speech or language disorder.

- The child doesn't talk.

- The child's speech is largely unintelligible.

- The child does not use two to three word sentences.

- The child uses mostly vowel sounds.

- The child talks in a monotone.

- The child sounds as if he or she were talking through the nose.

- The child doesn't answer questions, understand what is said, or follow verbal directions.

If any of the above signs are present over an extended period of time, it is a good idea to refer the parents to a speech pathologist, a specialist who can give the child a comprehensive language assessment and determine the child's skills and needs. The speech pathologist can suggest specific strategies to use at at the program and at home.

Applying Your Knowledge

In this learning activity, you select two children and observe their language skills over a one-week period. Use the form Observing Children's Language Skills to identify the skills you will be observing about each child. If possible, select one child who is learning a second language. Be sure to observe each child using language in various situations, such as indoor and outdoor choice time, a routine, while playing alone and with a group. Also, observe and record how each child uses language for different purposes, for example, to get information, give directions, or solve a problem. Begin by reading the example on the next page.

Observing Children's Language Skills
(Example)

Child: *Nadia*   **Age:** *4 years*   **Dates:** *March 2 - 6*

Listening and Talking Skills	Summary
Uses words to communicate thoughts and ideas.	*Nadia uses short sentences to express herself. She is more likely to talk to a teacher one-on-one than in a group situation.*
Uses words to negotiate, solve disagreements, and express strong feelings.	*This skill was not observed. Nadia is quite shy so she tends to play alone more than with other children.*
Uses language creatively; makes up words; enjoys nonsense words and rhymes.	*During small group time I taught the children a new fingerplay. Nadia smiled and quickly learned the hand and finger movements. She took longer to learn the words.*
Uses language in dramatic play situations.	*Again, her shy nature leads her to play alone rather than with others.*
Asks and answers questions.	*Answers questions with a single word. Rarely asks questions.*
Participates in conversations with teachers and/or children.	*Rarely starts conversations with adults or with other children.*
Makes mistakes that show an understanding of standard rules of grammar.	*I did not observe this.*
Needs to work on specific language skills.	*She has a very soft voice, so it's difficult for others to understand what she's saying.*

Observing Children's Language Skills

Child #1: Dan   Age: 3   Dates: nov, 1998

Listening and Talking Skills	Summary
Uses words to communicate thoughts and ideas.	Dan uses short sentences and sometimes pronounces words the wrong way
Uses words to negotiate, solve disagreements, and express strong feelings.	Dan tries very hard to negotiate w/ words but gets frustrated.
Uses language creatively; makes up words; enjoys nonsense words and rhymes.	Dan sometimes creates his own words
Uses language in dramatic play situations.	Dan tries to speak as less as possible
Asks and answers questions.	Asks many questions but doesn't answer many.
Participates in conversations with teachers and/or children.	Dan tries very hard to conversate w/ teach + children
Makes mistakes that show an understanding of standard rules of grammar.	—
Needs to work on specific language skills.	Dan does have a language problem, but we are working w/ him on this.

Observing Children's Language Skills

Child #2: Emma   Age: 3   Dates: Nov 1998

Listening and Talking Skills	Summary
Uses words to communicate thoughts and ideas.	Emma is a very talkative little girl.
Uses words to negotiate, solve disagreements, and express strong feelings.	Emma always uses her words to solve problems w/ the children
Uses language creatively; makes up words; enjoys nonsense words and rhymes.	~~Emma~~ I haven't seen Emma make-up any words.
Uses language in dramatic play situations.	Emma loves the dramatic play area + enjoy playing different roles
Asks and answers questions.	Emma always asks + answers questions
Participates in conversations with teachers and/or children.	Emma is the one who usually initiates conversations
Makes mistakes that show an understanding of standard rules of grammar.	~
Needs to work on specific language skills.	Emma's language is developmentally appropriate for her age.

Discuss your completed charts with your trainer.

III. *Encouraging Children to Listen and Speak*

> **In this activity you will learn to:**
>
> - Use the environment to encourage communication
> - Help children learn how to participate in conversations

The more opportunities children have to listen and speak, the more skilled they will become. A room in which children feel free, relaxed, and encouraged to communicate is not a quiet room. Teachers must be willing to accept a certain level of chatter and noise to encourage language development.

Many of the strategies for creating a learning environment found in Module 3 will encourage preschool children to practice and expand their language skills. Here are some specific ideas.

An interesting environment promotes listening and talking.

- Set up interest areas where children can work and play in small groups.

- Offer interesting materials—an old radio to take apart or funnels and plastic tubing for the water table—that encourage children to explore, ask questions, talk about their ideas, and play with each other.

- Provide dramatic play props that encourage children to listen and speak. Two or more telephones can lead to many lively conversations. With menus and tablecloths in the house corner, children can set up a restaurant with servers and customers.

- Plan some group projects, such as painting a mural or making bread. Help the children plan projects together and carry out their ideas.

- Take trips and walks in the neighborhood to expand children's experiences and give them new things to talk about.

- Offer materials that promote language use, such as puppets and flannel boards.

- Eat family-style meals at small tables where five or six children and a teacher can take part in interesting conversations.

- Ask parents to make audiotapes of children's favorite books. Place the books and tapes in plastic bags and display them in the library area near the tape player and headphones.

Help children feel comfortable and relaxed.

Most children will express their ideas and feelings more freely if they feel comfortable and relaxed. They may need to get to know you and the other children, learn to follow your predictable schedule, explore new and unfamiliar materials, remember what to do during routines, and master their feelings about separating from their families.

You've probably noticed that the most verbal children tend to make friends easily. It's especially important to be aware of shy children who may require your help to feel accepted by their peers and to learn how to express themselves. Similarly, children are more likely to respond to your questions and share their thoughts after they learn that you will accept them as they are.

Accepting children's efforts to communicate means:

- encouraging both verbal and nonverbal attempts to communicate;

- never degrading what a child says;

- waiting patiently until a child is ready to speak;

- getting down to the child's level and listening carefully and patiently.

The rules of conversation are complex.

To be effective communicators, children need to learn how to participate in conversations. Here's how two children might use conversation rules while talking with each other.

Conversation Rules	Example
You can start or join a conversation by saying something to another person and waiting for a response.	*"What are you doing?"* *"We're building a zoo with lots of different animals."*
People take turns in conversations. It is your turn when the other person has finished talking. You should finish what you are saying so the other person can have a turn.	*"Will there be monkeys in the zoo? I like them the best because they're so silly."*
"Look at and listen to the person speaking. Keep the conversation going by taking a turn saying something else about the topic.	*"Yeah, we can have monkeys. I like the snakes, because they're scary."*
If you don't understand what someone said you can ask a question.	*"Do you like scary things?"* *"I only like them when they're locked up."*
Let the other person know that you are leaving the conversation.	*"I'm leaving now. I'm going to paint a picture now."*

You probably know both children (and even adults) who find it hard to follow these rules. It can be very difficult to give someone else a turn to talk or resist the urge to interrupt. Helping children learn to be equal partners in conversations is a gradual process.

Teachers can engage children in one-on-one conversations during transitions, while completing chores such as washing paint brushes, or at the beginning or end of the day when it's easier to provide undivided attention. By talking with children, teachers can model conversation rules. Here are some suggestions for beginning a conversation.

Try these suggestions.[1]

Join in children's play so you will both have something to talk about. "I like green peppers on my pizza. What do you like on yours?"

Say something interesting that invites children to respond. "The prism hanging in the window is making rainbows on our floor."

Ask an open-ended question that narrows the topic. Some open-ended questions are so broad, children have no idea how to respond. For example, ask, "What did the clowns do?" instead of "What did you see at the circus?"

Once you have begun a conversation with a child, use these strategies to keep it going.

Ask questions that encourage the child to provide more information. "Did your dog get sick after he ate your whole ice cream cone?"

Comment on what the child says, then ask a question to keep the conversation going. "Your plant is much taller than last week. What did you do to make it grow so fast?"

Ask for clarification when a message is unclear. You might say, "Could you repeat that, please?" "Tell me again what you did."

Redirect children back to the topic. "Can you finish telling me about what happened at the dentist?"

In addition to helping children learn the rules of conversation, you can introduce new words and model standard use of language. Here are some suggestions.

Help children expand their vocabularies and understanding of language.

Talk to children about how things feel, smell, taste, or sound. Because they use all their senses to learn, children tend to be aware of the sensory characteristics of objects. Encourage them to describe what they experience. "Yes, this rock feels smooth. Is it as smooth as ice?"

---

[1] Based in part on Elaine Weitzman, *Learning Language and Loving It: A Guide to Promoting Children's Social and Language Development in Early Childhood Settings* (Toronto: The Hanen Centre, 1992), pp. 121-135.

Ask open-ended questions that encourage creative thinking. "What could we use this for?" "What might happen if?" "What would you do . . . ?"

Name things. Describe toys and materials a child is using, something a child is wearing, or what a child is doing. "You are wearing bumpy corduroy pants today." "I see you're using all the yellow pegs first." "What a long road you made with the blocks!"

Use full and complete sentences that describe details. If a child asks where something is, rather than pointing and saying, "Over there," take time to say, "The markers are on the art shelf next to the drawing paper."

Use a soft tone of voice. A harsh voice makes children tense. A loud voice makes them talk louder and creates unnecessary noise in the room.

Teach categories as you talk to children. "That *color* is blue." "We're having apples today for snack. What *fruits* do you like?" "Here are some *farm animals*: a horse, a cow, and a pig."

Describe the specific characteristics of objects or actions. "Roll the *rubber* ball to me" rather than, "Roll it." "Put the *paint* brushes in the sink" rather than, "Put the brushes here." "Look at how *fast* Kris is riding the tricycle" rather than, "Look at Kris." "See how *high* the bird is flying—up to the *top* of the tree" rather than, "See the bird."

Take time to talk about feelings. Help a child who is upset to use words to express his or her feelings. Sometimes you have to provide the words. "I can see you're having a hard time waiting for your turn. It feels like your turn will never come, but it will."

Applying Your Knowledge

In this activity you draw on your observation notes from the previous activity to plan some strategies and activities for encouraging the listening and speaking skills of the same two children. You can use the suggestions in this learning activity and some of your own. The first step is to review your notes to identify each child's skills and needs. Then decide what strategies and activities you will try with each child. After implementing your plans for two weeks, report on the results. First read the example that follows.

Encouraging Children to Listen and Speak

(Example)

Child: *Nadia*   **Age:** *4 years*   **Date:** *March 10*

After reviewing your observations of this child, what language areas do you want to work on?

Nadia rarely starts conversations with other children. She speaks so quietly it's hard to hear her.

Nadia responds to questions with one word. She rarely asks questions. When she talks, it's with many short sentences.

What strategies and activities will you try?

I will use puppets with Nadia to try to get her to talk more. I will invite her to join a child with more advanced language skills in play and help them get started. I'll be sure she sits near me at mealtimes so that I can help her talk to other children.

I will help Nadia learn about conversation. I can describe what she is doing, extend her sentences, show interest in what she has to say, and respond to her comments in ways that encourage her to say more. Nadia usually arrives early, so I'll use those times for one-on-one conversations.

What results do you notice after trying out your strategies/activities for two weeks?

The puppets were a big success. I was able to involve another child, and Nadia started talking to her. I saw the two children playing together several times.

Nadia and I have had more frequent conversations. She often seeks me out when she arrives in the morning. It's still hard to hear Nadia. When she is more comfortable using language, I will help her learn to speak louder.

Encouraging Children to Listen and Speak

Child #1 : Dan   Age: 3   Date: Nov. 1998

After reviewing your observations of this child, what language areas do you want to work on?

Dan has a hard time w/ all areas of language. I would recommend speech for Dan so a specialist could work w/ him.

What strategies and activities will you try?

I would read more often to Dan, and I would be available in the Dramatic play area for him - because in this area, the children do alot of talking.

What results do you notice after trying out your strategies/activities for two weeks?

I have been working w/ Dan all semester and I have noticed a bit of improvement w/ him but still think speech would be good for him.

Encouraging Children to Listen and Speak

Child #2 : Emma   **Age:** 3   **Date:** Nov, 1998

After reviewing your observations of this child, what language areas do you want to work on?

Emma seems to have a problem w/ language only when she's upset and is trying to talk fast.

What strategies and activities will you try?

I would work w/ her on slowing down her speech when she is upset.

What results do you notice after trying out your strategies/activities for two weeks?

Emma has been trying to slow down - but when she gets upset she is still talking fast + I think this is normal for 3 yr. olds.

Discuss this activity with your trainer.

IV. Reading Books with Preschool Children[2]

In this activity you will learn to:

- Choose books that are appropriate for the children in your class
- Read to individuals and small groups of children

Children develop a love for reading when they are regularly read to and exposed to the power and pleasure of words. Teachers who genuinely enjoy reading, who like to tell stories, and who appreciate the rhythms and rhymes of poetry, can instill the same feelings in children. When you carefully hold a book while reading with a child, share a tidbit from a story to excite a child's interests, repeat a particularly appealing description because you like the way the words sound, and read a story with great enthusiasm and expression, you convey how wonderful you think books are.

Selecting Appropriate Books

Books written for preschool children can help them learn more about themselves and the world around them. When books depict familiar experiences—a new baby at home, making friends, starting a new school—children can better understand and deal with their feelings. When children discover that the experiences of characters in books are similar to their own, they seek out books for reassurance.

In selecting books for your classroom, seek ones that match children's skills and interests and depict their cultures, ethnic groups, families, and abilities in positive ways. Offer books in children's home languages and English.

Young preschool children like to identify with the characters in books.

Young preschool children (threes and early fours) are very centered on themselves, their families, their homes, and their friends. They like stories about characters with whom they can identify. Books that are appropriate for young preschoolers have the following characteristics:

- a simple plot about familiar experiences

- colorful and bold illustrations

- realistic illustrations that children can understand

- lots of repetition in the story

---

[2] Based in part on Diane Trister Dodge and Laura J. Colker, *The Creative Curriculum for Early Childhood, 3rd. Edition* (Washington, DC: Teaching Strategies, Inc., 1992), pp. 221-234.

- happy endings that encourage a sense of security

- rhymes, nonsense words, repetition, and good language

Older preschool children (fours and fives) tend to enjoy books with more complex plots. They can sit for a longer period of time and appreciate humorous and imaginative characters and events. Books that are appropriate for older children have the following characteristics:

- a plot they can follow

- humorous characters and events, and perhaps a surprise ending

- imaginative stories

- stories that extend their understanding of the world around them

- colorful, detailed illustrations

Older preschool children are ready for more complex stories.

Provide five to eight books per child in your class. Offer an inventory that includes books from categories such as the following:

- everyday life (for example, making pancakes)

- self-awareness (what makes each of us a unique person)

- simple, predictable text with lots of repetition (so children can "read" to themselves)

- real experiences, feelings, and problems (for example, adjusting to a new baby)

- wordless (pictures tell the story)

- big books (enlarged versions of popular books)

- non-fiction books tied to current themes and interests (buildings, dinosaurs, trains)

- poems, rhymes, fingerplays, and songs

- basic concepts (counting, alphabet, opposites)

- references (simple dictionary, nature guides, software manuals, cookbooks)

- nonsense and fantasy (silly words, characters, and stories)

Offer children many different kinds of books.

It is important to vary the selection of books throughout the year. Always include some familiar books, while adding new ones that respond to children's growing skills and changing interests. You can also add books to different interest areas to reflect and extend current themes and activities.

Use the library as a resource when selecting books.

The children's librarian at your local library can be an excellent resource on choosing appropriate books for preschoolers. If you describe the children's skills and interests, the librarian can direct you to books that are just right for your group. While at the library, look for books that were nominated for or won awards such as the Caldecott medal for picture books. Also, review book lists from the American Library Association and the International Reading Association. Your library may carry journals that publish reviews of new children's books, such as *The Horn Book*.

Setting Up a Library Area

Every preschool room should have a library area—a place where children can sit comfortably while exploring many different kinds of books. The best location is a quiet corner, away from noisy activities such as blocks and the house corner.

Try these suggestions for creating a library area.

Make it soft and comfortable. Put a rug on the floor, as well as some large pillows. Include an overstuffed bean-bag or rocking chair. Use a mattress covered with attractive and cheerful fabric.

Include a table and two or three chairs. Provide for children who like to sit at a table to look at books. Cover the table with a colorful cloth and decorate with a small plant.

Display books attractively. Use a shelf that allows books to stand alone with covers in view. Keep books in good repair—not torn or marked up. Preserve the attractive covers on new books using clear Contact paper.

Decorate the area. Hang book covers and posters. Display photographs of children and adults reading books. Create a display related to a favorite book.

Provide good lighting. Locate the area near a window so natural light is available. Provide a standing lamp or ceiling fixture if additional light is needed.

Invite children to help repair damaged books.

As with other materials in your classroom, well-loved books can wear out. Keep in mind that worn-out books signify that children are learning to love books and reading. If you pay too much attention to keeping books in new condition, some of the more active children in your class may be discouraged from reading.

On the other hand, you do want to encourage children to take care of books. Ask the children to help you set a few simple rules such as "Write on paper, not in books" and post them in the library area. Offer frequent reminders to help children remember how to treat books. Point out how you take care of books. "I'd love to read to you. First, I have to wash the paint off my hands. I don't want to get paint on the book."

Remove damaged books so they can be repaired. If pages are missing, there is little you can do; however, you can erase pencil marks and tape torn pages or covers. You can create a book repair kit in a shoe box or basket stocked with items such as transparent and cloth tape, erasers, correction fluid to cover ink and crayon marks, and scissors. Involve the children in helping you fix the books. Older preschool children will soon learn to fix books on their own. Younger children will be more likely to report "hurt" books and ask for your help.

As adults, we rely on books and other printed materials for many different reasons—to look up a recipe, answer a question, explore a special interest. Children learn about the many different purposes for reading when teachers include books and other reading matter in all interest areas and outdoors. Here are some examples of the kinds of reading materials children could use in different areas:

Encourage reading in all interest areas.

- **Blocks**: books about buildings, farms, and bridges

- **House Corner**: magazines, catalogs, and junk mail

- **Art**: books about famous artists and artwork

- **Music and Movement**: song books

- **Cooking**: cookbooks and recipe cards

- **Computers**: software manuals and books made by children

- **Outdoors**: a basket of books to look at while sitting on the grass

Reading with Children

Reading aloud to children helps them discover that reading is an enjoyable activity. They begin to understand the connection between spoken and written words, and they gain meaning from the words and story. When teachers take time to read to a group of children, they bring children together for a meaningful social experience. Children often react to the story and comment on a picture or what is happening. Sometimes they will correct you if you miss a word or leave something out of a familiar story. The ability to remember the words in a story is an important step in the process of learning to read.

During choice time, you may see some children looking at a familiar book and telling the story to themselves. They may not know the meaning of all the words on the page, but they will probably demonstrate their understanding of several reading principles: books are read from front to back; the words on each page are read from left to right and top to bottom; words and pictures tell a story.

Individualize reading times to meet children's needs.

Teachers can read during a scheduled story time as well as in response to children's requests throughout the day. You might read to two children in the library area, a small group seated under a shady tree outdoors, one child curled up with you in the easy chair, or a group of ten gathered around your chair. Young children can generally listen to a story for five to ten minutes. Older children can listen a little longer—between ten and fifteen minutes. Some children find it difficult to sit for a group story time of any length. Allow them to leave and find something else to do if they lose interest in the story. Later, you can read to the child one-on-one. Reading to one or two children at a time allows you to gear the story to their special needs and interests and share a special time of closeness. As children grow older, they will remember these times, and continue to associate reading with feelings of warmth and security.

Prepare for small group story times.

Begin by carefully selecting the books you will read. Use the criteria suggested in this module and consider the interests and abilities of your group. If children particularly enjoy a book, read it again. If you plan to introduce a new story, read it to yourself several times so you can become very familiar with the words, characters, and plot. As you think about the children's possible reactions to the book, consider the following questions:

- How long will it take to read? Can the children sit for that length of time?

- Can the children join in to repeat phrases or answer questions?

- Will any concepts or ideas be unfamiliar to the children? How can I explain them?

- Do the illustrations have tiny details or hidden surprises to point out to the children?

- How can I make sound effects (e.g., animal noises or sirens) part of the story?

- How can I vary my voice for the different characters?

- What props (e.g., hats or musical instruments) could enhance the story?

Introduce the story to capture children's interests.

The first step in reading a story is to gain the attention of a group of children and help them focus on the book. You want to give them a reason to listen. Here are some suggestions:

Explain how the story is tied to familiar feelings or a recent experience. "We all have angry feelings sometimes. If there's no room on the swings, or we can't find our shoes, we may feel angry. So I thought I'd read a book about feeling angry. It's called, *I Was So Mad!*"

Discuss the cover of the book or the first illustration. "What do you think these two girls are talking about?"

Share an object that is an important part of the story. "Here's a nice round stone I found outside. Do you think we could make soup from this stone? Let's see what happens in this book called *Stone Soup*."

Relate a new book to a familiar one. "Do you remember reading *The Very Hungry Caterpillar*? This book is by the same author. It's called *The Very Lonely Firefly*."

Varying your reading style will engage children's attention and hold their interest. Here are some suggestions:

- Make sure the children are comfortably seated where they can see the pictures.

- Start as soon as you have the children's attention.

- Hold the book to one side so the children can see the pictures.

- Make the characters and experiences come alive by changing your voice and facial expressions.

- Stop to talk about the pictures, answer questions, discuss what might happen next, and think about what the characters might be feeling.

- Change or paraphrase the words to help children understand the story.

- Invite children to join in with repetitive refrains and responses.

When you have finished reading the story, talk about the plot and characters and offer materials and activities that enhance children's enjoyment of the book. Here are some examples:

- Discuss what the characters did and ask the children to share their own experiences.

  "Have you ever felt like Andrew did? Did people not listen to you when you had something important to say to them?"

  "It was really hard for Frances when it was her sister's birthday. Did you ever feel like Frances?"

- Provide props so children can act out the story.

- Make flannel board cutouts of favorite stories so children can retell the story themselves.

- Display the books you have read prominently so children can enjoy them again and again.

Make story time an enjoyable experience.

Plan ways to extend children's experiences with the book.

Make sure every child has reading materials at home.

The more children are read to, the more likely they are to learn to love reading. Even the most busy parents need to find time to read regularly to their children. You might allow children to borrow books overnight or for a few days. Provide information to all families about your local library—hours of service, special programs, and lists of good books for preschoolers. Invite the children's librarian to a parent meeting to share tips for reading with children. Sponsor a book fair so families can trade used books or buy new ones. In short, do whatever you can to support family reading times.

Applying Your Knowledge

In this learning activity you select two books you think are appropriate for the children in your classroom. Choose books from your classroom inventory or borrow them from your library. Read one book to a small group of children and read the other to an individual child. Then answer the questions about your reading experiences on the blank forms. Begin by reviewing the examples that follow.

Reading to a Small Group

(Example)

Title and author: Everybody Cooks Rice *by Norah Dooley*   **Date:** *September 20*

Children (ages): *Leon, Dontae, Shiho, Zuri (4 and 5 years)*   **Setting:** *Outdoors under a tree*

Briefly describe this book and why you selected it.

This book is about a girl who learns that her neighbors, who come from various cultures, have something in common—they all eat rice. However, they do things in unique ways, and cook different rice dishes. The children in our class represent several cultures, so I think they will like this book. Also, we have just set up a cooking area.

How did you prepare for reading this book?

I read the book several times and thought of questions to ask the children. I brought in some pictures of rice dishes.

What happened when you read the book?

There were many interruptions as children recognized the rice dishes they eat at home. They added more information than was in the book. They weren't very interested in the pictures I brought in.

How did you extend children's enjoyment of this book?

I asked parents to share simple recipes for their own favorite rice dishes. We made several dishes in the cooking area. I put the book in the cooking area so children could explore it on their own.

Reading to an Individual Child

(Example)

Title and author: Owl Babies *by Martin Waddell*   **Date:** *September 23*

Child: *Nigel*   **Age:** *3 years, 2 months*   **Setting:** *Seated in the rocking chair in the library area*

Briefly describe this book and why you selected it.

This book is about three baby owls who wake up to find their mother gone. When she returns, they are very happy to see her. I chose this book because Nigel has been having a hard time saying good-bye to his mother each day.

How did you prepare for reading this book?

I read the book several times and thought about questions I could ask Nigel to help him handle his own feelings about separating from his mother.

What happened when you read the book?

The first time I read the book Nigel was very quiet. At the end of the book I asked him if he would like me to read it again. He said, "Yes," so I did. This time I stopped at key points to invite Nigel to talk about what was happening in the story.

How did you extend the child's enjoyment of this book?

I asked Nigel's mother to make a tape of herself reading this book. I provided the blank tape, book, and tape recorder. Now Nigel can listen to the story on his own.

Reading to a Small Group

Title and author: _____   **Date:** _____

Children (ages): _____   **Setting:** _____

Briefly describe this book and why you selected it.

How did you prepare for reading this book?

What happened when you read the book?

How did you extend children's enjoyment of this book?

Reading to an Individual Child

Title and author: _____   **Date:** _____

Child: _____   **Age:** _____   **Setting:** _____

Briefly describe this book and why you selected it.

How did you prepare for reading this book?

What happened when you read the book?

How did you extend the child's enjoyment of this book?

Discuss this learning activity with your trainer.

V. Supporting Emerging Literacy Skills

In this activity, you will learn to:

• Identify the skills and understandings that are part of emerging literacy

• Create an environment that supports emerging literacy

Most people would agree that children begin learning to listen and speak long before they talk in sentences. But if you ask people when children learn to read and write, they often say "in first grade." In fact, learning to read and to write starts in infancy as children are naturally exposed to spoken and written language and to books and other reading materials. Speaking, reading, and writing are related parts of literacy learning. Young children develop reading and writing skills at the same time. Many two- and three-year-olds can identify the familiar signs, labels, and logos they see at home and in the community. They also experiment with writing by making scribbles that are similar to the writing of parents and other adults. The gradual, ongoing process through which children learn to listen, speak, read, and write is called emerging literacy.

Young children construct their own knowledge about reading and writing. They figure out for themselves: "What is the difference between drawing and writing?" "What does it mean when my teacher uses a different tone of voice?" "What do the symbols in books have to do with the words that people say out loud?" Adults encourage children's emerging literacy by regularly exposing them to literacy activities at home and at the program. Children learn about the purposes of written language when they see adults reading (books, charts, a bulletin board) and writing (shopping lists, notes, recording a child's description of a painting).

The Foundation for Reading

Children who have been read to regularly in their early years and who are given a rich assortment of good books to look at are more likely to want to read to themselves. Children develop many important understandings by being exposed to books throughout the preschool years.

- They learn that books have a beginning and end and that (in English and many other languages) the words on each page are read from left to right and top to bottom.

- They learn that the print on the page represents spoken words. If the events and ideas in stories are relevant to children's life experiences, they will understand what they hear.

- They learn that reading books is an enjoyable and satisfying activity. This discovery encourages a positive attitude toward reading.

As in all areas of development, children go through predictable stages in understanding what reading is all about. Knowing about these stages will help you to recognize typical behaviors and encourage children's development. These stages are described below.[3]

Exploring books. Children imitate what older siblings and adults do while reading. They turn pages while retelling a familiar story. Children may ask to have a favorite book read again and again. They feel a sense of mastery when they know the story so well they can retell it. Predictable stories and those with repeated refrains are particularly useful in helping children remember what will happen next.

Understanding sequence. Children gradually learn that stories have a beginning, middle, and end. The more children are exposed to books and encouraged to retell stories, the more they can recall the details and correct sequence of events.

Recognizing that written words are symbols. Before children reach this stage they may ask you to read a page with no print or cover up the print on a page while asking you to read. More experienced children will say things such as, "Now you can start reading again," when you get back to a page with print on it. They realize that printed words function differently from pictures and that words stand for people, objects, and ideas.

Matching words with the printed text. At this stage, children may run their fingers along the text as you read. They may also point to individual words, though not necessarily the ones you are reading. This behavior tells you that the child is beginning to understand that each set of letters represents a word.

Recognizing printed words. Children at this stage are likely to ask questions about the print on the page. They may ask, "What does this say?" or "Where does it say that?" You may notice these children starting to pick out printed words in the classroom or while on neighborhood walks. They are developing a "sight vocabulary" as they learn to recognize signs, their own names, and sometimes the names of other children in the class.

The Foundation for Writing

Children learn to write by writing. They practice writing long before they can make recognizable letters or numbers. Using pencils, pens, crayons, and other writing tools, they imitate adult writing. If you make a shopping list, a three-year-old may make one. If you write a letter, a four-year-old may decide that he or she needs to write one, too. Just as in learning to read, children go through predictable stages in writing. These stages are described on the next page.

[3] Based on Diane Trister Dodge and Laura J. Colker, *The Creative Curriculum for Early Childhood, 3rd. Edition* (Washington, DC: Teaching Strategies, Inc., 1992), p. 227.

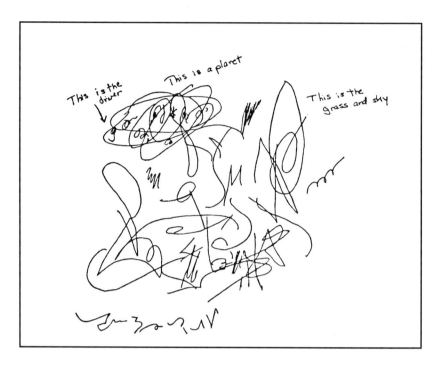

This is a planet

This is the driver

This is the grass and sky

The stages in learning to write are also predictable.

Writing scribbles. At first, young children imitate adult writing by scribbling. If you look closely, you will see that they can distinguish between drawing and writing. In the drawing above, which demonstrates this distinction, the child's writing is at the bottom left of the picture.

Making recognizable letters. As children gain more experience with writing, they begin making actual letters. These letters may be a part of a series of marks, some of which are not letters at all.

Organizing writing on the page. Children begin to realize that there are standard rules for how to place letters and words on the page. Rather than placing marks haphazardly, they recognize that, like the words on a page in a book, writing goes from left to right and there are spaces between words.

Connecting speech and writing. As children begin to recognize individual letters, they also learn that each letter represents a sound. At this stage they may begin writing words and making up their own spelling—for example, "kt" for "cat." There is no need to correct children's invented spelling; it is an important step in their understanding of reading and writing. Ask the child to read to you what he or she has written. You will soon understand the writing system the child has devised.

At each of these stages, children need small muscle skills to hold and manipulate writing tools. They can strengthen these muscles while enjoying a variety of materials and activities such as, rolling playdough, stirring raisins into muffin batter, buttoning and zipping, building with Legos, and using a computer keyboard.

Creating a Print-Rich Environment

Children's emerging literacy skills will develop naturally in a print-rich environment—one filled with books and written words that have meaning and are displayed at children's eye-level. As children see the many uses for print and have many opportunities to explore reading and writing materials, their own skills and understandings will grow. In addition to creating an appealing library area, there are many ways to expose children to the uses of print.

Use signs, labels, and charts as a way to share important information. Teachers can help children learn about the importance of print by using it to communicate in English and the children's home languages. Ask children to help you make print and picture labels for shelves and containers to show were materials belong. Label individual cubbies with children's names, and perhaps a photograph. Post picture and written versions of the daily schedule. Make helper, daily attendance, and birthday charts. Make signs for each interest area telling how many children can use it at a time and listing a few, simple rules. Create a system for taking turns with popular materials, by posting a piece of paper and a marker attached with a string. Children can write their names and cross them off after their turn.

Make experience charts with children. Ask children to describe what happened after a trip or a shared group experience. Write a story by recording their comments on a large piece of paper. As you and the children read the story aloud, point to the words and move your finger along each line. Post the finished story in the room.

Point out words in the environment. On a neighborhood walk, show children traffic signs and explain what they mean. Read aloud the signs posted in store windows and on the sides of buses and other vehicles.

Do your writing where children can see you and tell them what you are writing. "I'm writing this note to your dad to let him know that your sniffles are much better today." Ask children to help you make a list of things you need for a trip or an activity. They can draw what you need while you write the words next to the pictures.

Write a recipe or the steps in a simple activity on a large piece of paper, while children are watching. Talk about what you are writing. "This is the recipe for English muffin pizzas. First, we pull the muffins apart to make two pieces." Post the paper in the appropriate interest area.

Invite children to help you write a book about their activities. Illustrate it with photographs and bind the pages together. (Office supply stores are a good source for inexpensive but strong bindings.) Put the finished book in the library area.

Model using print to get information and talk about what you are doing. For example, while looking up the number for the Nature Center in the phone book, say, "The names in the phone book are listed in the same order as the alphabet. *Nature* starts with an *N*, so I'm going to look for it after *M* and before *O*."

Expose children to many different ways we use print.

Include games and materials with words and numbers. Children can learn about words and numbers while playing Lotto, matching games, and number games that have words and numbers as well as pictures.

Include opportunities for writing as a part of children's play.

If you provide markers, pencils, and crayons with plain drawing paper in all interest areas, children can incorporate writing in their play and activities. Items such as magazines, telephone books, and pads and pencils can be placed in the dramatic play area. Add props related to real-life activities along with reading and writing materials. For example, if playing doctor is a favorite theme, provide prescription pads, an eye examination chart, magazines for the waiting room, and office supplies for the receptionist. In the block area, provide a basket filled with index cards, markers, and masking tape so children can make signs for their buildings. Include props that have writing on them, such as wooden traffic signs.

Establish a writing center in or near the library.

Children will make good use of a writing center filled with the materials needed to write signs, stories, letters, cards, and messages. If space allows, locate the area near the library area to take advantage of the related nature of reading and writing. Furnishings for the writing center might include a desk or table and chairs, a shelf, and a bulletin board. The following materials can be included.

Tools for writing:

pencils (thick lead; colored)	markers (washable, non-toxic)
chalk (white and colored)	crayons

Surfaces to write on:

paper (lined and unlined, white and colored, different sizes, weights)	index cards
	cardboard
chalkboards	magic slates with pencils
ready-made blank books	

Miscellaneous materials:

junk mail	yarn
catalogs	typewriter
magazines	computer and software
erasers	envelopes
clipboards	blunt-edge scissors
paste and glue	file folders
stickers	hole punch
stapler	cardboard mailbox

A child's first exposure to print usually occurs within the home setting. Parents can continue to play a central role in promoting literacy. When your program receives donations of paper, pencils, crayons, or markers, share them with the families. If necessary, ask your director if it is possible to include money in the budget to purchase writing materials for children to use at home.

Make sure every child has writing materials at home.

Applying Your Knowledge

In this learning activity you observe a child's emerging reading and writing skills. Next, you complete a chart noting the materials in your environment that encourage children's emerging literacy and determine what items you want to add.

Emerging Literacy Skills

(Example)

Child: *Jennifer*　　　　　　**Age:** *4-1/2 years*　　　　　　　　**Date:** *June 1*

What emerging literacy skills did you observe this child using?

While looking at books:

With familiar books, she likes to turn the pages and tell herself the story. She occasionally goes to the library area and looks at favorite books. Sometimes she tells the story to another child.

When listening to a story:

When the teacher is reading a familiar story, Jennifer frequently corrects her if the text is not read exactly. She pointed to a page with no text on it and said, "There's no talking on this page."

During an activity or routine:

When she set the table for lunch she read each child's name aloud as she put the place mats down. When playing restaurant with several other children she asked the customers what they wanted and pretended to write down their requests using her finger and her hand.

While using writing tools (crayons, markers, pencils, paint brushes):

She writes her name correctly. In the block area, she likes to make signs for her buildings. She will ask a teacher to write down what she wants to say, and then she likes to copy it herself. Sometimes she adds letters to her paintings.

How you can you encourage this child's emerging literacy skills?

I can ask her to read a familiar story to me and encourage her efforts. I can add writing materials to the dramatic play area to support the restaurant play theme. I can ask her to tell me about the letters she adds to her paintings and write down her descriptions of the paintings, if she likes.

Emerging Literacy Skills

Child: _____ Age: _____ Date: _____

What emerging literacy skills did you observe this child using?

While looking at books:

When listening to a story:

During an activity or routine:

While using writing tools (crayons, markers, pencils, paint brushes):

How you can you encourage this child's emerging literacy skills?

How Does the Environment Encourage Emerging Literacy?

After each example, list ways that your indoor environment encourages children's emerging literacy skills.

Signs, Labels, and Charts

Picture and written versions of the daily schedule

The Many Ways to Use Print

A photograph of the winner of a pet show, with the caption

Opportunities to Write While Playing

A grocery store dramatic play kit with props featuring print and materials for writing

Games and Materials with Words and Numbers

Alphabet lotto

Writing Center

Junk mail

Review your chart, then list five new ways to support emerging literacy skills. Make the changes, observe children's reactions, and summarize what you saw and heard.

1.

2.

3.

4.

5.

How did the children react to the changes in the environment?

Discuss this learning activity with your trainer.

Summarizing Your Progress

You have now completed all of the learning activities for this module. Whether you are an experienced teacher or new to the profession, this module has probably helped you develop new skills in promoting preschoolers' communication.

Before you go on, take a few minutes to summarize what you've learned.

- Turn back to Learning Activity I, Using Your Knowledge of Child Development to Promote Language Skills, and add to the chart specific examples of what you learned about promoting children's language skills while you were working on this module.

- Next, review your responses to the pre-training assessment for this module. Write a summary of what you learned and list the skills you developed or improved.

If there are topics you would like to know more about, you will find recommended readings listed in the Orientation.

Your final step in this module is to complete the knowledge and competency assessments. Let your trainer know when you are ready to schedule the assessments. After you have successfully completed these assessments, you will be ready to start a new module. Congratulations on your progress so far, and good luck with your next module.

Answer Sheets

Encouraging Children to Listen and Speak

1. **How did Ms. Kim know what Jerry wanted?**
    a. *She interpreted his nonverbal communications—tapping her shoulder, pointing to the block corner, nodding, leading her there.*

    b. *She went with him to the block corner and asked questions about what had happened.*

2. **How did Ms. Kim help Jerry use words to express his feelings and thoughts?**
    a. *She stated what she thought he meant by his nonverbal gestures.*

    b. *She told him what to say to David.*

    c. *She respected his desire to make his own garage.*

    d. *She repeated what he said using a complete sentence.*

Helping Children Use Language in Meaningful Ways

1. **Why did Mr. Lopez suggest that the children write a story?**
    a. *They had a lot to say when he asked them about their walk.*

    b. *They seemed excited about their experience.*

2. **How did Ms. Nolan help the children use language in meaningful ways?**
    a. *She asked what their story said.*

    b. *She offered to write down their words as they dictated them to her.*

    c. *After recording their words, she read them aloud.*

Providing Materials and Opportunities that Support Emerging Literacy Skills

1. **What did Ms. Williams do to interest the children in hearing the story?**

    a.   *She reminded children that they were familiar with the story.*

    b.   *She introduced the story and asked questions to help children recall the plot.*

    c.   *She showed the children the cover of the book.*

    d.   *She let the children share what they remembered about the story before she began reading.*

2. **How did Ms. Williams use the group story time to support children's emerging literacy skills?**

    a.   *She read the story with lots of expression to enhance children's enjoyment of the story.*

    b.   *She paused frequently to let the children recite familiar phrases.*

    c.   *She asked a motivating question before starting to read.*

Using Your Knowledge of Child Development to Promote Communication Skills

(p. 297)

What Preschool Children Are Like	How Teachers Can Use This Information to Promote Communication Skills
They use language to think, learn, imagine, plan, make requests, direct others, and solve problems.	*Plan activities and provide materials in each interest area that allow children to use language for different purposes. Talk and listen to children and encourage them to talk and listen to each other. Expect that the classroom will be filled with children's voices.*
They tell stories about imaginary and real experiences that take place in the past as well as in the present.	*Offer to write children's stories to be hung on the wall at their eye level, or in books that children can illustrate. Invite children to act out their stories for others. Ask questions to help children tell stories with a beginning, middle, and end.*
They participate and take turns in conversations with peers and adults.	*Use mealtimes as opportunities to model and directly teach the rules followed in polite conversation, such as talking one at a time, responding to what was said, staying on the topic. Talk with individual children about topics of interest to them.*
They make up and act out scenarios with plots and different characters who solve a problem or do something specific.	*Provide props, dress-up clothes, and accessories that stimulate children's imaginations. Observe children's play and offer new materials that will encourage them to expand their play or take it in a different direction.*
They can retell favorite stories, sometimes in correct sequence.	*Read favorite stories often, and plan activities that build on the story's characters or plot.*
They ask many questions and can answer open-ended questions that have no right or wrong response.	*Answer children's questions directly, or let them help you find the answer by using a book or other resource. Ask questions about what children are doing to engage them in conversation.*

Using Your Knowledge of Child Development to Promote Communication Skills
(p. 298)

What Preschool Children Are Like	How Teachers Can Use This Information to Promote Communication Skills
They learn most rules of grammar without direct instruction. They may make mistakes because there are exceptions to a rule.	*Accept children's use of language without pointing out mistakes. In your response, restate children's words using standard language. Serve as a model for standard use of language.*
They may be learning one language at home and another at the program.	*Learn a few useful phrases in the children's home languages. Make labels and signs in both English and children's home languages. Provide books and other print materials in the home languages. Ask parents to help you include their home language in your materials and activities.*
They are learning that printed words are symbols for spoken words and convey messages.	*Print and post signs, job charts, bulletin boards, and stories to provide important information. Label cubbies, containers, shelves, and interest areas. On a neighborhood walk, point out traffic signs and signs on buildings. Offer writing materials in a separate area and in all interest areas.*
They scribble and write invented letters and words.	*Ask children to read what they have written so you can understand what they know about writing. Accept their writing without pointing out mistakes or making corrections.*
They like a wide variety of books.	*Offer a variety of fiction and nonfiction books in English and children's home languages that are appropriate to the children in your group. Include books about familiar characters and experiences and books that introduce new people, places, and ideas. Offer poetry, alphabet, and counting books and simple dictionaries in English and children's home languages.*
They can memorize songs, poems, rhymes, and books with repetition.	*Read books with repeated words and phrases again and again, until children know what comes next and join in. Ask parents to share their favorite poems, songs, and rhymes. Make up songs and rhymes about the children and classroom life.*

Glossary

Communication

The act of expressing and sharing ideas, desires, and feelings.

Conventional reading and writing

Reading and writing that follows accepted standard rules for language use.

Emerging literacy

The developmental process through which children gain listening, speaking, reading, and writing skills.

Language

A system of words with rules for their use in speaking, reading, and writing.

Nonverbal communication

The act of conveying feelings or ideas through gestures and body language.

Predictable books

Those with plots that allow children to guess correctly what happens next.

Repetitive books

Those that repeat certain words and phrases.

Standard language

The form of any language that is usually taught in an educational setting, and follows specific rules for speech and writing. There are many forms of a language (dialects) other than the standard spoken and written forms.

Notes

Notes

Notes

Notes

Notes

Notes

Notes

Notes

Notes